Simon Collin

The Essential LAN Source Book

McGraw-Hill Book Company

London • New York • St Louis • San Franc~
Bogotá • Caracas • Lisbon • Madrid • ~
Montreal • New Delhi • Panama • ~
São Paulo • Singapore • Sydney ~

Published by
McGRAW-HILL Book Company Europe
Shoppenhangers Road, Maidenhead, Berkshire SL6 2QL, England
Telephone 01628 23432
Fax 01628 770224

British Library Cataloguing in Publication Data
Collin, Simon
    Essential LAN Source Book
    I. Title
    004.68

    ISBN 0-07-707881-0

Library of Congress Cataloging-in-Publication Data
Collin, Simon.
        The essential LAN source book / Simon Collin.
            p.   cm.
        Includes index.
        ISBN 0-07-707881-0
        1. Local area networks (Computer networks) I. Title.
    TK5105.7.C65 1995
    004.6'8--dc20   94-30166
                                                                              CIP

      998765

          Local Image Ltd, London
          bound in Great Britain by Biddles Ltd.

Contents

4 The Server   48

12 Connecting Networks 149

13 Interoperability 157

14 Protecting Your Data 165

Preface

Local area networks (LANs) are big business. They are taking hold in almost every office across the world. They can also be difficult to deal with and the market is moving so fast; it is a full time job just keeping up with the latest standards.

That is why I wrote this book—to help you get to grips with the whole LAN market. If you are an expert in one field, I hope this book will inform you about all the others from tips on linking LANs to tuning servers.

This book covers current software standards, including Novell's NetWare 3.12 and Windows NT/AS (which includes LAN Manager), together with open standards such as CMIP and hardware standards including FDDI and SCSI-2. New standards, just coming onto the market, including Windows/NT, the Pentium CPU, FDDI-2 and NetWare 4.0, are also detailed.

I wrote this book as a guide to help anyone concerned with LANs get to know the whole subject. The first chapter gives any newcomer to the subject a condensed run through the field. The rest of the book will supply you with the information that you need to select and install, then upgrade and tune your network. I hope this will become your source book for any questions related to PC-based networks. I have covered every area in detail, with buying tips and selection hints, and explained the technology in detail. But I have written it in an accessible style that shouldn't baffle anyone with a basic understanding of computers.

ABOUT THIS BOOK

Are you a network supervisor, in charge of managing the installation or running of a local area network? If you are, this book is for you. Whether you are an experienced PC consultant or have just been told to find a network, I think you will find this book indispensable.

In the following chapters, I have tried to include all the information a supervisor will need to boost the reliability, productivity, and performance of their network. This book also covers in detail all the aspects of linking LANs, setting up WANs and new technology such as the benefits of SCSI-2, T1 links, or tuning NetWare 3.12—which will be useful for any experienced LAN administrator who wants to learn more about a particular subject.

Perhaps your company is growing and you have to link two offices or upgrade your file server. I have provided all the information you need to help you understand your choices and then point you in the right direction for a solution that works, at a low price. I have included information that will move you from forward planning, to selecting the correct equipment for your installation, through to installing and maintaining your PC-based LAN.

If you are about to face the job of choosing, installing, and maintaining a new network, don't worry. We have included step-by-step guidance that carries all the technical details a professional supervisor will want, explained in a language anyone with a basic knowledge of PCs will understand.

To cover the wide field of networking, I have included detailed information that will help if you are still selecting hardware and software for small office networks or country and international-wide systems, or about to integrate your LAN with mini and mainframe computers. There is information to help you deal with interoperability between PCs, Macintoshes, minis, and mainframes—and stay sane.

Detecting problems before they arise is covered in depth, with current and future network management standards examined. Comprehensive information on how to protect your data, tuning your server and workstations, and installing application software is written in a style that is easy to understand, without compromising technical content.

This guide is based mainly around Novell's NetWare operating system, but I have included specific examples that will help any administrator who is running a LAN based on Novell's NetWare 2.2, 3.12 or Personal NetWare; Windows for Workgroups, Windows NT/AS, Microsoft's LAN Manager 2.1; or Artisoft's LANtastic.

Local area networks are the computer industry's fastest growing sector, so the chances are if you are not already in a networked office, you soon will be. If you are involved with LANs, you will gain a lot from this guide. I will tell you how to select, install, tune, and protect your LAN with tips and tricks to save time, cut costs and boost the performance of your network.

List of trademarks

The following are the companies and the products registered as trademarks that are used within this book:

Apple
AppleTalk
LocalTalk
Macintosh
Artisoft
LANtastic
Banyan
VINES
Beyond Corporation
BeyondMail
Borland
dBase
Paradox
Compaq
PageMarq
SystemPro
D-Link
LANsmart
DataProducts
LZR2080
daVinci
daVinci Mail
DEC
Pathworks for OS/2 v1.1
Digital Research
Multiuser DOS
Eagle
NE1000
Finansa
WinMail
Hewlett Packard
JetDirect
LaserJet 4
IBM
LAN Server
OS/2
PROFS
Intel
LANProtect

NetPort Express
Lotus
Ami Pro
cc:Mail
Notes
Microsoft
Excel
LAN Manager
Mail
MEMAKER
MS-DOS 6
Schedule
SMARTDRV
Visual Basic
Windows
Windows for Workgroups
Word
Word for Windows
Novell
MHS
NetWare 2.2
NetWare 3.11
NetWare 4.0
NetWare Global MHS
NetWare Lite
Personal NetWare
QMS
PS1700
Sage
MainLAN
SCO
LAN Manager for Unix
SPI
Invisible LAN
InvisibleNet
Symantec
VirusScan
XTree
ViruSafe/LAN

The following are companies whose names are also trademarks:

Cabletron
CIX
CompuServe
David Systems
MCI
Mitac

NetFrame
Olivetti
Proteon
Synoptics
3Com
Tricord

1
A Condensed Introduction to LANs

This first chapter is a condensed guide to the whole topic of networking aimed at anyone installing their first network. In this book, I have tried to cover all the areas that are important to a network supervisor, but if you are new to networking, you might find the concepts alien and the language a little intimidating (although I have tried to write it in a user-friendly style).

This chapter will bring you up to speed on the subject of local area networks (LANs). It will give you a broad overview of the topics together with plenty of information you will find useful when choosing and installing your first LAN. Once you are familiar with the basics introduced in this first chapter, you will find that you will be able to make better use of the tips and information in the rest of the book. If you are an experienced networker, but want to know more about a particular area, skip this first chapter, which is designed for new supervisors, and move on to the section covering your relevant field.

YOUR FIRST NETWORK

So you have just been told you have to install the new office network . . . now what do you do? Maybe you want to make your office more productive, so you have turned to a network. Whatever the reason for choosing to network, and however experienced you are with PCs, you had better ready yourself for a new onslaught of jargon and standards. This book will help guide you through the minefield; this chapter will get you started with a basic grounding in networking.

How do you start? If you set out a complete plan for your requirements, you will save yourself considerable bother later on. The first step is to total the number of users that you will want to connect together and then calculate the growth expected and the time frame for this expansion.

Next consider the applications that each is likely to use. There are two main types of networks available, and the combination of number of users and type of application will determine which network you should buy (Fig. 1.1).

First are peer-to-peer networks such as Artisoft's LANtastic, Novell's NetWare Lite, SPI's InvisibleNet, Microsoft's Windows for Workgroups, and Sage's MainLAN. As the name suggests in this design all PCs are equal. You do not need

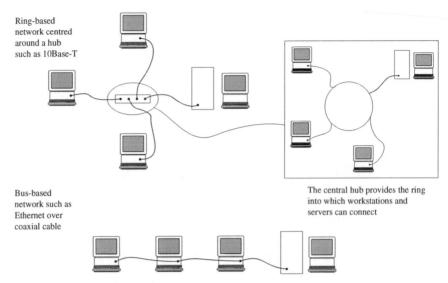

Ring-based network centred around a hub such as 10Base-T

Bus-based network such as Ethernet over coaxial cable

The central hub provides the ring into which workstations and servers can connect

Figure 1.1   Ring and bus topologies

to purchase any extra PCs or a central server. Instead, the network tasks are shared out among the workstations. Peer-to-peer networks are ideal for small numbers of users with low demands.

An office with less than 10 users, all running spreadsheet, wordprocessing, or simple database applications would be well served by a peer-to-peer network. Artisoft's LANtastic is the fastest of the bunch, and is capable of supporting up to 100 users. It also lets you transmit voice messages (using a microphone) and is well supported by third-part software and hardware vendors.

Novell's Personal NetWare (the successor to its NetWare Lite peer-to-peer product) is compatible in look and operation to the bigger NetWare products— such as NetWare 3.12 and 4.0. Personal NetWare comes bundled with DR-DOS, a version of DOS compatible with MS-DOS. Personal NetWare is designed to provide a seamless upgrade path to anyone who wants to start small but expects their LAN to grow and so move onto a server-based network. Personal NetWare is also very fast—almost as quick as LANtastic—but does not include any electronic mail utilities like MainLAN.

SPI's InvisibleNet sticks to proprietary hardware, while LANtastic can support any standard Ethernet network cards—which are easily available from most dealers starting at £100. Sage's MainLAN, like LANtastic, supports standard network hardware. All three are available in starter-packs which include all the software and hardware (cables plus network interface cards) needed to connect three users together. Be careful, most bundles are available in two options: proprietary cards that are cheap or industry-standard compatible cards that are more expensive. Check the hardware that your network software can support— LANtastic, for example, is available in two versions. The standard version uses proprietary cards and you will have to buy Artisoft cards if you ever want to expand your network. The second version is compatible with industry-standard NE1000 cards from Novell. This means that you can shop around when you need to expand your LAN; you are not stuck with one supplier.

When setting up a peer-to-peer network, one PC is designated as the print-server: this simply means that this PC has a shared printer attached and any data waiting to be printed is temporarily stored on this PC's hard disk until the printer is ready. This looks after the print queue, storing unprinted files on the local drive until the printer is ready. Another PC would typically be designated as the mail-server. In this case, the PC provides the storage for electronic mail messages. All messages between users are stored on the server's local drive until they have been read. Just because a couple of PCs are called servers does not mean that these PCs are dedicated to the tasks. No, these tasks work in the background and the PCs can be used as normal workstations running any normal PC software.

The main advantage of peer-to-peer networks is their relatively low initial cost: you can, by shopping around, get away with spending around £180 per PC, including all hardware and software. Peer-to-peer networks are designed for small, two to four users, to medium sized, five to ten users, network installations.

To install a peer-to-peer network you also need to add special hardware to your PC —a network adapter card. If you are worried about opening up your PC, or need to attach a laptop to the LAN, you should pick a parallel port adapter (also called pocket adapters). These plug into the PC's printer port and are a lot slower in operation than a normal internal adapter. They are also more expensive, but are much easier to install (Fig. 1.2). (See Chapter 3 for a more detailed explanation of the different types of network adapter.)

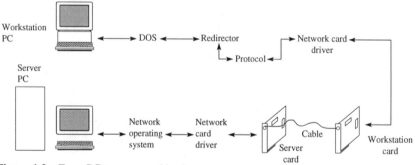

Figure 1.2   From PC to server and back

Performance can be surprisingly good, often equalling the data transfer rates of a local hard disk. Effectively, this kills any ideas you may have that networks are slow. A user who has just connected their elderly PC/XT to the network is going to see at least a 25 per cent speed improvement when accessing remote files compared to accessing the local disk—simply because the LAN can move data faster than an old disk drive system. Disk performance has now improved and transfers are in the order of 1 megabit per second (Mbps), while network cards are still limited to a rate of around 500 kilobits per second (Kbps).

Peer-to-peer networks are ideal for situations where you want to share data files

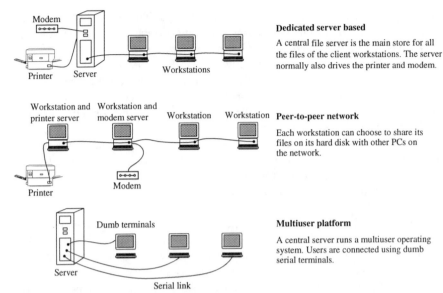

Dedicated server based

A central file server is the main store for all the files of the client workstations. The server normally also drives the printer and modem.

Peer-to-peer network

Each workstation can choose to share its files on its hard disk with other PCs on the network.

Multiuser platform

A central server runs a multiuser operating system. Users are connected using dumb serial terminals.

Figure 1.3 Types of network installations

between users, and want to achieve this as cheaply and efficiently as possible. You do not need to buy any extra PCs, and the RAM lost on each PC will be between 10 and 100K. Peer-to-peer networks begin to reach their limits with large networks of 10 users or more. The reason lies in their foundation (Fig. 1.3).

These networks rely heavily on DOS. Each PC on the network runs DOS and, in addition, runs a terminate and stay resident (TSR) program that takes between 10 and 100K of RAM. This program makes sure that commands go to the correct resource. For instance, if you want to read from a remote drive, then the TSR program diverts the request away from DOS and on to the network adapter card, to the remote PC. However good this software, the basis is still DOS, which is not very efficient at handling very large amounts of data, or at executing more than one task at a time.

For this reason, server-based networks were developed and remain a more popular choice for large installations with over 10 users. These differ in one main respect: one PC is dedicated to serving the needs of the PCs connected to it.

All network traffic goes through this central server and the network operating system software it runs looks after security, user accounts, and printing. To be able to handle instructions from dozens of workstations, the server runs a multitasking operating system. Network operating systems such as Novell's NetWare 3.12, NetWare 4.0, Banyan VINES, or Microsoft's Windows NT/AS (previously called LAN Manager) are all capable of multitasking. They also improve on DOS by storing and retrieving files from disk far more efficiently than DOS can. In a server-based network, only the server needs to run the multitasking operating system. The workstations connected to it can still run DOS.

The normal scenario is to use the server as a telephone exchange. Each PC runs

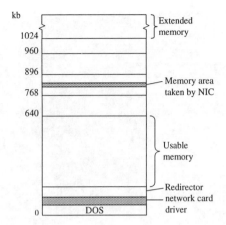

Figure 1.4 Memory map of a networked PC

a small resident program, taking up between 40 and 100K, called the redirector. Just like the resident program in a PC connected to a peer-to-peer network, the redirector sends requests for remote files on to the server, while keeping those meant for the PC's local resources (Fig. 1.4).

Minimizing how much RAM the redirector takes can be crucial if your users need to run big DOS applications. If the workstations are 386-based, utilities such as 386-Max and QEMM386 can remap your PC's conventional RAM to leave as much of the original 640K to DOS programs. DOS 5 and DR-DOS 6 are both able to load resident network redirectors high into any available EMS memory (see Chapter 7 for more details).

SECURITY

When you start to connect your users together, the one thing most will begin to worry about is security. Network security measures have improved considerably over the last few years to prevent hackers breaking in, as well as minimize problems with viruses. You should expect your network operating system software to be able to support either or both types of share-level and user-level security.

Share level is standard on very cheap peer-to-peer networks and can be a useful addition to high-end network systems. It relies on the theory that people can trust each other—at least to a degree. The network supervisor can set up a share name that is allocated to a particular disk drive, directory, or printer. Anyone connected to the network is allowed access to this resource. The security is minimal, but it is an easy security system to set up for small and medium sized installations (Fig. 1.5)

For larger networks, user-level security offers better control for a supervisor to monitor who is doing what and where. Each authorized user is given an account. This carries a username, password, and groups of rights. In addition to users, the supervisor can set up groups; these carry rights to use files, printers, and drives. Individual users can then be added to a group, making user management far easier.

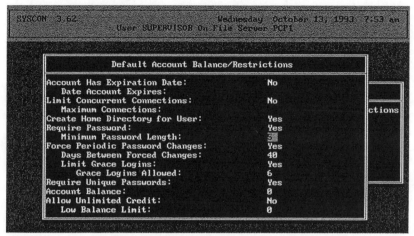

Figure 1.5   Access restrictions using SYSCON utility on Novell Netware 3.11

The rights assigned to a user or group should provide restraints to user reading and writing to a file as well as dictating whether a user can run a program. These rights can be extended to cover a directory or whole drive as well as a single file.

If you install user-level security, you should ensure that it remains effective. From the set-up or administrator screen, you can set up how the first line of defence is implemented: a user's password. You should set a password to have a minimum length of six characters (this provides 4.3 billion possible combinations with ASCII characters).

To remain effective, passwords should be changed every couple of months. Either enforce this softly by asking politely, or set the network software to keep a track on the age of passwords and force a user to change their password every two months.

When you are connected to a network, who else can see your letters and personal information? It depends on how the network has been set up and on your working methods. If you save all your work onto your local C: drive, then another user will only be able to see the data if you publish the drive. Publishing a drive means issuing an explicit command to the network operating system to include your disk drive as a shareable, network resource.

If you save your work to a network drive then it is conceivable that any other user could access your files. The main method of protecting your data from unwanted eyes is to create and use a private subdirectory on a network drive. By only assigning yourself rights of access to this drive, you can protect your data from everyone except your network supervisor—who has god-like rights to see and change anything.

As a network supervisor, rather than a user, the importance of security is to prevent unauthorized copying and make sure viruses are not spread around all the more easily. The surest way to prevent anyone copying important or company-sensitive information onto a floppy is to remove the floppy drives from everyone's PC. To go one step further, you could remove the hard disk and the floppy drive from every user's PC. The PC is booted up to run DOS using a ROM chip on the network adapter card. When the PC is first switched on, the ROM makes a call to the server and asks for the main DOS files to be downloaded. DOS is downloaded and, as far as the PC is concerned, it is running DOS from its local drive.

Although no use as a deterrent, your network software should include the ability to keep an audit trail—an excellent detective when tracing the cause of a mishap. As each user logs in and out, a record is kept of which workstation they logged in from and, if you specify this detail, which files were used.

Viruses can spread very quickly over a network, so precautions must be taken. The harshest is simply to keep the entire network as a separate autonomy, away from any links to the outside world. This means removing floppy drives from all PCs and cutting out any modem links. A more practical and socially acceptable method is to install virus-checking software such as products from McAfee, S&S, CheckIt LAN from Touchstone, or Intel's LANProtect as part of your network strategy.

Every time a user logs in, the virus checker will scan their local disk drives and the remote network drives. The virus scanner will then stay resident, taking around 10K of RAM and keep tabs on any unauthorized disk accesses that could be generated by a virus.

LICENCES

A problem that soon crops up with network installations is how to share information efficiently. If you install an application such as a wordprocessor onto a shared drive, anyone can run the program. It is also possible for several users to run the same program simultaneously. Of course, unless you have bought a multi-user license this is illegal. Unless otherwise specified, applications bought off-the-shelf are for a single user.

You are faced with a dilemma if you are installing a new network and want to keep the same software. If your office used 10 copies of a wordprocessor, you can upgrade your single-user licence for a fee (normally around half again of the original cost per user). Unfortunately, you are scrapping your original investment. There is little to be done about this unless your dealer is particularly generous. You can get around this by keeping your software installed on each separate PC and just sharing your data files over the network.

Installing multi-user software varies little from installing its single-user version. There are two ways of going about it; either install it on a central machine and every user runs the same, shared copy. Alternatively, install a single-user version on each machine and simply share the data files, as mentioned above. This latter move keeps the licensing simple if you already use the package in a stand-alone way, but means that you waste disk space on each PC.

The main advantage of special multi-user software is that it has been written to ensure that file sharing is carried out correctly—a major problem when sharing data files over a network. If one user opens a document to make a couple of changes to the text and then, before they have saved the changes, a second user opens the same document, there is going to be a problem. When the first person saves the changes, these will be overwritten when the second user saves their changes.

Multi-user applications, specifically written for a network environment, will try to get around this problem by alerting the second user to the fact that the document is already open, or even preventing them opening it at all.

PROTOCOLS

With the two network systems described above, the method of installing both software and hardware varies little for your users' PCs. The main difference comes in installing the server—we will deal with this later. The users' PCs are physically connected by cabling that completes an electronic circuit. Data to and from a PC is turned into signals and squirted along the cable. The signals are generated by adapter cards fitted into one of your PC's spare expansion slots. There are three main standards defining these signals: Ethernet (which includes many types of cabling), ARCnet, and Token Ring.

Ethernet

Ethernet dominates with over 60 per cent of the installed base. There are two types of Ethernet that use a bus and coaxial cabling. The first has a greater range and uses thick coax cable—hence Thick-Wire Ethernet or 'thick Ethernet'; the second uses thinner coax cable, is easier to handle, cheaper, but has a shorter range: it is called Thin-Wire Ethernet—often termed 'Cheapernet' or 'Thin Ethernet'. The IEEE name for it is 10Base-2. The cable consists of a central, solid, copper core surrounded by insulating a layer of plastic which is then covered in a third layer of metal mesh. The whole is wrapped in a plastic sheath. The central copper core makes this type of cable susceptible to being bent to extreme angles. A chair leg or sudden bend in the cable can often snap or, worse, crack this core (Fig. 1.6).

If the core is snapped, nothing works. If it is cracked the fault is intermittent and can be a pain to find. The length of cable ends with a BNC plug. The adapter card fitted to each PC will have one BNC socket sticking out. A T-piece is fitted to this

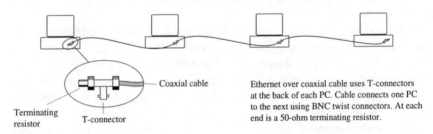

Coaxial cable

Terminating resistor

T-connector

Ethernet over coaxial cable uses T-connectors at the back of each PC. Cable connects one PC to the next using BNC twist connectors. At each end is a 50-ohm terminating resistor.

Figure 1.6   Standard Ethernet

and the cable from the previous workstation plugs in one side of the T-piece, with a second cable going off to the next PC in line (see Fig. 1.6). Make sure that you use reinforced T-pieces with an additional metal band around the centre. If you do not, this could lead to flexing inside the connector resulting ultimately in either cracks or a snapped conductor within the T-piece.

Ethernet's wiring scheme is very straightforward. A single cable links each of the PCs in daisy-chain fashion. At the extreme ends of the cable, a terminator is fitted. This is simply a 50-ohm resistor built into a BNC plug, but without them, you will get nothing.

Thin coaxial Ethernet cabling can be bought in pre-made lengths with BNC sockets already attached, normally in 1, 3, or 5 m lengths. If you are planning to install more than 10 users, you will find it cheaper and more flexible to build your own cables. A stripping tool is used to cut away the coaxial cable's insulating layers and the BNC connector can then be fixed using a crimping tool. Solder joints should be avoided—they can crack or oxidize with time which could lead to faults.

At the back of the Ethernet adapter cards you will often notice a 15-pin connector. This is for a Thick Ethernet cable connection—rather similar to laying heavy hosepipe around your office. It is good for installations with long distances between nodes but often proves too expensive and intrusive compared to Thin Ethernet.

The last type of Ethernet connector, 10Base-T, is the newest and most convenient to use. This uses thin cable (called unshielded twisted pair, UTP) which is similar to telephone cable with a pair of wires running inside rather than a single core as found in coax. Cables connect to network cards using RJ-45 connectors, which look like telephone sockets (Fig. 1.7). 10Base-T solves one of Ethernet's big disadvantages. To add a new PC into your Thin Ethernet system you need to disconnect one T-piece connector, and add a length of cable and another T-piece (Fig. 1.8). Breaking the circuit that makes up the bus of the network will crash the network—everyone does this the first time they install a new workstation. The repeated violence from users should ensure you do not do it again. Using RJ-45 connectors means you can plug in PCs without disruption. The reason is that 10Base-T uses a star topology. A central hub has a single cable running out to each workstation; if one workstation stops or breaks, it does not affect the others (this is rather similar to the Token Ring network in physical appearance in which a central concentrator houses the ring, and cables run out to each individual workstation).

If you are installing your network into a small office, without any heavy

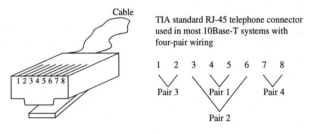

Figure 1.7   RJ-45 10Base-T connector

Figure 1.8   Ethernet BNC T-piece

industrial equipment which could cause electrical interference, then you should stick to Thin Ethernet cabling. It is the cheapest and most widely available system, so spares are easy to come by. If you have the luxury of specifying your office wiring from scratch, opt for floor boxes with BNC connectors fitted. Alternatively, route the Ethernet cable along the sides of walls and preferably under the carpet or through rubber floor ducts. Someone tripping up on a loose cable is not a good advertisement for a network.

Names and standards

Thick-Wire Ethernet	also called Thick Ethernet.
Thin-Wire Ethernet	also called Thin Ethernet or Cheapernet. IEEE name is 10Base-2 (10 MHz transmission over the baseband with approx. 200 m limit per segment).
Twisted-pair Ethernet	IEEE name is 10Base-T (10 MHz transmission over baseband using twisted-pair cable).

Token Ring Network

The second main choice you have when wiring up your network is called Token Ring. Just like Ethernet, it uses a ring of cable, but again it does not look like a ring. The trick that Token Ring uses is called a concentrator or multiple access unit (MAU). This is a box with 8 or 16 ports fitted. Inside the box is the ring of cable, connecting together, daisy-chain fashion, each of the 8 or 16 ports. Into each port plugs a cable that effectively stretches the ring to the PC (Fig. 1.9).

Ethernet, as we mentioned, suffers from a problem that its common bus is broken every time a workstation is fitted because one of the BNC connectors must be undone. Token Ring solves the problem using relays within the concentrator box. If there is no extension cable plugged into a port, a relay snaps shut and keeps the ring intact. When a cable is inserted, the relay opens and includes the cable as part of the ring. The relay will also close when the PC is switched off—otherwise the ring would, again, be broken. If you use Token Ring and sit near the concentrator, you might hear clicks. This is nothing to worry about—just the relays opening and closing as people switch their PCs on or off.

Token Ring cabling is more expensive than Ethernet, as are the connectors. It is

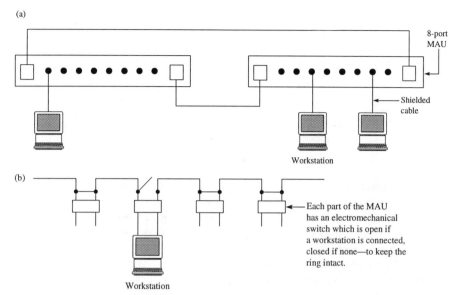

Figure 1.9 (a) Token Ring. Using shielded Token Ring cable allows a maximum of 260 workstations or up to 12 MAUs to be connected. (b) How a MAU works.

usual to buy the cable ready made with connectors fitted, simply because there are nine wires within the cabling to solder to the connector at each end. Token Ring cabling is, however, far more robust than Ethernet and is not as likely to crack or snap.

Token Ring adapter cards fit into a free expansion socket in your PC and connect to the network through a 9-pin D-connector. A new cabling alternative if you have set your heart on Token Ring is UTP. Just like 10Base-T for Ethernet, UTP uses telephone cabling and telephone sockets for a cheaper solution that is less obvious and disruptive as you rewire your office. The one disadvantage of UTP is that you will need an adapter between the card's 9-pin D-connector and the telephone socket—these cost an additional £90–150, considerably pushing up the total price per workstation.

ADAPTER CARDS

The missing link between your PC and the cable is a network adapter. There are two types of network adapter—internal or external. External adapters plug into the parallel port of PC and are limited by the parallel port's throughput—generally they are around 30 per cent slower than an internal adapter. An alternative to an external adapter that is now gaining popularity with many laptop vendors is a PCMCIA adapter. PCMCIA adapters are roughly the size of a credit card, several millimetres thick. The card has a connector at one end and plugs into an interface built into the laptop. PCMCIA slots can transfer data in 16-bit chunks, so performance is far better than with a parallel port adapter.

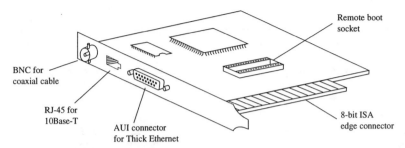

Figure 1.10   Standard 8-bit Ethernet card

Internal adapters, by comparison, fit into an expansion slot and, accordingly, can carry 8, 16 or 32 bits of data. If you expect a PC to be used for wordprocessing and other simple office tasks, you can get away with fitting an 8-bit adapter (Fig. 1.10). In theory, you should decide on the type of adapter according to the data throughput the adapter will have to handle—you can get a good idea of throughput by considering what the workstation will be used for.

Ethernet adapters for PCs are available from dozens of makers. The big names are Eagle, Intel, 3Com, and Hayes. Prices start at around £120 for an 8-bit card. A remote-boot ROM for these cards is an additional £45. Token Ring cards are available from Madge and IBM; Madge cards offer more features, but IBM cards can often be found at rock-bottom prices of £200.

PCs that will be used as front-ends for intensive database application, CAD workstations, or any application that warrants a fast 386-based PC should be fitted with a 16-bit adapter. This can transfer data between the cable and the PC's processor twice as fast as an 8-bit card. The most popular standard for 8-bit Ethernet cards is based on a Novell/Eagle design called the NE1000. The original from Eagle costs £245, while its 16-bit brother, the NE2000 costs accordingly more at £445. Compatible clone cards from other vendors are available for under £100.

If you are setting up a peer-to-peer network, for simple file sharing, then installing 8-bit cards on each of the PCs will not impair the performance. If one of the PCs in the network is being used as a print-server, and you do a lot of printing, then it would be sensible to boost its performance by fitting it with a 16-bit adapter.

Within a more complex installation with a central PC dedicated as a server, the policy for distributing adapters is different. The server should be fitted with the fastest adapter card you can afford. If it is a 386-based PC then the fastest adapter will be a 32-bit card. Powerful operating systems, including NetWare, Windows NT/AS, and VINES, can support more than one adapter in the server. By fitting two adapters, you are halving the load on each, effectively doubling the rate at which data is transferred around the network.

For EISA-bussed systems, 32-bit bus master cards allow the fastest data transfers from the system's RAM to cable. Eagle's NE3200 card costs £1150. If you are fitting Ethernet to Macintoshes and PS/2s, 3Com makes network cards for all three platforms.

A network card communicates with the PC using an area of memory and an interrupt. Whenever data has arrived over the network, the card sends an interrupt signal to the PC and normally stores the data at a particular location in the PC's memory. This simple method of communications runs into problems if you have any other cards fitted into your PC. Chief among the troublemakers are VGA and disk controller cards. To make sure that your network adapter does not clash, you will have to set the address and interrupts it uses. Older technology cards use little DIP switches to set these. Current technology provides automatic configuration or includes a utility program that allows you to examine the switch settings and change them under software control.

Installing the adapter cards into every user's PC is just a part of the total installation process. We have included the following checklists for the items you should have ready before you start the installation, either for a peer-to-peer network or a server-based system.

CHECKLIST

You will need the following for each workstation:

For Ethernet

1 Two lengths of coaxial cable, with a BNC connector at each end.
2 One T-piece.
3 One Ethernet network adapter card.
4 Software redirector supplied with network software.
5 Software driver for your particular adapter card.

In addition, you will need two terminators.

For Token Ring

1 One length of cable with MAU connection one end, 9-pin connector at the other.
2 One Token Ring network adapter card.
3 Software redirector supplied with network software.
4 Software driver for your particular adapter card.

In addition, you will need a concentrator (or MAU) box.

If you are planning a schedule for the installation, fitting the network adapter card into a PC will take approximately 30 minutes; installing the software will take a similar time. If you are setting up a peer-to-peer network, then the only other time considerations are cabling and setting up each user. A typical small, four-user LAN can be installed in around three hours.

For a network based around a central dedicated server PC, you will also need to install the new operating system onto the server. For NetWare, this will take between two and three hours for a newcomer. For LAN Manager, you must first install OS/2 (around 45 minutes) then LAN Manager itself—another 90 minutes. Novell has simplified installation considerably by supplying its top-of-the-range NetWare 4.0 product on a single CD-ROM. you will need a CD-ROM drive attached to your server, but installation is very quick.

WHEN IT ALL GOES WRONG

The last topic that must not be ignored is what to do when it all goes wrong. Users expect networks to go wrong, and when they do, you will be surrounded by people nodding sagely that this was anticipated.

The vulnerability of networks will soon make itself apparent. If you use a peer-to-peer network and the PC operating as print-server breaks down, no one can print; another PC would have to be redefined as print-server and the printer plugged in. It is worse with a central server; if the server goes wrong, no one can access any of the files stored on it.

To minimize accidental damage, such as a cleaner knocking it or switching it off by mistake, the server should be kept away from general office traffic—if possible, in a locked room. Because the server is going to be on 24 hours a day, the room should be kept cool and the power supply regulated.

Write up a record of your LAN's installation and keep the book safe. Include a drawing of the wiring route through the office. Follow this information with a checklist of exactly how each user's PC is setup, and what software you have loaded. Ideally, all PCs should be the same, with the same CONFIG.SYS and AUTOEXEC.BAT files. List the contents of each file.

Lastly, detail step-by-step instructions on how to reconfigure a PC to work correctly, what special driver software is needed and where it is kept. Link this with instructions about what to do if there is a power cut —typically how to restart the server. Everyone should be told that this book exists, and where it is kept. If you have an accident or are on holiday, then someone else will be able to keep the system going by following your step-by-step instructions.

Backup is often overlooked as a needless expense. But think pessimistically: if you lost all the data stored on the network, how long would it take someone to type it all back in again? Typically, this runs into years, which can be tens of thousands in salary. Save yourself the bother with a tape backup device, which costs around £400.

If you plan your needs, follow the instructions in the network manuals, and tackle each PC individually, preferably when there is no pressure—ideally over a weekend—then you will find installing a network is not difficult. Adding a backup device, writing a disaster recovery manual, and making sure that security is correctly setup will cut the impact of any future problems, whether malicious or not.

2
Effective Network Management—What You Can Gain

This guide is about effective network management. How to pick the correct equipment, and then ensure that its reliability and performance are at an optimum. With good network management, your network will become more productive and more reliable.

Reliability is particularly important for your users. They will grow to hate you and your network if it is always going wrong. Your goal, and this book will help, is to make your network more reliable. The most important step is to plan every change. If you implement a new piece of software or a special backup procedure, you must plan the operation and then document the changes. This might seem like a tedious chore if you have only got a half-dozen users, but you should still follow it through. Without good documentation, you will find yourself spending more time keeping the network running that improving the service to users.

For example, if you did not bother drawing a wiring diagram when you laid the LAN's cable, how can you hope to find a broken piece of coaxial if you cannot remember where the coaxial runs? But enough of the preaching, the real benefits of good network management will be a better network that works well and reliably.

Before you start changing any of your current equipment, or upgrading to a new version of the software, consider what you are likely to want from the LAN in a year's time. It is pointless buying a new hub without a network management agent built in (or that is upgradable) because in a year's time you will want to monitor the hub from your desk. Or worse, your company might grow and you will have four or five hubs and no effective management in place.

Be careful before you plunge into any new standard that has been developed. FDDI is the standard defining very high-speed networks running over fibre optic cables; it is very fast, but still very expensive. As an alternative, if a couple of users want more performance, why not fit a second adapter card into your server just for their segment? If your whole department is complaining, then installing FDDI as a backbone linking servers rather than individual workstations might be an answer (see Chapter 3 for more on FDDI).

Once the basic blocks of the network are in place and you have established a working, and reliable, backup procedure, then you can start experimenting with performance tricks. In this guide I will tell you what is worth spending your money on and what is not. There is little point in spending £1000 on a cacheing disk controller for your NetWare 3.12 server, since NetWare implements its own, very effective cache algorithm in software; in fact, you could actually slow down its operation. You would be wiser to spend the money on a second adapter card or more RAM.

If you plan ahead, you can soon pinpoint your system's bottlenecks and find the best way of removing them. With a LAN, remember that you will have to up the performance as new, more demanding software is developed or required by your increasingly sophisticated users. You will also have to add new users as your company grows—or connect to other computers. By bearing in mind the future expansion when you are choosing your basic equipment now, you can make your life easier.

FORWARD PLANNING

If you are currently choosing new hardware or software for your LAN, or are considering upgrading or expanding your existing network, you should take into consideration what your future needs will be. What is your company's likely growth and how should you spend your budgets?

Before you start buying any equipment, you should do a quick survey of your users. What sort of mix of applications do they currently run? Will you keep to this mix, or do you want to try and standardize on a suite of software? Will you be running Microsoft's Windows or OS/2 instead of plain MS-DOS? Does your company have to stick with a particular piece of custom-written software or can you pick and choose from standard off-the-shelf applications?

You should take into account how computer-literate your users are. Will they not only resent being provided with a fixed menu of applications, but do they also have the knowledge to circumvent this and install their own software?

Before you can install any software, you must first decide on the basic type of network architecture to install. There are two main choices: to use a dedicated PC as a central server or to spread the load equally over all the PCs within a peer-to-peer network.

3
Network Hardware

This chapter describes the methods of linking your computer to a LAN. We will cover in detail the different network interface adapters that fit in a PC or Macintosh and the types of cable that link them. There are a number of different signalling schemes that describe how data is sent over the cables—Ethernet, 10Base-T, Token Ring, ARCnet, and FDDI—and there is a lot of confusion about the compatibility and standards that should be used. We will also look at how to choose the best system for your installation, how to pick the right equipment, and how to cable up. Anticipating the worst, this chapter ends with a discussion of what could go wrong with each cabling system and how to go about avoiding and solving problems, together with a guide to test equipment.

NETWORK INTERFACE CARDS (NICs)

In order to connect your computer to a LAN, you need to install a network interface card (also called a network adapter). This card is normally plugged into a free expansion connector inside your PC or Mac. It takes the data from the computer's internal bus and converts it into standard packets of information that it then sends along the cable. These packets are defined by the signalling scheme; for example, a Token Ring card sends different types of packet and represents the data on the cable with different voltage levels to an Ethernet card. (We describe these signalling schemes later in this chapter.) The main function of a network card, then, is to take the data from the computer and add a header. This header contains: the address of the computer that the data is destined for, the sender's own address, and error-correcting data. It then sends this packet of data off along the cable.

When receiving data, the reverse happens. The network adapter looks at each packet and checks the destination address in the header. If it recognizes its own address, it strips out the data, checks it has no errors using the error-correcting data in the header, then signals to the CPU (using an interrupt) that there is data ready to be processed.

Before you select a network adapter, there are several things you should consider. The first is to decide on the signalling method you will use—you cannot connect a Token Ring and Ethernet card to the same piece of LAN cable. Further factors include the type of cable that will connect the LAN together, although this is influenced by the choice of signalling method, and the topology and layout of the network. Lastly, your choice of network card will be dictated by the type of computer you want to fit it into. PCs—i.e. IBM compatibles—have several different types of expansion connector (which are described in Chapter 5), some of which are compatible.

ISA Adapter Cards

Early PCs with an 8088 processor used an 8-bit bus as the expansion connector. Data travelled along in 8-bit parallel chunks. Adapter cards that fit into an 8-bit ISA connector are the cheapest available, and the slowest: data is passed between the processor and the network adapter card in 8-bit chunks, which is four times as slow as an expansion bus that sends data 32-bits at a time (such as EISA or MCA).

With the arrival of the 80286 processor fitted to AT-compatibles, the expansion connector had to be enlarged to carry the 16-bit wide data bus of the newer, more powerful processor. AT-compatibles were first fitted with a 16-bit ISA bus. This still accepts old 8-bit cards, but for higher performance, 16-bit NICs were designed that would transfer data in 16-bit wide chunks to the CPU. For all but the most basic of workstation users, 16-bit NICs should be used. The extra cost over 8-bit cards is minimal and the speed increase is between 30 and 80 per cent depending on the CPU and the application (Fig. 3.1).

If you want to make sure that there is no bottleneck between the main processor and the NIC, then you should fit an adapter card that can accept data in the same word size that the CPU is using. For example, PCs with a 32-bit processor like the 80386, 80486, or Pentium would ideally use a 32-bit expansion bus such as EISA or MCA. If your 386-powered PC has an ISA bus, then it is limited to 16-bit transfers, which will slow data throughput.

EISA and MCA expansion buses are designed for 32-bit, high throughput data transfers and are vital in a server or power-user's workstation. EISA has one major advantage over MCA: you can still plug your old ISA adapter cards into an EISA bus; MCA is totally backwards incompatible. MCA does, however, offer slightly better throughput (see Fig. 3.1).

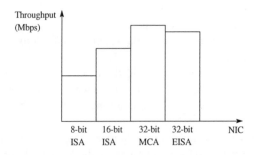

Figure 3.1   Graph of throughput vs NIC type

Improving still further on throughput, and designed to get rid of any lingering bottlenecks, is Local Bus. This offers even higher data throughput than EISA or MCA expansion buses, but is currently still hampered by a number of conflicting and proprietary standards. The aim of Local Bus is to allow high-performance expansion cards, such as fast network adapters, to talk directly to the computer's CPU. All other buses have layers of decoders and buffer chips between the adapter card and the CPU—which slows down data throughput.

Adapter I/O: How Data Is Transferred Between NICs and the CPU

Once data is received by the network card it is stored in memory before being dealt with by the central processor. There are four ways of transferring data from the adapter card to memory; you should be aware of them since they can affect performance and can cause problems with other cards in your PC, such as a scanner or SCSI adapter.

Shared memory

Adapters fitted with shared memory are one way of getting around the limitations of programmed I/O and direct access memory (DMA) data transfers. The network adapter card carries buffer memory that is accessible to the computer's processor. The processor can read or write data to the on-board shared buffer memory at full speed; high-speed RAM chips are used so that no wait states are required from the processor. Although the most expensive, it is the second fastest of the four techniques, with bus-mastering coming first, shared memory has one major drawback—memory conflicts.

A typical PC's memory map has little spare room. It is packed with the PC's BIOS, system RAM, and extended memory. The few gaps that are available are normally used by graphics adapters (VGA and S-VGA cards also have their own on-board memory). This makes it likely that your shared memory network card will conflict with a memory address used by some other device. You should always check a card with the application software you will be using before you buy a batch of adapters. If your PCs are packed with expansion cards, you might find that you have to disable your NIC's on-board shared memory in order to use the card at all, so losing the speed benefits of shared memory.

Programmed I/O

Adapters using programmed I/O offer an efficient way of transferring data if you are using newer PCs with at least an 80286 processor. With programmed I/O transfer, the adapter has an on-board processor which transfers data to a predefined area of the computer's system memory; the computer's processor does the same. Each time either processor has written new data to the area of memory, it signals to the other processor that data is available.

Many slower processors generate a wait state to carry out each read or write to the area of memory, slowing down the transfer speed. A second problem is that the older 8088- and 8086-based PCs cannot use programmed I/O because their instruction set does not contain the relevant instruction for this process: it is only included in 80286 processors and above. For PCs with a minimum of an 80286 processor, programmed I/O can be an efficient transfer mechanism.

Direct memory access (DMA)

Many of the network adapters on the market use DMA to transfer data between the card and the processor. The computer has a DMA controller which takes over the bus and directs data from the network card to an assigned area of system memory. The advantage is that the computer's processor is not involved in this data transfer and can carry out some other task, thereby increasing efficiency.

DMA's main disadvantage is down to historical reasons. The original PC/XT used a DMA controller that was clocked at 4.77 MHz, as a result, all DMA controllers still move data at the same rate to ensure backwards compatibility. With high-speed 50 MHz processors, operating 10 times faster than the DMA controller, this option suddenly looks an inefficient way of moving data if you are using a fast processor. For old PCs using a 8088 or 8086, this is an efficient data transfer method. For newer PCs with fast processors, there are more efficient methods.

Bus mastering

We have talked so far about the network interface card receiving data from the computer's processor or passing data to it. Each time there is a data transfer, the processor is interrupted and the processor has to do a lot of work just looking after the data transfer needs of the adapter card. If there is a lot of data movement, the adapter will be taking up most of the processor's time with requests for data or passing on received data. Unless you have a fast processor such as an 80386 or better, your users could notice quite a reduction in the speed of their applications.

The answer is to give the network interface card its own processor which can transfer data from the network adapter to the main system RAM without having to interrupt the central processor. These cards are called bus-master cards—they have the processing capability to manage the computer's bus by itself. However, only two of buses we have discussed can cope with bus-master cards: EISA and MCA.

WHICH ADAPTER IS RIGHT FOR THE JOB?

There is little point fitting a 32-bit bus-master NIC into a workstation that is used for wordprocessing. The user will notice almost no difference and there will be no benefit to the rest of the LAN.

To improve your performance in one move, you should fit the highest performance NIC into your server. In a server-based LAN, the central server has the highest throughput of data—every user's data passes through its NIC—so a network card that can transfer data to and from the server's processor and disk as efficiently as possibly will benefit every user. Even with a small network of four users, you should fit a 16-bit adapter. For a dozen users, a 32-bit adapter in an EISA or MCA bus is a minimum requirement, and for larger networks or high performance, fit a 32-bit bus-master card.

In a peer-to-peer network, you should fit higher performance (with wider bus width) adapters into the PCs that carry the most traffic—typically the print server or the PC used to store most shared files.

DRIVING THE ADAPTER

Even with the network card fitted, you cannot access the LAN until you install the driver software on the workstation and server. Each maker of NICs will, unless they are manufacturing a clone card, specify its own set of commands used to control the card. This can cause you problems if you do not check on the availability of drivers for your particular card running different operating systems.

There are two main sections to the software you will need before your local operating system will talk to the LAN. The first is the driver, which is specific to the NIC. The second is the redirector, which intercepts commands typed in by the user or sent by an application and meant for the network, such as changing to a remote drive letter, and redirects them over the LAN (Fig. 3.2).

Under the Novell operating systems, the network card needs a special Novell driver file. If you use the traditional Novell way of working, then this driver is linked with Novell's IPX (internetwork packet exchange) file to create a resident program that acts as a bridge between the NIC and the Novell redirector. Be aware

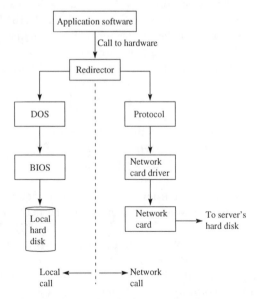

Figure 3.2 The route through a workstation's network software

that you will need different Novell drivers for each version of NetWare. This type of redirector is no longer recommended by Novell—it has developed ODI (open data-link interface) drivers as a replacement.

In order to avoid the bother of joining two files to create a workstation-specific network driver, Novell developed ODI. An ODI-compliant driver is supplied by the manufacturer of the card, and Novell supplies a redirector and protocol stack that can talk to the card via the standard ODI interface. If you are using ODI drivers, the ODI driver is a separate EXE file that must be loaded first, followed by the IPXODI resident protocol stack.

If you are fitting the NIC to a NetWare server, the drivers it requires will be different from those used in a workstation. Older workstation drivers normally have the extension OBJ, newer drivers conform to the ODI standard described above. Drivers for a server have an extension of LAN; the two cannot normally be mixed.

Microsoft's NT/AS and its protocol stack talks to the hardware through an NDIS driver that is rather similar to ODI in theory. The adapter manufacturer supplies an NDIS-compatible driver and the redirector talks directly to this. Windows NT/AS servers can use the same NDIS-compatible driver files that are used on a workstation, but check if you are using NT/AS for a Unix (LMX) server to make sure that it will run with NDIS drivers or if specific LMX drivers are required.

Both Microsoft and Novell have developed new software drivers that allow several protocol stacks to be loaded. The driver provides a standard interface to the adapter's hardware and the protocol defines the way the data appears on the cable. Microsoft's DPA (demand protocol architecture) allows two protocol stacks to be loaded at once—letting your PC talk to both a NetWare server using the standard IPX protocol and to a NT/AS server using its NetBEIU protocol. Novell's rival driver, ODI, allows several protocols to be loaded at once—including TCP/IP to connect to Unix servers and mainframes, as well as IPX and NetBEIU.

In many cases, especially for the most popular cards, the network operating system will supply drivers with the software. Drivers for Novell's NE1000, NE2000, and NE32000 range of NICs are normally supplied with most operating systems. If you are buying a new NIC or one from a smaller manufacturer, make sure that it can supply standard drivers for your network operating system software.

If you are worried about incompatibilities, stick to big name manufacturers such as 3Com, Intel, or Eagle, or use cards that are clones of industry standard cards. Almost all software will drive a Novell NE1000, NE2000, or 3Com EtherLink card, so you should have few compatibility problems if you use a clone of one of these adapters.

Whatever type of driver you are using, or the protocol it requires, you will need a NIC driver for each workstation and server within the network. Drivers for a workstation are either loaded in as device drivers in the CONFIG.SYS file or loaded by running an EXE file. Whichever method, the driver stays resident until the PC is reset—thus taking up RAM.

In some operating systems, the driver on each workstation can take upto 120K of system RAM so it is worth trying to minimize this by loading the driver into extended memory or removing some options—such as NetBIOS support under

NetWare. (We deal with this topic more fully in Chapter 5.) If you are running MS-DOS 5 or above, or using a memory manager on a 80386-based PC, you can load almost all the network software into high memory, keeping the base 640K area free for applications.

ADAPTER INTERRUPTS AND MEMORY LOCATIONS

The driver software supplied with the network adapter will need to know how to communicate with the NIC before any part can work. You will normally have to specify the interrupt the NIC responds to, its buffer memory location, and, depending on the method of data transfer (discussed earlier in this chapter), the DMA address it uses. PCs have a limited number of interrupts, expansion slots, DMA addresses, and free memory locations so it is very likely you will have to change the factory settings on the NIC to avoid clashes with other adapters fitted in your PC (Table 3.1). If you install an adapter into an EISA or MCA slot, you can set these details using your PC's setup software.

To make sure you avoid running into problems with adapters that use the same address space or interrupt as another card, record how each PC is configured. If possible, configure each PC the same way; it will make your life as a support engineer far easier. You might find it useful to stick a label inside the PC's case and write on it the interrupt and memory settings of each new card as you install them. This way, you will instantly spot any potential conflicts.

The interrupt and memory settings of network cards are changeable, but are set

Table 3.1 Table of interrupts

Device	IRQ
IRQ timer	0
Keyboard	1
IRQ cascade	2
COM1	4
COM2	3
COM3	4
COM4	3
LPT1	7
LPT2	5
Floppy disk	6
Real-time clock	8
IRQ cascade	9
Maths coprocessor	13
AT hard disk	14

to standard defaults by the factory. In almost all cases, these defaults will work in without a problem, and it is best to try and stick to the factory defaults. If you do encounter problems, the manual normally lists a couple of alternative settings. (We also cover specific problems of each signalling method later in this chapter.)

SETTING UP YOUR NETWORK ADAPTER

Older network cards designed for ISA expansion connectors tend to use jumpers to set the interrupt and address used. You can change the setting by moving the small jumper from one pair of pins to another—see your manual for details. Alternatively, some cards use DIP (dual inline) switch banks. The settings are changed by flicking the miniature switches on or off.

Newer ISA cards and those for EISA or MCA systems use software setup. This simplifies installation and troubleshooting enormously; plug the card in, refit the computer's case, and run the install program. You can set the interrupts from a menu of choices or, if the software is sophisticated enough, it will scan your PC and suggest the best settings that do not conflict with any other adapters it detects.

Almost all network adapters now come with a default setting of interrupt 5. In a current, standard PC, INT5 is nominally assigned to servicing the second parallel port, LPT2. However, since few computers have two parallel ports, it is safe to use INT5 for a network card. One warning: this will work fine in most AT-machines, but will not work if you are planning to fit the adapter into an older XT (using the 8088 CPU)—it will clash with the hard disk controller.

- In some computers, if you set the NIC to INT5, the PC's BIOS will assume that a second parallel port has been fitted. It can then take matters into its own hands and try and poll what it thinks is a printer port—wrecking printing operations and stopping the network card's activity. If you cannot disable this feature of the BIOS using the PC's setup utility, then the only solution is to use a different interrupt setting.

There are some other interrupts that you should watch out for. Be careful if you are using INT2. In an AT-bus machine, this triggers the high interrupt controller. The PC knows that an interrupt within the high range has called for action and switches control to the high interrupt controller. Unfortunately, if it was the NIC that signalled for attention, its cries will have been ignored as the high interrupt controller tries to work out which of its peripherals generated the interrupt.

You will normally also have to set a default I/O address for the card and, if it is fitted with one, the address space of the remote-boot ROM. Network cards normally come with an I/O address set somewhere within the range 2E0h to 380h. This memory area is out of the way of the address areas used by a standard keyboard and hard disk, but you must make sure that your NIC does not clash with the secondary serial or parallel ports. COM2 is located at 2F8h to 2FFh. 300h is normally free to be used by a network adapter, as is the memory block above 380h. LPT1 takes the range of memory space just preceding this: from 378h to 37Fh.

If your network adapter is one of the few that uses a DMA channel, you will also have to set the DMA channel during installation. According to Novell, a workstation's DMA channels 1 and 3 are normally reserved for network cards. Channel 1 is often used for SDLC cards (used to connect a PC to a mainframe) and so this channel can normally be used for your NIC. It is worth bearing in mind that channel 0 is reserved for memory refresh in an XT, channel 3 is reserved for the hard disk controller in an XT, and floppy drives use channel 2.

Once you have made the changes to the hardware, you must install the driver software. The driver software has to be told the interrupt and memory location that the card is using, or it will not be able to communicate with the card. This is sometimes done by using command-line switches. Novell, with the introduction of its ODI drivers, requires the settings to be in a text file called NET.CFG (which can be edited using EDLIN or any DOS editor). The driver software looks in NET.CFG when it is loading.

EXTERNAL ADAPTERS

Laptop and notebook owners have a tougher time getting onto a network. Laptop computers rarely have space within the case to fit a normal, full size NIC. Some companies, such as Digital, do offer an internal network adapter option, but most laptop users have to turn to an external adapter.

External adapters normally connect to the PC's parallel port (although some Toshiba and Compaq machines have a proprietary bus interface connector which is used by some manufacturers). Xircom and D-Link both produce external Ethernet, Token Ring, and 10Base-T adapters. These devices are the size of a pack of playing cards and normally require a mains adapter lead as well as the network connection.

Normally, a parallel port is a one-way device, capable of sending data, but not usually accustomed to receiving it. To work as a network adapter, the manufacturers supply driver software that reconfigures the parallel port to allow a two-way data flow.

External adapters are unusual enough in design and software driver requirements not to conform with standard *de facto* network adapters, such as Novell's NE1000. This means that you must be sure the adapter is supplied with the drivers you need for your network.

If you are currently shopping for an external network adapter, check the specification of the laptop it will eventually connect to. If the laptop uses enhanced parallel port (EPP) technology, then make sure your external adapter does to. EPP was developed by Zenith Corp. and Xircom Corp. as a means of relieving one of the major drawbacks of parallel port adapters—their low throughput.

A standard parallel port is only capable of transferring data at between 2.4 and 4 Kbps. This has never been a problem when the parallel port was used only for printers, but it drags down performance when connected to a network that is capable of 10 or 16 Mbps. When two EPP capable ports are connected, they can boost throughput up to 16 Mbps.

PCMCIA Adapters

PCMCIA is a technology that was defined in the late 1980s, but has taken many years to bring products to market. PCMCIA defines a peripheral that is the size of a fat credit card which carries a 68-pin connector at one end. The card is slipped into a PCMCIA slot in your PC and acts as a normal peripheral. Originally developed to house memory and software, PCMCIA has now developed to include miniaturized modems, network adapters, and hard disk controllers into its credit card-sized confines.

It is no longer rare to see a laptop computer with PCMCIA slots and the importance of PCMCIA to laptop users will grow. PCMCIA network adapters, such as the DE650 produced by D-Link, pack all the control logic into the main card, with a media coupler (a BNC plug or RJ-45 plug for 10Base-T) attached by a short piece of cable. Configuration and setup is automatic and the benefits considerable. When you leave the office, you do not have to leave your expensive external network adapter lying on your desk, instead you leave just the media coupler. The expensive controller is snug in the PCMCIA slot.

REMOTE-BOOT ROMs

One option that is standard on almost all network cards (the exceptions being pocket and PCMCIA adapters) is an empty chip socket ready to accept a remote-boot ROM. This ROM, bought separately but from the same vendor as the card, forces a PC to look at the network for its DOS startup files. Instead of reading system files from a floppy or hard disk, a workstation with a remote-boot ROM will download a disk image of a system disk from the network server. This means the workstation needs neither floppy nor hard disks—which cuts out a possible security risk and saves money. Buying and fitting a remote-boot ROM does not guarantee that everything will work—the network operating system must also be able to support boot ROMs. The bigger network operating systems, such as NetWare, NT/AS, and VINES do, but only a few peer-to-peer network systems support boot ROMs.

CONNECTORS

When choosing a network card, you will obviously choose one that has the correct connector for your wiring scheme. However, most network cards have two or more connectors—and these can be important if you want to future-proof your investment.

Standard Thin Ethernet uses a BNC connector on the NIC to connect its thin-coaxial cable. 10Base-T uses telephone-style RJ-45 plugs with a similar socket on the NIC. Lastly, your Ethernet NIC might carry a 9-pin D-connector. This is an attachment unit interface (AUI) port used originally for Thick Ethernet connections. An AUI port also allows you to fit a transceiver device. If your NIC is fitted with a BNC and AUI port and you change your wiring to 10Base-T or fibre, you can still use the same NIC by attaching a suitable transceiver to the AUI port.

CHECKLIST TO CONSIDER WHEN BUYING A NETWORK ADAPTER

- Is the NIC for a workstation or server?
- What bus architecture does your PC use (8-bit ISA, 16-bit ISA, EISA, MCA)?
- If the NIC is for an EISA or MCA-bus server: (i) try and buy a 32-bit card (EISA or MCA), (ii) find a NIC that will do bus mastering, (iii) check that it comes with drivers for your network, (iv) check it has the correct connector for your LAN.
- If the NIC is for a workstation:
  —You will save time if it is software configurable.
  —If it is Token Ring, check it supports 4 and 16 Mbps.
  —Does it come with the correct drivers for your network operating system?
  —If you want a secure LAN, are remote-boot ROMs available?

ETHERNET

The Ethernet standard you are most likely to come across is Thin-Wire Ethernet, which uses thin coaxial cable and has a limited range. Thick-Wire Ethernet uses thicker coaxial cables—it is dealt with later in this section.

Thin-Wire Ethernet or Cheapernet (officially called 10Base-2) uses a bus-topology implemented using coaxial cable with BNC connectors to connect the stations to the main bus.

A new derivative of Ethernet is called 10Base-T; this uses cable with a pair of conductors running inside. The connectors are RJ-45 telephone-style connectors and the cable is thin and flexible. 10Base-T uses a central hub from which a cable runs to each workstation, so it has a star topology compared to the bus topology of Thin-Wire Ethernet.

The Ethernet Specification

Ethernet is a standard that allows several stations to share a common bus medium. It uses carrier sense multiple access with collision detection (CSMA/CD) as its media access method.

The previous paragraph describes the theory behind Ethernet, but is a little dry. In reality, this means that an Ethernet network cable has a definite beginning and end (unlike a Token Ring network, which is a ring). The CSMA/CD describes how data is put onto the cable by the network card. As the acronym describes, the card

Figure 3.3   A standard Ethernet packet

picks up the signal carrier (a constant, high-frequency signal), when it cannot see any other data on the carrier—i.e. there is a quiet period—the network card sends its message in serial form, one bit at a time. If two stations try to send at the same time, a collision of data occurs. Both stations back off for a short time then start the process again, waiting for a quiet period.

Each network card sends its data within a standard packet format. This packet includes six fields that carry a destination address, a source address, the data itself, and error-checking information. The main packet can be variable length between 72 and 1526 bytes (Fig. 3.3).

Every Ethernet network adapter has a unique address hardwired into it by the manufacturer. This 48-bit address is used by the NIC to work out if it is supposed to read a particular packet of data on the bus.

Ethernet's Speed

The IEEE definition covers a range of transmission speeds from 1 to 20 Mbps in the anticipation of different cables and transmission medium. Standard Thick- and Thin-Wire Ethernet use a transmission carrier rate of 10 Mbps.

The Ethernet CSMA/CD method of putting data onto the cable usually provides the fastest throughput compared to other signalling methods. In principle, any workstation can access the cable immediately and send data without delay. If the network traffic is not heavy (less than 60 per cent) then collisions are unlikely to occur and the network will operate efficiently at high speed. As traffic increases, Ethernet's effective throughput quickly drops as stations have to wait after collisions. If very heavy traffic is expected, you could improve throughput using a Token Ring network which has a lower transmission efficiency, but maintains it almost constantly regardless of load.

Ethernet Cable

Many Ethernet cards will work with either Thin- or Thick-Wire Ethernet cable. The trend is towards including an RJ-45 connector on the adapter to connect to 10Base-T twisted-pair wiring (this is covered in the following section on 10Base-T). The most popular cable used for Ethernet is thin coaxial cable. This looks like the cable used between your television and the aerial, but it is of a higher grade.

Coaxial cable is made up of concentric layers. A copper core, twisted strands in a thin cable and a solid core in Thick Ethernet cable. The central core is surrounded by a plastic insulating layer around which is a woven copper braid or metal foil. Covering this is the final, outside insulating layer made of tough plastic. The two conducting layers, the central core and the braid, have the same axis,

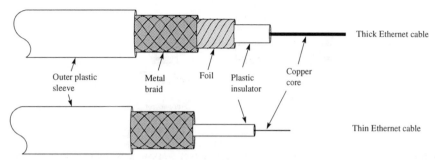

Outer plastic sleeve Metal braid Foil Plastic insulator Copper core Thick Ethernet cable Thin Ethernet cable

Figure 3.4   A comparison of Thick and Thin Ethernet cable

hence the cable's name. Thin Ethernet cable is around 5 mm in diameter, while Thick Ethernet cable is between 10 and 15 mm thick (Fig. 3.4).

Coaxial cable is popular for all sorts of applications, so make sure that you have the correct grade of cable. Thin coax cable for Ethernet should be marked as grade RG-58, while coax for ARCnet installations is marked as grade RG-62. Do not use television coax cable as a replacement.

Thick-Wire Ethernet cable is expensive, heavy, and difficult to bend, which makes it hard to route it around corners to a desk. It is, in its favour, very rugged and offers excellent protection against interference from other electrical devices which might cause voltage spikes in thinner, less shielded cable. It is also capable of supporting greater distances between repeaters (500 m).

Thin-Wire Ethernet cable is cheaper, lighter and easier to handle than Thick Ethernet cable. It is less prone to electrical spikes than twisted pair cable, but is not as good as thick coaxial cable. It is not capable of supporting as long spans between repeaters or stations as is thick cable (recommended maximum of 185 m).

Ethernet connectors

A typical LAN in an office is wired up using Cheapernet, i.e. thin coaxial cable running daisy-chain style between each computer. In keeping with the definition of Ethernet, which requires bus-topology cabling, the daisy-chain is the bus and each computer taps into the bus.

Thin coaxial cable connects to Ethernet cards using BNC connectors. These carry a gold-plated central connector protected by a solid case with a locking ring. The method of implementing this wiring scheme is as follows (see also Fig. 3.5):

- A separate T-connector (with one BNC socket, two plugs) is connected to each network adapter's BNC plug.
- A length of coaxial cable, with BNC sockets at each end, is connected between each network adapter, daisy-chain fashion.
- The T-connectors of the first and last PC in line have only one cable attached, and a terminator must be fitted.
- For example, if you are installing a three-user network, you will need three T-connectors, two cables, and two terminators.

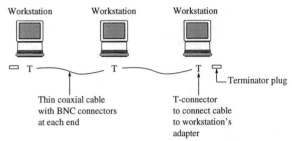

Figure 3.5   Requirements for cabling three Ethernet workstations: two termulator plugs, two lengths of coaxial cable and three T-connectors

Making your own cables

Coaxial cable is available either in a reel or pre-manufactured to lengths (normally 1, 3 and 5 m lengths). Pre-made lengths of cable already have BNC connectors fitted on each end, which accounts for the extra you have to pay.

If you are installing a small network, you will probably find it simpler to use pre-cut lengths of cable with connectors already fitted. If you are installing lots of computers or are running long cables, you will probably find it cheaper and more convenient to cut your own cable lengths and fit your own connectors. This process only takes a couple of minutes for each cable, and will save you money.

There are two methods of fitting BNC connectors, one is to use a solder join, the second is to use a crimp join. Solder joins last longer, but you have to be sure that the solder join is perfect otherwise you will find intermittent faults appearing. A second problem with solder joins is that if the connector is knocked, say if a PC is pushed back against a wall, the solder could crack—again leading to intermittent faults which can prove very difficult to trace.

Crimping is the simplest way of attaching BNC plugs to coax cable. You need a special crimping tool, which looks like a pair of pliers, together with a coax wire-stripper and a supply of crimp BNC connectors. Good crimping tools and silver-plated BNC-connectors (avoid unplated connectors) cost extra, but it is better to spend and be sure you have made a good cable than have another element that could bring your network down.

T-Connectors and terminators

T-Connectors attach to the BNC plug on the back of your network card and provide two BNC connectors. Onto these two connectors join the cables that link this computer to those on either side in the chain. You should not skimp when spending on T-connectors; if they are poorly made or unplated you cannot trust them to make a good, secure connection.

You might think that there is little to choose among T-connectors—you would be wrong! Normally, their shape is like a T, but this can sometimes be inconvenient depending how close your cables are to a wall or other obstacle. T-connectors are available that look more like an L with the coax cables attaching vertically.

The join between the cable and T-connector is going to be under a lot of stress:

the weight of the cable is normally supported by this small area. If possible, try and tape a small section of cable either side of the T-Connector to relieve the strain on the crimped join.

Terminators are used to complete the circuit between the central core and the outer copper braid within a coax cable. They are BNC plugs with a 50-ohm resistor built in. You will need two per Ethernet LAN; without them, the network will not work. With the wrong sort of resistor, signal reflections will be propagated and wreck the carrier signal.

Ethernet Topology

Ethernet was originally specified using a common bus transmission topology, but in practice its topology can be arranged either as a bus or a star (as in 10Base-T). It is most commonly arranged in a bus topology with the cable linking computers, daisy-chain fashion.

Thick-Wire Ethernet topology

Standard Ethernet cable is thick coax. Computers connect to this wiring system via transceivers. The main cable is cut where you want to add a workstation, and a transceiver plugged in. From the transceiver, a thin AUI cable runs to the 9-pin D-connector on an Ethernet card in the workstation. The usual scenario for this type of wiring is to hide the thick coax cable in a wall or in ducts with the transceiver as the access point. At the two ends of the thick Ethernet cable you need to fit a terminator box (Fig. 3.6).

The thick coax cable has marks every 2.5 m to indicate where a transceiver can be inserted. This backbone cable has a maximum length of 500 m. If you want to extend it beyond this length, you should use a repeater. The AUI cable that runs between the transceiver and the workstation is limited to 15 m.

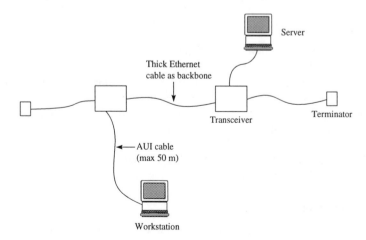

Figure 3.6 Typical Thick Ethernet installation

Thin-Wire Ethernet topology

Thin coaxial is easier to handle than thick coax, so it can be extended right to the desktop without the need for transceivers. Each computer in the LAN has a T-connector connected to the BNC plug on its Ethernet card. This T-connector has two cables plugged, forming a daisy-chain link between the workstation and its two adjacent neighbours. At the two ends of the physical cable you need to fit a terminator plug (Fig. 3.7).

If you want to add a new workstation to the LAN, you need to add two lengths of coax. To do this, you need to break the daisy-chain, which breaks the LAN and could crash your server or workstations (depending how they are configured). Novell's NetWare 3.12 is tolerant of a break if it is no longer than a few seconds. Microsoft's NT/AS is better: it will keep persistent connections and try to reconnect workstations if it finds they are no longer responding. If you break the bus for too long, the software running on the workstation will time out waiting for a signal from the server and you will have to reset each PC.

- When adding a workstation, try and do it out of normal office hours or, if that is impossible, gather all the connectors you need and do it as quickly as possible.

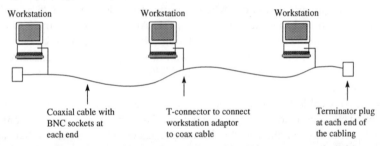

Figure 3.7   Requirements for coaxial cabling of an Ethernet network (with a maximum recommended segment length of 200 m

What can go wrong?

Cheapernet uses thin coax in a bus configuration, as we have just described. If a break occurs anywhere on the bus the connection to all the workstations will be severed. For this reason, you should be careful where and how you cable up. Avoid leaving coils of coax on the floor—someone could trip up and wrench one of the connections. Worse, a chair or desk on a cable could fracture the central core causing an intermittent fault that is hard to trace.

- If nothing works, are you sure that you fitted both terminator plugs to the last T-connectors at each end of the chain?

When it goes wrong

At the end of this chapter, we look at the testing tools that you should buy or hire when installing a large network—you will save time finding cabling faults if you have the right tools. If you are installing Thin and Thick Ethernet cabling, described above, there are a few guidelines you should stick to.

To run over the basics for Thin Ethernet, or Cheapernet, again. Each workstation is connected to the cable using a T-connector that twists onto the BNC plug on the back of the network adapter. The thin coaxial cable runs between each T-connector. This leaves two unconnected ends. You must fit a 50-ohm terminating resistor plug to each end of the network.

Try and avoid running the coax cable near to any heavy machinery that could cause electrical noise (such as a lift, generator, or motor). If you cannot, it is worth ensuring you have got a good ground connection by running a piece of wire between the T-connectors and a ground connector.

If nothing works, check the terminating resistors. Does the cable form one long 'bus', connecting each workstation in a daisy-chain fashion—it should. Make sure the cable is not running under any heavy desks or chairs, which could crack or break the copper core (causing intermittent errors that are difficult to trace). Make sure that any bends in the cable are not too severe—the tightest recommended corner is a 5 cm radius bend in the cable; any tighter and you could crack the cable's copper core.

Make sure you have the correct grade of cable. Thin Ethernet uses RG-58-type coaxial cable that has a 50-ohm impedence and is $\frac{3}{16}$ in. in diameter. Do not use bits of old television or 3270 workstation coax cable; you could crash the network or cause intermittent errors.

If you are making your own cable segments, you will find it easier to get a more reliable joint from twist-on crimp BNC connectors rather than solder joints. Solder joints, if made properly, are excellent, but if not are prone to brittle connections that could cause intermittent errors.

If you do get faults, you will find a time domain reflectometer (TDR) the best tool. It will pinpoint the location of a cracked cable or connector fault. It will also help you check you are not running too close to the maximum recommended length for an Ethernet system (the maximum segment length is 185 m).

10Base-T

The previous section dealt with Ethernet over coaxial cable. This is how it is most often used. In 1990, the IEEE defined a new standard that allowed Ethernet-type signals to run over UTP cabling instead of the original coax cable. The 10Base-T standard defines a signalling speed of 10 Mbps (the same as standard Ethernet) using a baseband signalling scheme over twisted-pair cabling. The big difference is in the topology: Thin-Wire Ethernet uses a bus topology; 10Base-T uses a physical star topology (Fig. 3.8).

10Base-T uses the same signalling technique as standard Ethernet, CSMA/CD, and runs at the same speed of 10 Mbps. It differs in cable; two thin wires are lightly twisted to give a degree of protection against electrical interference. The connectors are, in keeping with the telephone-style wiring, modular phone plugs that are easy to snap in and out.

The main claimed benefit of 10Base-T is that it uses twisted-pair wiring, the same as is already installed into many offices to support the phone system. In

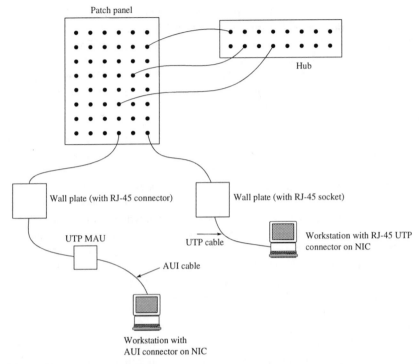

Figure 3.8   A Typical 10Base-T network showing one workstation able to connect to UTP cable and a second requiring a MAU to convert to AUI thick cable

reality, this is a minor advantage, since the installed phone cable you might have is unlikely to be of the correct quality, unless it has been installed within the last couple of years. The two major points in favour of 10Base-T are the lower cost of the cable, and the reliability advantage of a star topology over the traditional Ethernet bus topology.

Unlike standard Ethernet in which one workstation is connected to its two neighbours, one cable runs to each workstation from a central hub. This makes it much easier to add, replace, or repair workstations since there is no chance of disrupting the network. As we will discuss in Chapter 10, a hub-based star topology can improve data security.

Most Ethernet adapter cards are now fitted with a BNC connector to accommodate the older Cheapernet cabling together with an RJ-45 modular phone-style socket for 10Base-T wiring. If your Ethernet card precedes this development, but has a 9-pin AUI connector (previously used for Thick Ethernet), you can attach a media filter to convert the AUI output to the levels of 10Base-T. (This device is sometimes called an unshielded twisted pair MAU.)

10Base-T cabling costs less when compared to standard Ethernet cable, but the length of cable you need is very likely to be greater. All cables run to the wiring closet or server room rather than just to the next computer. A second initial cost premium is the price of the hub.

Network management with 10Base-T

With the 10Base-T standard defined, any compatible equipment can be mixed or added to the network without worry. Any hub can be used and linked to any Ethernet card with a modular socket.

It soon becomes evident that the hub is vital to the reliable operation of the network. Because of its position as the centre of the star, the hub sees all network traffic. This puts it in an excellent position to oversee all network activity. By adding a processor to the hub, which can control each port to each computer, it becomes very easy to implement a powerful network management system. You should always try and stretch your budget to a hub with the capability to run a management agent. Normally, this would be an SNMP (simple networking management protocol) agent—avoid any proprietary management protocol standards.

Hubs take many different forms, from rack-mounted systems that offer excellent expansion capacity for large networks, to a card that fits inside the server. The latter, marketed by 3Com, provides an eight-port hub (which can be expanded) combined with a standard Ethernet card as one large expansion card. The actual physical RJ-45 connectors of the hub are situated outside the server and attached to the card using a wide ribbon cable.

What can go wrong?

The combination of 10Base-T and a high-end operating system like NetWare is tough to crash. You can often swap out hubs, boards, and single workstations without losing the logical connections—they reconnect when the device is plugged back in. However, it is not worth the risk of swapping out your equipment too often. Because of the star topology of 10Base-T, you can crash a workstation or pull its connector out without effecting the rest of the network. The problems start when your hub fails. Ideally, you should place your hub near to the server so that it can share the server's UPS. This will protect it from spikes and blackouts.

If just one or two workstations are not responding, check the status lights on the hub to see which workstations are dead, then look at the status lights on the transceivers or adapter cards fitted to the workstation. Many adapters and transceivers have status lights that indicate errors such as collisions, jabbers, or card failure. Before you turn to the cabling, make sure that the software has loaded correctly on the workstation—for NetWare that means that IPX and NETx both report that they have loaded correctly.

You should now start to suspect the cable, a bad hub, bridge, or router. Pull out your network wiring diagram and use COMCHECK (supplied free with NetWare) to see if the workstation is receiving any data at all from the server. You should now move to the wiring from server to workstation. There are simple twisted-pair wiring testers (at around £100) that will display if a length of cable is faulty. Unlike TDRs, these simple tools will not tell you where the fault lies. This means you will have to check each segment of cable right to the workstation. If your budget stretches to around £700, you should invest in a TDR that can work with both coax and twisted-pair cabling.

Lastly, make sure when adding new workstations or expanding your LAN that you are using the same standard of wiring connection. There are actually three standards that define how the RJ-45 plugs can be wired up, and mixing standards will cause you a lot of down time.

TOKEN RING

The Token Ring system you are most likely to meet is defined as IEEE 802.5—often called IBM's Token Ring. Token Ring adapters for PCs have only been available since around 1986; they offer advantages and disadvantages over other systems such as Ethernet. The main difference is that a logical Token Ring LAN is, essentially, a circular network around which a digital token circulates. Each adapter card plays an active part in the network and acts as a repeater to the signal, unlike the broadcast method used by Ethernet which is simply received by all adapters.

Thanks to the IEEE 802.5 standard, Token Ring can form part of an Open Systems network taking the place of, for example, Ethernet. Token Ring was originally specified as running at a speed of 4 Mbps over shielded cable. By 1989 high-speed versions of the adapter cards were available and running at 16 Mbps (and normally switchable back to the slower speed of 4 Mbps). Now, Token Ring can run at 16 Mbps over UTP cable. The future will see Token Ring running over optical fibre with a standard currently known as 802.5F.

How Token Ring Works

Token Ring could not be more different from Ethernet. A Token Ring network is arranged as a logical ring, while Ethernet workstations are daisy-chained together using a bus topology. To transmit, an Ethernet adapter blasts out its message; if it detects that another adapter is also trying to transmit, they both back off and try again (Fig. 3.9).

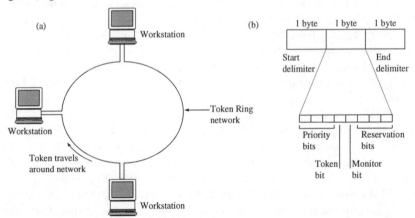

Figure 3.9 (a) A token travels around the Token Ring network; workstations can only transmit if they are holding the token. (b) Token structure made of 3 bytes of control data

Like a car driving around a race circuit, a digital token travels around a Token Ring LAN. If a workstation wants to transmit it must catch a ride with the token. First, the workstation waits until the token reaches it, then the adapter checks to see if the token is available to carry data. If it is, it appends its data onto the back of the token and changes a flag on the token to say it is busy. The token continues around the circuit now carrying a load. The data packet includes a destination address, the address of the sender, and the data itself.

When the token passes through the workstation adapter with the correct destination address, the data is copied off and the token is sent on around the circuit. The whole transaction is completed when the original sender receives the token back and removes its message. The token is now free to be used by another station. This may seem like a protracted and long-winded scheme but it has its advantages. The main one is that, although a 4 Mbps LAN sounds much slower than a 10 Mbps Ethernet network, Token Ring will maintain almost the same speed whatever the load and, in practice, Ethernet is not as fast. This ability to maintain a predictable response time is particularly important for real-time applications. In the case of 16 Mbps Token Ring, it is not unusual to find a benchtest being completed in one-third the time it takes a 10 Mbps Ethernet system.

The Token Ring Specification

Token Ring LANs were originally specified at a data rate of 4 Mbps; this data rate has been improved to the current standard of 16 Mbps. Your LAN can only operate at one speed or the other, and if you have got old adapters fitted, you are likely to be limited to the slower, 4 Mbps rate. New Token Ring adapter cards should be able to switch between either rate.

The token that travels the LAN is a 24-bit packet of data that carries a number of flag bits to indicate if it is currently carrying information. Unlike Ethernet, the ring tolopogy used by Token Ring means that all the token passes through each adapter card. This can cause problems if you want to add or remove a workstation; how can this be done without breaking the circuit? The answer lies in the physical wiring method used.

Despite using, in theory, a ring topology, Token Ring networks are normally wired in a physical star topology. A central wiring hub carries the logical ring and each workstation can be plugged into a spare port to extend the ring out. The trick to allow workstations to be inserted or removed without disrupting the ring is to use relays. Each port within the hub has a bypass relay fitted. If the workstation is unplugged, the bypass relay snaps shut and the ring remains complete. Wiring hubs are often called Multistation Access Units (MAUs)—their IBM brand name—not to be confused with Ethernet's Medium Attachment Unit.

By their nature, each Token Ring adapter has an active part to play; the signal passes through the adapter. If a computer is switched off, the adapter no longer works so, again, the relay in the hub snaps shut. If you sit near a Token Ring hub, you will hear the relays clicking open and shut as users switch their PCs on and off.

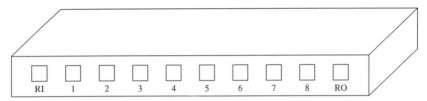

Figure 3.10   Token Ring 8-port MAU showing RI (ring in) and RO (ring out) sockets to daisy-chain multiple MAUs

Token Ring's great advantage, like 10Base-T and ARCnet, lies in its physical star topology: if one PC breaks down or a cable is damaged, just one single link is broken. In a bus-topology Thin-Ethernet network, the whole LAN would break down.

A typical wiring hub has eight ports with two additional ports labelled 'RI' (ring in) and 'RO' (ring out). These ports allow hubs to be daisy-chained together to extend the LAN (Fig. 3.10). By using media adapters or repeaters, it is also possible to extend a LAN's logical ring across different transmission media.

Token Ring Cable

The original specification for Token Ring, set down within IEEE 802.5 defined transmission speeds of 1, 4, and 16 Mbps. The 1 Mbps used UTP cable while the 4 and 16 Mbps systems used shielded twisted-pair (STP) cable. Until 1992, STP was the recommended cabling for a usual 4 or 16 Mbps installation. STP cable consists of two pairs of twisted wires covered by a metal foil shield.

It is not unnatural that the market wanted to wire Token Ring using the cheaper and more easily handled UTP cable. It is possible to use UTP by fitting a media filter to the 9-pin D-connector on the back of the computer's network adapter card. This can cause problems due to electrical interference and has proved difficult and sometimes unreliable in practice. The problem occurs because of signal distortion at high speed over UTP. In order to run at 16 Mbps over UTP, the token and bit signals have to be checked for stability and retimed to prevent distortion and jitter. Currently, two groups of manufacturers are disputing how this should be done. IBM claims it is better to put the retiming circuitry into the hub, while a rival group claim it should be built into the adapter. Until the IEEE has settled on one standard and properly defined it, you could risk losing part of your investment if you install 16 Mbps Token Ring on a UTP LAN.

Token Ring Connectors

IBM dominates the Token Ring market and so the cables and connectors you are most likely to come across are those from IBM. Typically, you would wire each adapter card to the hub (called MAU by IBM) using a cable around 7mm thick. One end carries a 9-pin D-plug to fit in the back of the adapter, the other a dual-gender plug that fits into any port in a MAU.

If you are wiring up a Token Ring network with IBM equipment, it is worth investing in the IBM 8228 Setup Aid—a small, battery-powered tester that plugs into a port in a MAU and checks that the bypass relays are working correctly.

Token Ring Wiring Hubs

In common with other physical star-wired LANs, Token Ring requires a central wiring hub. The hub offers an excellent place to locate network management hardware. This becomes particularly important due to one drawback of Token Ring. If one single adapter becomes faulty or unstable, it will corrupt the token and throw the whole ring's operation. To get around this, hubs from manufacturers such as 3Com and Synoptics Corp. are available that will monitor ports and workstations and report back to a central SNMP or similar terminal.

Counting the Cost of Token Ring

Token Ring is expensive to install. Compared to Cheapernet, there is the additional expense of a hub, and expensive pre-manufactured cable with equally expensive connectors. The network adapter cards have, until recently, been around twice the price of the cheapest Ethernet cards. (IBM has recently licensed its chip-set to other manufacturers so 3Com and Madge can now produce IBM-clone adapters at a more competitive price.)

In the defence of Token Ring, it will sustain a very predictable and regular throughput without any drop if more stations are added.

Token Ring is often described as the only way to connect PCs and LANs to a mainframe, which is untrue. In Chapter 12 I discuss how to connect an Ethernet LAN to a mainframe without a Token Ring card in sight.

ARCnet

If you want a cheap alternative to either Token Ring or Ethernet, ARCnet is a safe bet. ARCnet (the acronym ARC stands for Attached Resource Computing architecture) was developed by a gang of engineers from Datapoint Corp. ARCnet uses a transmission method similar to that of Token Ring, with 'transmission permission' messages controlling traffic and access to the medium.

The one thing that is holding back ARCnet is a lack of IEEE certification. If ARCnet was another IEEE standard, like Ethernet and Token Ring, it would be a serious challenge. As it stands, it is used mostly by small networks of fewer than 10 users. For them, it provides all the functions of its big brothers, but without the cost: ARCnet adapters are available from around £50 each.

How ARCnet Works

ARCnet sits somewhere between Ethernet and Token Ring when it comes to operation. ARCnet uses a broadcast-type logical bus in which all stations receive a transmission at approximately the same time. Coupled with this, the signalling method uses what can be loosely described as token-passing to moderate bus access. In a Token Ring LAN, a token passes around the LAN from one station to the next. In an ARCnet LAN, one station broadcasts the token to the others on the network.

This token, called a 'transmission permission' signal, is transmitted together with the station's unique ID number. Both Token Ring and Ethernet adapter cards carry an internationally unique ID number hardwired into the circuitry by the manufacturers. Numbers are assigned to manufacturers from a pool. ARCnet adapters carry no such number. Instead, the installer sets each adapter's ID using a bank of DIP switches on the card. ARCnet is limited to a maximum of 255 connected workstations, so each must be assigned an ID number between 1 and 255. Station address 0 is reserved and used when broadcasting. The adapter's ID number does not define its position in the LAN nor function—it is just an identificator.

When all the workstations are first switched on, each adapter broadcasts its ID number. The workstation with the lowest ID number becomes the controlling station. The controlling station moderates data transmission over the LAN. It sends out a transmission permission token to the first workstation which can then transmit any data waiting to be sent or keep silent. The controlling station then sends the token to the next workstation in turn.

If a new workstation is switched on, or another added to the network, all the workstations have to reconfigure to again check who has the lowest ID number and is therefore the controlling station. This RECON signal is generated by the new workstation that has just switched on, and lasts just under 3 msec. When the workstations have reconfigured, which in practice takes around 1/10th of a second, operation continues with the new controlling station.

Speed Isn't Everything

ARCnet uses a data rate of 2.5 Mbps and limits its maximum data packet size to just 508 bytes (compare with Ethernet's 1526 bytes). The designers stuck to this small packet size because they had discovered on their test network that 90 per cent of all traffic used little packets of data.

If you are beginning to find yourself limited by the low data rates of ARCnet, there are a couple of possible solutions. The first, which is explained in Chapter 7, is to fit multiple ARCnet adapter cards into the server PC. Each of the ARCnet cards then drives its own small ring of workstations. Effectively, you are reducing the load and keeping the same bandwidth. A more radical solution is to upgrade to the new ARCnet Plus standard designed by the ARCnet Trader's Association—it runs at 20 Mbps.

ARCnet Components

ARCnet was designed to operate with almost all types of media—coaxial cable, UTP, and fibre—and adapters and cabling are available. Typically, RG-62/U (93-ohm) coaxial cable is used. Each end of the coax is fitted with BNC connectors.

(RG-62 coax is also commonly used within an IBM 3270 mainframe site to link terminals to the mainframe. In order to save rewiring, many companies choose ARCnet simply because they already have a compatible, star-wired cabling system installed.)

An ARCnet LAN has a maximum size. Not only is there a limit of 255 workstations per network, but the maximum length of cable from one end of the LAN to the other is also limited to 20 000 feet.

There are two main components within an ARCnet LAN: passive and active hubs. Active hubs have the same role as a repeater in other networks—they amplify and regenerate the signal. An active hub normally has eight ports; the maximum cable length between active hubs is 2000 feet.

Passive hubs typically have four ports fitted and carry BNC connectors. Because there is no active circuitry inside a passive hub, unused ports have to be terminated with a terminator plug; these unpowered passive hubs can support up to 100 feet of cable and must not be connected in-line to another passive hub or the signal attenuation will be too great.

ARCnet Topologies

ARCnet is normally installed in a physical star topology. This gives you the security against one connection failure outing the whole network. An active hub works in the centre of the star and workstations are either connected directly to one of the hub's ports or via a passive hub (Fig. 3.11).

ARCnet Cable Limitations

From	Max distance (feet)
One end of the LAN to the other	20 000
A network station to an active hub	2000
A network station to a passive hub	100
An active hub to an active hub	2000
An active hub to a passive hub	100
A passive hub to a passive hub	forbidden

ARCnet can also be used in a bus topology with up to eight workstations daisy-chained to each other. The cabling is again RG-62/U coax and the maximum distance from one end to the other is 1000 feet. Workstations connect to the bus using BNC T-connectors, and each end of the bus must be terminated with a 93-ohm terminator plug—very similar to Cheapernet.

It is also possible to mix star and bus topologies; for example, one end of the bus connects to an active hub while a star network runs from the other ports on the hub. To use active hubs to extend a bus-based layout is also legitimate. Each of the hub's eight ports can support a bus with eight stations. If multiple hubs are used, one port in each is used to connect to the next hub. A maximum of 64 hubs can be connected in this way.

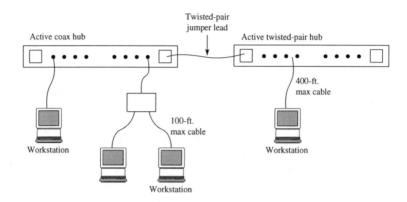

Figure 3.11   Typical ARCnet installation using two active hubs

The Future with ARCnet Plus

With the arrival of ARCnet Plus, running at 20 Mbps, this networking method poses a real threat to Ethernet and Token Ring. ARCnet Plus is totally downward compatible with the older ARCnet, and yet is eight times faster.

ARCnet Plus has an effective data transfer rate of 16 Mbps, well in excess of Ethernet and Token Ring. It will talk to other ARCnet Plus adapters at 20 Mbps, but will automatically switch down to 2.5 Mbps for older cards. The new standard also allows bigger packets of 4096 bytes for a more efficient transfer and IEEE 802.2 addressing can be used, making it easier to tie ARCnet Plus in with Ethernet or Token Ring networks.

ARCnet is a cheap alternative to the two main players, and combines the low-cost cabling of Cheapernet with the security of 10Base-T and the maintained performance of Token Ring. It is a safe and economical way to network.

ARCnet Rules and Tips

- Active hubs can connect to either another hub (active or passive) or a workstation.
- Passive hubs can only connect to either an active hub or a workstation.
- Any used ports in a passive hub must be terminated.
- Keep a record of which adapter is set to which ID number.
- Try and group the adapter numbering into a tight bunch; do not spread numbering over the whole 255 range as this will slow performance a little.
- Set your most powerful PC as station ID 1; being controlling station takes some CPU cycles and it will be felt less by the user of a powerful PC.
- Do not create a loop within a LAN; a cable running from one hub through other hubs must not be connected back into the original hub.
- If you are mixing ARCnet Plus and ARCnet, use ARCnet Plus active hubs, otherwise the high-speed data will be filtered out as noise.

FDDI

FDDI (Fibre Distributed Data Interface) is a high-speed transmission method that runs at 100 Mbps: 10 times the speed of Ethernet. By using fibre optic cables, and transmitting light signals, FDDI cannot be tapped by hackers and is almost impervious to external conditions. It is, unfortunately, still very expensive to rewire an office with fibre, and adapter cards still cost over £600 each. Since its launch, FDDI has changed its role and, while the load carrying capacity has not changed, the applications have. FDDI is now seen to have two main uses. The first is as a high-speed backbone and the second is as a complete LAN tranmission medium. Because of its ability to drive signals over 100 km of fibre, FDDI also has specialized applications to connect LANs to form a wide area network.

How FDDI Works

FDDI is based on a token-passing access similar to that used in IEEE 802.5 Token Ring. There are two basic topologies used with FDDI, both of which are rings. The first, a full FDDI configuration, consists of a dual ring of optical fibre. This dual ring consists of concentric primary and secondary rings; the primary ring is used for data transfer, the secondary ring is used as a backup in case the primary fails. Autosensing circuits will switch in a section of secondary ring where a primary ring has failed. This level of fault-tolerance could be vital to your business. However, only workstations that have a dual-attachment adapter (i.e. they are linked to both rings) can make use of the fault tolerance. Cheaper single-attachment adapters only connect to one ring and do not offer such good fault tolerance.

PCs are rarely connected directly to an FDDI ring. The FDDI circuit is normally used as a backbone to link a number of smaller LANs, servers, or workgroups.

The Future of FDDI

FDDI has arrived, well almost. The standards for its operation over fibre cables is laid down and well adhered to by vendors. However, its main drawback is its price of close to £1000 per workstation. To try and counter the high cost of laying new cable, two new standards have been proposed to transmit data at the same speed and in the same format, but over copper cable instead of fibre cable.

The two proposed standards are as follows. The first is backing TPDDI (twisted pair over copper) with the cable defined as 150-ohm STP as is currently used in 802.5 Token Ring networks. Its encoding method is the same as standard FDDI, so it can use the same chipsets. The only requirement is a modification to the transceiver to ensure that it will not be damaged if it is accidentally plugged into a Token Ring installation instead of a TPDDI system. The main vendors behind this standard are National Semiconductor and Cabletron.

The second standard is being proposed by the UDF (unshielded twisted-pair development forum), which includes Apple, AT&T, Fibronics, and Ungermann Bass. As the name suggests, UDF is proposing to run FDDI signals over UTP cabling. The only drawback is that the UDF scheme requires a different encoding scheme to standard FDDI that could mean new chipsets are required in the adapter cards. Both proposed standards are limited to an effective cable length of 100 m.

FDDI II—the next release of the current FDDI—will be backwards compatible with the existing FDDI but add support for new types of data streams, notably digital video and digital voice. FDDI II will also use an interleaved data structure within each frame which provides the ability to carry data from multiple applications within a single frame.

CONCLUSIONS: CHOOSING A STANDARD

One of the dilemmas facing network managers who keep a lookout to the future of LANs is how to specify the network for today. Which standard should they choose now that will provide enough future-proofing to protect the investment over the next few years? The best bet at the moment is probably to wire using UTP. It has the broadest range support from three different protocols: Ethernet, Token Ring, and CDDI (copper distributed data interface, FDDI over copper cable). Using a choice of these protocols, it is possible to bring data rates of up to 100 Mbps right to the desk.

UTP is also well supported by multimedia hubs that can bridge or route between the three protocols. As long as you pick a large vendor with a good reputation, these hubs should be well supported into the future and, if the design is modular, it should be easy to upgrade to allow support of new protocols.

If you are planning a backbone infrastructure, then the advice is slightly different; instead go for dual attached, fibre-based traditional FDDI. Of course, network management agents should be included in every hub and SNMP is the industry standard that you should stick to. This gives you the option of choosing a separate SNMP management software suite to run on your PC, safe in knowledge that it will run with your intelligent hubs.

TEST EQUIPMENT

Once you have ensured your cabling is correct and your LAN is working as it should, you want to try and keep it that way. There are three possible paths to minimize your downtime. The first is an effective network management plan (discussed fully in Chapter 10). The second step is to invest in a network monitor which is used on a continuous basis to provide statistical information about your LAN and the traffic it is carrying. The third is to buy a network analyser to detect what is the real problem with a dead network.

As you can see, each of the three steps is used at a different time for a different purpose, so ideally you should have all three. An effective network management strategy will ensure that all your hubs (if you are using 10Base-T or Token Ring) are intelligent and can report back to a monitoring station. This will give you control over the network connections and provide a useful indication of overall network traffic.

A LAN monitor (either a hardware or software device) is rather similar to a car's dashboard. Without a dashboard, you could still happily drive your car, but you would be blissfully unaware that it was overheating or running low on petrol. A LAN monitor should be able to generate alerts that will fire off an e-mail message or pop-up a window on your PC if some preset threshold is exceeded. Typically, you would set thresholds for the number of packet collisions, lost frames, or load.

A LAN analyser often confuses the issue by providing monitoring facilities. An analyser, costing up to £15 000 compared to a monitor's typical price tag of £3000, provides detailed analyses of protocols and data packets.

Plug in an analyser and you can single out the packets generated from a particular workstation or packets going to a particular location. You can then examine the packets, and check that the parity bits and other defined parts of the packets are correct. Finally, you can display the contents of the packet. For example, you can easily 'spy' on what a user is typing at the workstation or responses back from a server. Some network operating systems, such as Microsoft's NT/AS, include the option to encrypt the data within packets, but most operating systems transmit plain ASCII. The one exception is when transmitting passwords, which are always encrypted.

More usefully, an analyser should be able to record packets for a certain period of time and then analyse them. To justify the extra cost, they should be able to spot any problems within the packets and display a possible cause and solution. Data General's Sniffer adds an expert knowledge base and a little artificial intelligence to provide real-time analysis of packets. It will point out to a supervisor which packets he or she should worry about. The information is stored in a database and the Sniffer 'learns' about the LAN and its typical traffic with each analysis.

Novell markets a more sophisticated product, called LANalyzer, that will continuously monitor the network, then when it detects unusual traffic or a possible problem situation, it will run a number of applications to try and determine the cause and location of the problem. Once it has spotted a problem, LANalyzer will suggest you step through various software or hardware scenarios (shutting down, then starting up different pieces of hardware or software within the LAN) until it works out which is causing the problem. LANalyzer tops the competition when it comes to helping a LAN supervisor through a broken LAN and finding a solution without requiring the supervisor to be an expert on protocols, packets, or network hardware.

Modelling Your Network

Before you expand or reconfigure your network, you might find it worth using a modelling tool. These software applications allow you to apply 'what-if' scenarios to a network model and see whether your server could cope, where best to place routers, and to try new methods to minimize bottlenecks. Some modelling applications, such as LANsim from Phoenix Datacom, also allow you to feed in real data captured by a Data General Sniffer. This way, your modelled network will be a very accurate representation of the real LAN. You can then change adapter cards, protocols, wiring topologies, and users within this virtual LAN and see the results. The drawback is the price of around £9000. Cut-down software modelling tools start at around £1500.

Cable Testers

Before you can start to worry about software problems and configuration of hardware, you have to make sure that your LAN's cabling is working. If your LAN is beginning to behave oddly or crashes when a particular application is started, then you should look at LAN analysers and management tools. If nothing works when you first switch on your LAN or if a few workstations cannot access the server, it is more likely that your cabling is faulty.

Trying to trace faults, such as a cracked or snapped copper core within hundreds of metres of underfloor cabling might seem an horrific task. It is, unless you have a cable tester and a TDR (time division reflectometer). Cable testers are available for Ethernet and Token Ring and work regardless of any protocols or software. They simply test the physical cabling.

A simple cable tester will tell you that your cabling has a break in it. A more complex tester will tell you exactly where the break is. This detail and ability to work out the location of a break is done using a TDR. The tester sends out a signal and measures how long it takes for an echo to come back. It can then work out the distance along the cable. With a TDR you can pinpoint the problem segment and, together with your wiring plan, mend the cable with minimal disruption.

For twisted-pair cabling, you can buy a simple continuity tester which is useful when testing lengths of cable, but can only tell you if the cable works or doesn't. It cannot pinpoint where on the cable a fault might lie.

Extra functions that you should look for in a twisted-pair cable tester include near-end crosstalk which measures distortion that poor cable might introduce. In addition, it is worth getting a tester that can measure cable attenuation and background noise—especially if you are running cable near heavy machinery or a lift. Ethernet cable testers with a TDR that can test coax or twisted-pair cables cost around £1200—e.g. LANcat's model 1500. Bytex's Token Ring tester provides similar TDR functions for either 4 or 16 Mbps Token Ring installations and costs around £1000.

Key Points to Look for in Test Equipment

When buying a piece of test equipment such as an analyser, cable tester, or a monitor, check the following features:

- *Packet capture*—Any LAN analyser should be able to record packets being transmitted over a LAN. Unless the analyser's processor is capable of capturing all the packets, you will not be able to carry out comprehensive analysis. The monitoring or analysis tool should be able to trigger alarm events if any of the captured data exceeds preset thresholds.

- *Protocol decoding*—To detect any possible errors with your LAN's protocol, an analyser should be able to decode all the layers within your LAN's protocol. It is also useful if it can handle all seven layers within the OSI model. Ideally, the analyser should aim to provide some form of artificial intelligence that can sweep through the mass of data and retrieve possible problems within the protocol.
- *Filters and triggers*—Filtering in its most basic form will sweep through a captured data stream pulling out packets that meet certain criteria—perhaps to a particular destination, from a named source, or with an identifiable problem. Filtering can cause the analyser to miss some of the packets during recording unless the filtering can work at the same speed as the packet transmission over the wire. Triggers allow you to generate warning messages, audible alarms or e-mail messages if certain thresholds are crossed. Typically this would include triggers linked to excessive data transmission, packets that are too long or too short, or collisions.
- *Load generation*—Simulating network traffic is a feature within monitors and analysers that can be very useful when pushing your LAN to its limits and recording the limits and any problems that appear. You are in control when you can specify exactly the load and type of packet that is being transmitted rather than relying on standard use. It also allows you to test and stress elements such as a router or bridge.
- *TDR*—Time division reflectometry is the best way of detecting cabling faults and pin-pointing the exact location of the cable fracture or breakage. TDR works either over copper cable or over fibre (called OTDR—optical TDR); a TDR meter transmits a signal along the cable then measures how long it takes to be reflected back. It can then calculate the distance between the end of the cable and any fracture.
- *Echo tests*—Echo tests are used to check remote workstations. A test packet, such as the ISO test packet, is transmitted to a workstation, which responds with its supported protocols and configuration. Echo tests are used to establish if a workstation or node is working and that it supports and recognizes the protocols it is supposed to.

Conclusions: Test Equipment

Test equipment is vital to any network manager. With the correct tools you can cut down time dramatically and prevent problems by reallocating resources. You can only do this if you have a good information feed. Network monitors are very useful for any large network installation. For smaller LANs, the utilities provided with the network operating system might suffice (such as NetWare's MONITOR). Analysers will help you pin point what is going wrong with the information transmission—they allow you to view and analyse the packets carried by the LAN. Lastly, however small your LAN, a cable tester will save you time when someone kinks a cable or rests a desk on a connector.

4
The Server

INTRODUCTION

LANs can be split into two categories. Client–server LANs use a dedicated PC as a central file store; the network operating system runs on the file-server and all users are connected to the server. In a peer-to-peer LAN there is no central server PC, instead each machine shares its resources with the other PCs. Peer-to-peer LANs typically support a dozen or fewer users, while client–server LANs are normally specified for larger installations.

Although a peer-to-peer network, such as Artisoft's LANtastic or SPI's InvisibleNet, does not need a dedicated server, one machine in the LAN will normally be allocated as a print server, another as the mail server. This places an extra workload on the PC's processor, so the user might notice a performance drop.

Novell's NetWare 2.2 and 3.12 both run on a central, dedicated server PC—as does Banyan's VINES. Microsoft's original LAN Manager and IBM's LAN Server are based on the OS/2 operating system, which is a multitasking system, so the server can be used both as a server and workstation simultaneously, although in practice this is not to be recommended for security and performance reasons.

CHOOSING A SERVER

Within a central-server based LAN, the performance users experience depends on the power of both their own workstations and the server. With tens or perhaps even hundreds of users connected to one server PC, that one PC must be fast and efficient in handling multiple requests for data.

The most important choice is to select the bus architecture of the PC. There are four main choices: ISA, EISA, MCA, and proprietary.

The ISA Bus Specification

The least powerful and worst choice for a server is a PC based on the old ISA (Industry Standard Architecture) bus; this 16-bit bus was used in the earliest

PC/ATs and carries data in 16-bit chunks. The ISA bus speed can vary between manufacturers but is normally 8 or 10 MHz. The data-carrying ability of an ISA bus is limited by the bus speed and word size to (16×10). ISA has a second disadvantage: it is very basic. By this I mean that all peripherals talk to the central processor through the bus and all peripherals are, to some degree, controlled by the CPU. With the arrival of 32-bit CPUs, such as the 80386 and 80486, the 16-bit ISA bus acted as a bottleneck and limited the speed at which data could be transferred to and from the CPU, which began seriously to harm performance.

EISA and MCA

To remove the bottleneck created by ISA, two new bus architectures were developed. A group of nine manufacturers developed EISA (Extended ISA) while IBM introduced its MCA (Microchannel Architecture) design. Both buses are 32-bit and allow a feature called bus-mastering, but EISA has gained the greater market share by virtue of backwards compatibility: old ISA cards can still be used in an EISA-bus PC. For a server, this is of little consequence since you should always fit 32-bit cards to take advantage of the 32-bit bus. Compaq (one of the original nine manufacturers to specify EISA) uses, unsurprisingly, an EISA architecture in its SystemPro range of servers, while Apricot has chosen MCA as the system bus for its FT range of servers.

Bus-mastering sets EISA and MCA ahead of ISA by giving more control to the adapter. An adapter can take over control of the bus from the CPU and pass data directly to system RAM without adding to the CPU's workload.

You should not use anything less than either an EISA or MCA-bussed PC as your server. EISA has the advantage in data-carrying capacity: the bus operates at up to 33 MHz and uses 32-bit words for a throughput of 32×33 Mbps; MCA is slightly faster. One last consideration is that because of its greater market share, it is easier and cheaper to buy EISA adapters than MCA adapters.

The Proprietary Bus Option

The fourth option is to choose a server computer that uses a proprietary bus. These are normally included for a reason, typically because the server can support multiple processors. Tricord, for example, uses its proprietary high-speed bus to link multiple standard 80486 CPUs with a standard EISA bus expansion slots. This way you get the best of both worlds: compatibility with existing adapter cards and no comprise to the system's performance.

Which Processor?

Servers are required to cope with very high data throughput from all the users. This places a strain on the network adapter, the bus, and the hard disk. The processor in a server is relatively under-used in comparison to the battering the storage system receives. This does not mean that you can specify a server that uses a 16-bit 80286

CPU, but it does mean that you should pay more attention to as fast a hard disk as you can afford.

Novell's NetWare 2.2 is one of the few client–server network operating systems that can run on an 80286 processor. Others, such as NetWare 3.12, VINES, and LAN Server, require an 80386 or better. The oddity is Microsoft's NT/AS running on OS/2—in theory this can work on a 80286 platform, but the performance would be so slow as to be unusable.

It is worth taking some time choosing the type of processor your server needs. The 32-bit 80386SX, for example, was developed by Intel to be pin-compatible with the older 16-bit 80286. This means that the 386sx, although executing 32-bit instructions internally, transfers data to memory in two 16-bit chunks; it takes twice as long to carry out a data transfer compared to a 80386DX (which has both 32-bit internal and external data paths).

The 80486 is, like its predecessor the 80386, available as an SX or DX model; both are 32-bit, but the DX has an extra internal maths co-processor. Both 486 models have a small internal cache that can be boosted with external RAM chips to increase performance. The newest CPU from Intel is the Pentium. This is backwards compatible with the 486, but offers greater speed thanks to a RISC-based architecture. Currently, few manufacturers are still selling 386-based PCs, nearly all have turned to the 486. One particular benefit of the 486 is that it can, using a technique called clock-doubling, run at up to 66 MHz for the most demanding applications (see later in this chapter).

Selecting the Correct Processor

Each processor was created for a specific reason and purpose. Unfortunately, the best application for each is obvious neither from the chip-makers' designations and claims, nor the retail prices of PCs made from them. The differences between the chips are often subtle, often seemingly designed to add to the confusion. As a result, finding the right chip to power your PC is hardly a trivial task. But if you want to find the right PC for your own purposes, it is a question you must confront.

The economics of 8-bit external circuitry was a prime reason IBM chose the 8088 as the centrepiece of its first PC. The 8088 also let IBM claim its PC was a 16-bit computer (because of the chip's 16-bit internal registers) when nearly all other small business computers used 8-bit chips. The PC's success guaranteed Intel's success.

In 1982 Intel introduced its next-generation, the 80286. Although still a 16-bit chip, the internal circuitry of the 286 was designed to operate at higher speeds and to use fewer clock cycles to carry out each instruction. Four additional address lines gave it direct access to 16 Mbytes of RAM. Virtual memory techniques (i.e. using disk storage to emulate solid-state RAM) gave the 286 access to 1024 Mbytes of total memory—16 Mbytes real, 1008 Mbytes virtual.

The 286 maintained compatibility with its predecessor by operating in two modes: real and protected. Real mode was fully compatible with 8086 code and operations and limited memory addressing to 1 Mbyte. Protected mode allowed direct access to memory beyond the 1 Mbyte addressing limit of the 8086 (it also allowed hardware to protect the memory used by one task from interference from other tasks, hence the name).

When the design specifications of the 286 were set, neither the PC nor PC DOS existed. Consequently, Intel's engineers made no provision for opening protected mode to DOS programs. Moreover, they apparently believed that once you discovered the virtues of protected mode, you would never want to switch back— the 80286 was designed to boot up in real mode, then, on software command, shift to protected mode. It could not switch back without being reset, i.e. booting up all over again. DOS programs could not run in protected mode because of the incompatibility of the addressing schemes used in real and protected mode. The extra memory of the 286 was essentially beyond the reach of DOS.

By the time Intel began work on the successor to the 286, a product now known as the 386DX, DOS had become an accepted standard. Consequently the new chip, first released in 1987, included special provisions to make it compatible both with 286 software and DOS applications.

The 386DX incorporated 32-bit registers, which are also addressable as 16- or 8-bit registers connected to the outside world through a full 32-bit data bus. Although the 386DX understands (and carries out) the 8- and 16-bit instructions used by earlier Intel chips, it also has its own 32-bit command set. A 32-bit address bus allows direct control of 4096 Mbytes of physical memory and up to 16 384 Mbytes of virtual memory.

As with the 286, the 386DX has both a real and protected mode, but the chip allows shifting between them at will. In addition, it sports a new operating mode, virtual 8086 mode, which allows the 386DX to partition its memory into multiple simulations of 8086 microprocessors, each operating in real mode—each one a virtual PC capable of running DOS programs in complete isolation from the others.

The 386 also allows greater versatility in memory handling. Segmented memory is optional in advanced modes—the entire addressing range can be addressed contiguously or it can be divided into segments of any length (in 4K increments). The 386 also allows hardware memory mapping—the chip can redefine the logical addresses assigned to blocks of physical memory.

Although the efficiency of the 386 is about the same as the 286 using 16-bit code (the same number of clock cycles are required by each chip to carry out a given instruction), the 386 was designed with tighter rules that allow it to operate at higher speeds (about double that of the 286). Moreover, its 32-bit instructions load faster and do more in each cycle.

The 486DX was next and can run all 386 software. In truth, the 486DX is distinguished from the 386 by one flag, one exception, two page-table entry bits, six instructions, and nine control-register bits. Currently no major programs take advantage of these specific 486DX features, so nothing that runs on the 486 will not run on the 386 (and vice versa).

To the abilities of the 386DX, the 486DX adds four important performance-enhancing features: a 8K internal (or primary) memory cache using a four-way, set-associative, write-through design, an internal numeric coprocessor, tighter design rules allowing higher operating speeds, and greater efficiency allowing the 486 to execute instructions in about half the number of clock cycles as a 386. In other words, at a given clock speed, a 486 will get about twice as much done. The 486 architecture represents the current state-of-the-art in Intel-compatible microprocessor design.

386 derivatives

A number of microprocessors derived from the 386 architecture wear the 386 designation. First among these was Intel's own 386SX. As with the 8088 and 8086, the 386SX is the economical alternative to the 386DX. Instead of a 32-bit external data bus, the 386SX uses only a 16-bit bus. While the narrow bus means that moving data (and 32-bit instructions) in and out of the chip will take twice the time as with the 386DX, it also allows the use of less expensive motherboard designs. In other words, 386SX computers are generally cheaper and slower than 386DX machines. However, the 386SX will run all 386DX programs.

486 derivatives

The first chip derived from Intel's 486DX design was Intel's own step-down version, the 486SX. Unlike previous economy models, the 486SX differs from its high-performance predecessor not in external bus width but in the omission of internal floating-point circuitry. Otherwise, the 486SX is a 486DX in its register and bus configuration. In essence, the 486SX is an improved 386DX, capable of carrying out about twice as many instructions at a given clock speed. The 486SX is not, however, socket-compatible with the 386DX or 486DX.

Although initially a step-down version of the 486DX, Intel's 486DX2 and OverDrive chips hold the potential for being step-up products as well. This pair of chips offers the same functionality as the 486DX but has the unique feature of operating internally at twice the external clock frequency supplied the chip and are hence called 'clock-doubling' chips. By allowing motherboards to operate at lower frequencies, they follow in the philosophical footsteps of the 8088 and 386SX, although allowing manufacturers to reduce costs through the use of lower speed rather than narrower bus designs.

The 486DX2 and OverDrive chips are designed for different purposes. The 486DX2 is meant to be original equipment on new motherboards. The OverDrive series are upgrades, some to augment 486SX chips by plugging into coprocessor sockets (while electrically replacing the original microprocessor), others to substitute for 486DX chips as direct in-socket replacements.

Because of the speed disparity between their internal circuits and external connections, DX2 and OverDrive chips do well on internal operations but suffer in accessing memory and I/O devices. Overall, on typical applications they deliver about 80 per cent of the performance of a 486DX rated at the same speed. (Note that Intel rates these chips at their internal clock speed rather than their external clock speed which other chipmakers use for rating their 'clock-doubling' chips.)

Intel has announced the next generation of microprocessors, called the Pentium, which use 64-bit internal registers in a variety of configurations mimicking its present 386 and 486 offerings.

Table 4.1 shows the range of Intel microprocessors with their speeds and configurations.

Table 4.1 Intel microprocessor time line

Microprocessor	Mips	Bus (bits)	Speed (MHz)
8086	0.33	16	5
	0.66	16	8
	0.75	16	10
8088	0.33	8	5
	0.75	8	8
80286	1.2	16	8
	1.5	16	10
	2.66	16	12
386DX	5–6	32	16
	6–7	32	20
	8.5	32	25
	11.4	32	33
386SL	4.21	16	20
	5.3	16	25
386SX	2.5	16	16
	4.2	16	20
	5.25	16	25
486DX	20	32	25
	27	32	33
	41	32	50
486SX	13	32	16
	16.5	32	20
	20	32	25
486DX2	40	32	25/50
	54	32	33/66
Pentium	80+	32	60

Using Multiple Processors

The distinction between PC servers and super-servers is now a very blurred one. Compaq's SystemPro server can be fitted with two 80386 processors, and servers from Tricord, Mitac, Olivetti, and NetFrame push the definition of a PC still further. However many processors are fitted into a server, they will make no difference to performance unless the operating system can use them. NetWare has to be specifically ported to these new hardware platforms otherwise it cannot take advantage of more than one processor. For example, NetWare 3.12 on a Compaq

SystemPro will make use of just one processor, while the ported version of NetWare will operate across all fitted processors in a NetFrame machine. There are two distinct architectures that define how a computer with multiple processors operates and shares the tasks.

Asymmetric multiple processing

Asymmetric architecture is easier to understand and implement than symmetric multiple processing and is fitted into the NetFrame range of super-servers. The principle behind it is that one set of tasks is executed by one processor while a second set is executed by another processor. In practice, the most common arrangement is two processors: one for main program execution and a second to handle input/output (I/O). More complex designs use an additional processor for each I/O subsystem; one for disk drive, another for network adapter cards, and another for printing.

The argument runs that asymmetric processing allows the designer to optimize each processor for each task: for example, an I/O processor would be able to handle I/O data efficiently while the main processor would be better optimized for memory and numerical operations. This is also often reflected in an optimized price with asymmetric processing computers using cheaper, less powerful processors for less demanding tasks.

Symmetric processing

The symmetric processing design dictates that each processor should be equally capable of doing any task from handling I/O to executing part of a program. Compaq's SystemPro makes uses its two 80386 processors as symmetric multiple processors.

Symmetric processing requires that the system architecture has to be very open and the processors should, ideally, all be the same. The operating system arranges the tasks into queues; when a processor has finished a task, it takes the next available task from the queue and executes it. To optimize this, some computers use a master–slave design in which a master processor tries to share out the task load to even performance across all the slave processors. If this master–slave design is continued, the scheme begins to move towards an asymmetric processing architecture.

How Much RAM Do I Need?

As an example of the different effects of RAM fitted to a server, a 486-based server loaded with 20 users running NetWare 3.12 performs very differently when it has got 8, 12, or 16 Mbytes of system RAM. By halving the system RAM, performance in Mbps of throughput is reduced to a third.

The explanation of how much system memory you require is given in the NetWare installation manual as a multi-part formula. It should be borne in mind that NetWare operates in a slightly different way than other operating systems when it comes to memory allocation. After taking RAM for the kernel and to support the number of licensed users, NetWare uses RAM to hold the disk's directory entries and part of the bindery. This means that the bigger the disk you have installed, the more RAM it requires to hold its directory entries. Once all these operating overheads have been met, NetWare assigns all remaining RAM as cache RAM (although this can be modified).

To calculate how much RAM you should fit into your server, use the following Novell-supplied equation. Starting with the disk overheads: for any DOS volume in the drive, check the block size (normally 4 unless you have changed it).

$$\text{RAM\_DOS} = \frac{0.023 \times \text{volume size (in Mbytes)}}{\text{block size}}$$

For your NetWare volumes do the following sum for each:

$$\text{RAM\_NW} = \frac{0.032 \times \text{volume size (in Mbytes)}}{\text{block size}}$$

NetWare itself requires 2 Mbytes of RAM in which to operate, so the total system RAM required is:

$$\text{RAM} = \text{RAM\_DOS} + \text{RAM\_NW} + 2 \text{ Mbytes}$$

(This is subject to a minimum total RAM of 4 Mbytes.)

For example with a typical DOS segment of 30 Mbytes, and a 470 Mbyte NetWare volume, the calculation would be:

$$\text{RAM\_DOS} = 0.023 \times 30/4 = 0.1725$$
$$\text{RAM\_NW} = 0.032 \times 470/4 = 3.76$$
$$\text{NetWare} = 2 \text{ Mbytes}$$

giving a total of 6 Mbytes minimum in which your server could operate. If you fitted just 6 Mbytes, there would be almost nothing left as cache RAM for the drive. With 8 Mbytes fitted, the cache allocated by NetWare is 2 Mbytes, with 12 Mbytes fitted it is 6 Mbytes and so on.

To see how much cache RAM is being allocated, load MONITOR on the server's console and select the Resource Utilisation menu option. This displays statistics about the cache RAM in the top window. The important figure is the cache memory number—if this allocation is any lower than 60 per cent, your system performance will begin to suffer since NetWare is likely to run out of cache memory.

What Type of Disk Controller?

If you are worried about your PC's performance, forget the processor, look instead at the bottlenecks that form around the I/O system—particularly the network adapter and the hard disk system. Network adapter selection is covered in Chapter 4; in this section we will examine how to pick the best disk controller for your computer.

The more disk intensive your application, the more you will feel the effects of a sluggish disk system. Network servers are prime targets for a solution that will remove the data bottleneck from the hard disk drive interface. To get the best performance from an 80386 or 486 processor it needs an internal bus architecture that is capable of transferring large quantities of data at high speed between system memory, CPU, and peripheral storage.

EISA and MCA busses are both capable of transferring data in 32-bit wide chunks across the bus. ISA, in comparison, can only transfer data in 16-byte chunks. An ISA bus needs twice as many clock cycles to transfer the amount of data as an EISA system. EISA couples its wide data channel with a high 33 MHz clock speed; an ISA system is snail-like with a clock speed of just 10 MHz.

MCA, originally developed by IBM for its high-performance PS/2 range of desktops, has not been as widely accepted as the faster EISA bus and is generally only used in a few vendors' computers. Although the buying decision is similar for EISA or MCA computers, you will find you have a far wider choice of peripherals if you stick to an EISA-bus PC.

If you are specifying a new hard disk subsystem or upgrading from scratch, the most flexible technology that offers top speeds is SCSI (Small Computer System Interface). There is often considerable confusion surrounding the future of SCSI, but all disk manufacturers are committed to making it the main disk standard of the next few years. SCSI recently spawned a new version, SCSI-2. This enhances SCSI's control language and performance. Most SCSI controllers currently on the market are also compatible with the newer SCSI-2 standards.

Tear open the PCs in your company and you are likely to find that the majority are fitted with standard IDE disk systems. Thanks to its low price, this is the industry's prevalent standard: a 130 Mbyte IDE drive costs around £250, while a similar SCSI costs £450. IDE is normally limited to a maximum drive capacity of 330 Mbytes which is fine for most stand-alone PCs, but is a considerable limitation for network servers.

The ageing ESDI standard

To enhance the performance and drive capacity supported by the original ST-506 disk interface, the ESDI interface was introduced. Each controller supports a single drive with, like SCSI, disk capacities up to 2 Gbytes. But it is still slow; SCSI offers almost double the throughput at 40 Mbps compared to ESDI's 24 Mbps. ESDI matches SCSI in price, but not performance, and beats IDE in coping with high capacity but not price. As a result, production of ESDI drives is being phased out by many manufacturers and it is a poor choice for power users.

Disk cacheing

The basic idea behind a cache is that a small amount of fast memory holds the same data as some part of a slower storage device. This gives the processor faster access to the data when it needs it. This is the ideal, but putting it into practice is difficult. For a start, disk data cannot be accessed byte by byte. Instead, it must be accessed one whole sector at a time (typically 512 bytes). To be of any practical use, the smallest chunk of data that a disk cache has to deal with, called the line size, has to be several times greater than a sector.

A second problem for a disk cache is timing. Unlike RAM caches, there are different retrieval speeds for different data locations on a disk. The speed at which the data you request is delivered depends how far the read head has had to move and where, in relation to it, the last access was located.

Lastly, coherence or synchronization can be catastrophic if not properly addressed. If the contents of the disk do not match the contents of the cache, then security can be compromised, especially if your PC crashes before the cache has had time to update the disk. If you make a change to the file allocation table (FAT), and you switch off your PC before this is passed on to the disk, you could risk a totally corrupted drive.

Delaying write operations is the basis of write-back cacheing; it gathers together a number of write operations destined for the same sector or track and sends them as one packet. This optimizes disk write head movement, but unless precautions are taken, it is not as secure as a write-through operation which sends on all write operations as they are received.

Delaying write requests can cause problems when trying to maintain coherence. In Unix systems, it is common to run the 'sync' command before shutting down the operating system. This ensures any cached data is written to disk. Software and hard cacheing methods under DOS should trap the reset interrupt. By clearing up tidily before allowing a Ctrl-Alt-Del to work, they prevent disk corruption.

Write requests can be consolidated into groups addressed to the same disk sector to minimize disk head movement. In much the same way, disk reads can be minimized by using a read-ahead method. Instead of just reading in the 512 byte sector from disk, read-ahead caches pull in data from the subsequent sector. The assumption is that the application will want to look at the next sector in the future, and when it does, the cache can deliver data straight from RAM rather than waiting for disk.

Waiting for the disk is something that cacheing controllers are good at. By doing this as a background task, it relieves the operating system of the chore and lets it get on with other tasks. This is, unfortunately, difficult in systems which use the PC BIOS, since this is hardwired to wait. Software device drivers that avoid the BIOS can improve performance.

Performance of NetWare 3.12 and 4.0 can take a nosedive if you fit a hardware disk cacheing controller. The reason is that NetWare uses any spare RAM as a very efficient software cache and orders read and writes effectively in software. Add a hardware cache controller that is trying to do the same thing and it will certainly be redundant and could even work against the software and reduce performance. You should buy a fast, non-cacheing disk controller and spend the rest of your money on more RAM.

- It is wise to stick to write-through cacheing to prevent any chance of data corruption during a power failure or computer breakdown.

SCSI controllers

IDE drive controllers dominate the market thanks to low price, but SCSI has taken hold of the high-end market, ousting ESDI in terms of performance. SCSI is here now, but the next generation of controllers complying with the new SCSI-2 standard are already filtering through.

SCSI is capable of transferring data between drive and controller at 5 Mbytes/sec. SCSI-2 works at the same rate, so where is the benefit? Because it is backwards compliant, SCSI-2 has to match this mode, but it has two further modes up its sleeve. SCSI-2 Fast changes the timing clock and so doubles the synchronous data rate to 10 Mbytes/sec. SCSI-2 Wide adds a second data path boosting the standard 8-bit wide data path up to either 16 or 32 bits (depending on the implementation). This gives Wide a maximum transfer rate of 40 Mbytes/sec.

Wide SCSI has yet to find a firm footing and few controllers are able to run at data rates of 40 Mbytes/sec. With these two modes, you must remember that you need matching and compatible SCSI devices at each end. If you have a SCSI-1 drive, adding a SCSI-2 controller will work, but you will see no difference in performance. Upgrading both your drive and controller to SCSI-2 Fast, however, will double the performance of disk-intensive applications.

Hardware vs software cacheing

A hardware cache uses its own dedicated section of RAM located on the adapter card. This RAM, normally between 4 and 16 Mbytes, in the form of standard SIMMs, is only available to the cache processor; your applications cannot get to it.

The alternative is to use a software cache. For example, workstations running Microsoft Windows also use Windows' own SMARTDRV software cache, which is automatically installed during installation. This sets aside a chunk of standard system RAM for use as a cache store and hooks into the disk access interrupts. The disadvantage of a software cache is that it takes up valuable system RAM, but you can configure it very easily and release memory back to an application if you need to. In some circumstances, software cacheing can be faster than a hardware solution since the data transfer from cache RAM to system RAM (effectively, the same thing) can be handled by the memory management unit rather than the CPU. A hardware cache controller still must pass data from its own cache RAM over the system bus to system RAM.

For users running memory-hungry applications, a hardware cache frees up system memory and CPU time. For most users wanting a little boost, a software cache such as SMARTDRV, or products from Symantec, Fifth Generation, or Norton would provide more flexibility and a lower cost.

IDE vs ESDI vs SCSI

Simplicity vs flexibility is the key choice to be made when choosing a disk interface. Traditionally, the ST506 interface, invented by Seagate, was the standard way for PCs to access rotating storage. SCSI was confined mainly to other architectures such as the Apple Macintosh, and to external PC devices such as tape backup and other non-standard forms of storage.

The situation lasted until 1987 when Compaq, more a hardware standard-setter then than now, introduced the IDE (Integrated Drive Electronics) interface into its product line. The immediate reaction from some was that Compaq was attempting to hijack the disk interface standard and reduce the ability of its customers to choose the interface they wanted or to upgrade it if necessary.

All these fears have now been laid to rest. IDE is now firmly established as the standard PC hard disk interface. It was designed to deal with the burgeoning number of disk products; the standard PC BIOS has 47 disk types hard-coded into it but the growth of disk products meant PCs could not keep up with developments. IDE also provides greater simplicity and performance than ST506.

IDE is a development of the ST506 which moves the detailed work of requesting specific disk sectors from the adapter card onto the drive. The upshot is that instead of the PC BIOS needing to know the precise layout of the disk, the drive itself looks to the PC like an adapter card. Now hidden from the BIOS, it can therefore be any size and layout that the drive manufacturer chooses to make it. IDE also brings extra speed to the party with digital I/O requests compared to ST506's reliance on an analogue interface to pass commands between the BIOS and the disk.

From the manufacturer's and the user's point of view, IDE brings with a previously unheard of degree of standardization. You can plug an IDE disk into an IDE interface and be reasonably certain it will work. And it is cheaper. Standardization brings prices down, which increases volumes, thus further increasing downward pressure on prices. And there are minimal controller costs.

The disadvantages are that the underlying technology is still an 8-bit ST506 interface which is restricted to a maximum of two drives. So its attractive simplicity brings with it inflexibility.

ESDI, a go-faster development of ST506, has fallen out of use as IDE and SCSI have muscled in on its territory. It no longer offers any advantages that the two other main interfaces cannot supply.

SCSI, on the other hand, is more complex but it can speed up disk operations and has greater potential capacity. Although still only 8-bit—this will change as the 16-bit SCSI 2 becomes established—the host computer can dispatch its instructions to a SCSI disk and then carry on with other processing. The disk subsystem reports back on completion of the task.

This is not very useful under the single-tasking DOS as the operating system will wait for the results of its request. But run a SCSI disk under a multitasking system such as Novell Netware or OS/2, and the benefits immediately become clear. Instructions queue up and the host only becomes involved again when the disk subsystem reports the results are ready. Add to that SCSI's ability to daisy-chain up to eight devices—in reality seven since the host controller is included in this number—and SCSI opens up vast arrays of storage capacity.

SCSI's complexity also allows drive manufacturers to build in a number of performance enhancements such as segmented caches, which can further improve multitasking by effectively keeping a cache for each task.

SCSI-2 has now arrived and can offer at least a six-fold improvement in data transfer rates, and SCSI may be about to break out of its traditional corner. It is more of a standard than SCSI 1 ever was, even though it is unlikely that we shall ever see SCSI embedded on the PC motherboard as IDE is now. The future for SCSI looks very good. SCSI-3 is being developed and should improve further on performance and compatibility.

Table 4.2 lists the different drives together with prices for a range of capacities.

Table 4.2 Drive prices(£) and capacity

	IDE	ESDI	SCSI
90 Mbyte	130	320	170
130 Mbyte	250	554	350
400 Mbyte	500	800	600
1.2 Gb	NA	1100	990
1.6 Gb	NA	1800	1300

How Cacheing Works

Hard disks are typically 100 times slower than RAM so it makes sense to read and write to the disk only when it is necessary. If you are accessing a data file that is bigger than the controller's cache RAM, then the controller has to decide which data to keep, and which to discard. If it discards data, the next retrieve operation for that data will come from disk rather than from cache RAM.

A common technique to get around this is to implement a LRU (least recently used) algorithm. With this, the software keeps track of how recently a buffer has been used, and releases the buffer that has spent the longest time without being used. This free buffer can now be used to cache new data.

If the application software accesses data in a completely random order, typically found when using databases, then cache hits will occur in the ratio of size of the cache to size of data file. A 4 Mbyte cache would be expected to speed disks access to a 20 Mbyte database by 25 per cent.

In reality, you would expect better performance, as certain chunks of data are requested more frequently. The more clustered the requests to a particular area of the database file, the greater the chance of a hit and the better the LRU algorithm works.

If you are running a report which works its way through the data sequentially, record by record, then this cacheing method is hopeless. Similarly, with a C compiler or a process that copies large chunks of data around the disk, it will be a long time before the application asks for the same record a second time. By which time, the cache is likely to have discarded the record. In this situation, it may even slow the system down, as the cache algorithm ponders which buffer to cast out.

The opposite approach is that when a new buffer is needed, the cache mechanism picks a victim at random and uses that. This will counter the problem seen above, again giving benefit in proportion to the cache to data ratio. This method does less well when faced with smaller data sets, since it will frequently be throwing away data that has just been read and may be needed again soon. This will be especially true of those programs, such as compilers and databases, which make extensive use of temporary files which are written then, almost immediately, read in again.

If a little intelligence were added to the controller, it could switch between LRU and random—if it met less than 15 per cent of requests from cache, it would switch from one to the other.

Within most PC's the controller has no idea what sort of applications are running, or what their patterns of requests are likely to be, since to retain compatibility they emulate standard drive controllers. There is no standard method for a program to communicate with the cache controller, so it is up to the cache mechanism to guess future demands, based on past history.

With this in mind, the controller may adopt a method to weight certain buffers; one way is to increment a counter for each time a given buffer is used. For instance, under DOS, certain areas of the disk, such as directories, will be accessed more frequently, so would be given a higher weighting. Transient pieces of code, such as those from Windows or OS/2 .DLL files may also be weighted. When a new buffer is requested, it looks for the least used, and if there is more than one, the one accessed least recently.

This suffers far less when under heavy sequential access than an LRU algorithm and can be made at least as efficient as a random method. It is a more complex method, and thus needs more processing power on the controller, which pushes up the cost. It is also very sensitive to the method by which buffers that were once popular are demoted. If buffers are demoted too quickly, then you return to an LRU algorithm; too slowly and the cache never catches up with the current situation.

The focus so far has been on buffering reads. It is also possible to buffer writes: gathering together several writes before sending them on to the disk. Although writes typically only occur about one-quarter to one-fifth as often as reads, the potential to increase speed is still great. Lazy write cacheing can cause problems. If you switch off or crash your PC while data is still in the cache, the database and file system will not be up to date. This could result in loss of data, or the file system itself being corrupted.

In addition to the basic cacheing above, a good controller will try to optimize the disk head movement. A technique found is some cache software, called elevator seeking, which holds onto disk requests then tries to sort them into an order that enables the disk head to move in a clean sweep, as opposed to blindly moving backwards and forwards following whichever was the last request to come in. On completion, the cacheing mechanism reorders the data to present them in the correct order to the originating application.

WHERE TO PLACE THE SERVER

In any LAN with a dedicated PC working as a server, this PC is central to the LAN. If it goes down, so does the LAN. In mainframe installations it is common to see the mainframe situated in a separate room. This was mainly down to its size and cooling requirements, but it also helped security. The same is true of a PC server; to prevent accidental damage or tampering, it is safest to place your server in a separate locked room. If you are running a network servicing tens of users, you might already have a room dedicated as a wiring closet—again, powered hubs are vital to the network and it is best to keep them out of reach of any passer-by.

The extra convenience of locating all the central LAN equipment in a single room is that you can then, normally, adjust the air-conditioning in this room to compensate for the considerable heat the server and powered hubs generate. To mention the obvious, you should also locate the UPS in the same room, which allows you to provide standby power for the server and the hubs (see Chapter 13 for further details on UPSs).

Locking your server away presents a problem if you have a network printer attached to the server's parallel port. You have a conflict: easy access for users to pick up their printouts and limited access to protect the server. The best solution is to use a remote print-server. This is either a small box that links the printer directly to the network, or a PC running special software (such as Novell's RPRINTER utility) and a standard parallel printer connection.

CHOOSING A SERVER—A CHECKLIST

In this chapter, we have covered the main components of a server PC and described how you should specify your server. There are arguments for and against EISA or MCA-bussed PCs; perhaps you already have a good stock of high-performance MCA network adapters. Similarly with hard disk type: SCSI offers the most flexible solution with the best performance, but at a cost. The processor has become, especially in a network server, a less important detail; the bottlenecks have moved from the processor to the I/O systems such as the network cards and hard disk interface. Having said this, most high-end network operating systems operate using 32-bit code and so need at least a 386.

To summarize the main options and their advantages:

- *Processor*—Most operating systems require a minimum of a 80386. A 80386SX is a poor choice for a server, since it uses a 16-bit external data path. Although no software yet uses 80486-specific instructions, a 486DX includes an on-board cache that pushes performance past a 386DX.
- *Bus type*—ISA should be avoided for high-performance servers. Multiple network adapters are difficult to fit and throughput is very poor over this 16-bit bus. EISA or MCA are the only options you should consider for a server. Both

offer similar 32-bit data paths with bus-mastering. EISA has a greater range of third-party adapter cards available, while MCA has the backing of IBM.

- *Disk type*—The standard for most workstations will be IDE, which can be used for servers, but it proves difficult to find very large capacity IDE drives and throughput is poor. ESDI offers good performance at a higher price, but most manufacturers are phasing out production. SCSI and, if possible, SCSI-2 is the recommended storage system with high performance, good availability, and excellent expansion. Cacheing controller cards can slow NetWare servers and should be avoided, but can boost performance in operating systems that do not use their own software cacheing.
- *RAM*—In almost all cases, fit as much as you can afford. A recommended bare minimum for a NetWare 3.12 server would be 6 Mbytes, and you will see the greatest performance jump if you fit 16 Mbytes. For LANs with more than 20 users, consider 16 Mbytes as a minimum.
- *Network adapter*—Ideally, your server PC will have either an EISA or MCA bus backplane and you should fit 32-bit bus-mastering cards for maximum performance. However, if you are upgrading, you might find you get better performance by fitting multiple, cheaper, 16-bit cards. (See Chapter 4 for detailed description of network adapters.)

CONCLUSIONS

Your server's specification will effect overall network performance more than any other element in the network. Spending money upgrading workstations is likely to offer a less obvious performance boost than upgrading your server. Select your server's components carefully and pay just as much, if not more, attention to the peripherals than to the processor itself. Remember that in most modern 486-based servers, the bottleneck in data transfer is no longer a slow processor, rather it is the hard disk or network adapter.

5
Network Workstations

INTRODUCTION

Almost any type of computer can be attached to a network. If you have a standard PC or Macintosh, there are few problems and plenty of ways to connect to the LAN. If you want to network a specialized CAD station or dedicated computer, you may have more difficulty. In this chapter, you will see how to specify the best components for a workstation for a particular job, and how to connect it to the LAN and solve some of the common software problems that may trap you.

PCs AS WORKSTATIONS

There are far too many people who still think that networking is a black art and connecting a PC to a LAN should only be left in the hands of an expert. Well, it's not true. Any PC can be connected to a network. The way to do this is by adding a network adapter card (see Chapter 3 for more detailss). Most desktop PCs have expansion slots on the motherboard, and a network adapter plugs into a free slot. If you do not have a desktop or your expansion slots are either proprietary or full up with other adapters, you can always use a pocket network adapter that plugs into the parallel printer port.

The workstation itself needs to be nothing special. In fact, you could save money and increase security by specifying less. Diskless workstations (a PC with neither hard nor floppy disks installed) remove any threat of a user copying data and passing it on to a competitor (discussed in greater detail in Chapter 10). However, these are the exception rather than the norm. The norm for workstation PCs now is to specify a machine that can run Microsoft Windows and provide a reasonable degree of expansion for future needs.

A PC that is being used as a network workstation will need to have network driver software installed. This typically takes between 40 and 100K of memory. If you are using a 80286-based PC, then you will probably have 1 Mbyte of RAM fitted. To make the best of the memory, you should use a memory manager to move DOS into the high memory area above the 640K level and leave more free for applications. The network shell can also be moved into high memory. (See Chapter 7, Tuning your workstation, for more details on saving memory.) For a workstation that will run Windows you should go for a minimum of 4 Mbytes of RAM, preferably more (8 Mbytes is ideal), and a 32-bit processor such as the 80386 or 486. These are now so cheap that most manufacturers do not make 80286-based PCs any more.

Choosing Storage for a Desktop

The standard PC configuration has a minimum of an 80 Mbyte hard disk—with lower access times and higher reliability than ever before, and all in a package that is often smaller than the floppy drive. However, there are now two main choices for controllers and hard drives that are open to supervisors that are specifying for desktops (and, to a lesser degree, servers).

Hard disk technology has progressed slowly and steadily over the years, a new interface one year, lower access times the next, then smaller drives, higher capacities, and finally back to the start of the loop with another new interface. Few users worry about their hard disk until it breaks down or they need to upgrade it. If either happens to you, you will find that what was the tip of technological achievement is now commonplace or, more often, a defunct technology. For anyone who bought a PC just a couple of years ago, finding a new drive that is compatible with the old controller can be a nightmare. In this feature we look at the changing technology of hard disk drives and the new standards for disk controllers.

The changes in hard disk controllers are simple enough to follow; they correspond exactly to the requirements of the PC. Hard disk technology is less predictable, being governed by better manufacturing controls and new ideas. The original PC/XT was powered by an processor with an 8-bit bus. The expansion slots were 8-bit, so the controllers were 8-bit. Driving the hard disk in this setup was a controller conforming to the ST506 standard. It could transfer data between CPU and hard drive at up to 5 Mbytes/sec—there was little pressure from any of the components to go any faster—the CPU ran at 4.77 MHz and the drive pottered along with a stately 100 msec access time.

With the arrival of the PC/AT, powered by a 16-bit processor with a 16-bit bus, and 16-bit AT expansion slots, the disk controller had to change—it did, but only to the extent of coping with 16-bit data paths between controller and processor; it was still following the 8-bit data path between controller and disk drive: the ST506 standard with a 5 Mbyte/sec transfer rate. The arrival of 32-bit processors, like the first 80386 chips, brought a new popular standard for the controllers and drives— ESDI (Enhanced Standard Device Interface). ESDI was the first real attempt by the industry at producing a standard interface. Its main drawback was that it could only support disk drives—unlike SCSI which can drive a range of peripherals. Development of ESDI, and its lower-specification partner, the ST506 standard, have both died and are now very rarely seen except on old machines in for an upgrade. If you want to upgrade an ST506 drive, few manufacturers still supply this interface.

There are really just two current players in the controller-drive standards market

—SCSI (and its derivatives) and IDE. They have evolved over a number of years and are still being improved and enhanced. They have both prospered and developed not through smooth design—as you will see with the history of SCSI—but because of user demand. IDE offers an excellent solution for low-cost, single-drive desktop installations, and with local bus it can rival SCSI in transfer rates. SCSI provides a more sophisticated peripheral and multiple drive support required in redundant arrays and power workstations. The two differ fundamentally in their way they work: SCSI has separate controller and peripheral. The controller fits into an expansion slot and is sent instructions by the PC's processor. IDE integrates almost all the controlling logic onto the drive and hangs off the main system bus—which can include a local bus. Both interfaces are suited for different tasks and both have very different histories.

The SCSI interface standard

As far as bad reputations go, that of the SCSI standard must be difficult to beat. Originally developed by Shugart, and called SASI (Shugart Associates System Interface), it was designed as a parallel I/O bus to connect hard disks to a PC. In 1981, the ANSI committee took SASI as a basis for its proposed hard disk standard and renamed it SCSI. It was finally published as a standard in 1986. But SCSI already had problems, notably that it was designed for, and could only cope with, controlling disk drives. Users wanted a fast parallel controller that could cope with all their peripherals—hard disk drives, CD-ROM, plotter, scanners, and so on. Work began on a new standard, called SCSI-2, that would be able to drive multiple, different peripherals at the same time. Unfortunately, this new standard got bogged down and was withdrawn shortly before official publication in 1990—it was then rewritten and resubmitted. This only had the effect of adding to the suspicion surrounding SCSI.

The SCSI-2 specification was designed to handle different types of peripheral—the current standard can drive seven different types of device at the same time, daisy-chained off the same bus. SCSI-2 also improved on the vanilla SCSI standard in a number of other important areas: these were the addition of Wide-SCSI, Fast-SCSI, and multitasking. SCSI-2 was still beset with problems, but mostly these were because it was a very complex interface specification and because not all manufacturers followed it exactly or understood it completely. One of the problems commonly cited under SCSI-2 is associated with command queueing; SCSI-2 can accept up to 256 I/O commands from the host, and queue them, so freeing up the main PC processor. Unfortunately, the SCSI-2 standard did not provide enough error-correcting feedback when informing the host processor that each of the queued commands had been completed—but this will be amended in the new standard, SCSI-3.

The original SCSI specification started life when 8-bit data paths were the norm, and so SCSI used an 8-bit data path transferring data at 5 Mbytes/sec—the same rate as the doomed ST506 standard. SCSI-2 got out of this hole with Fast-SCSI which doubled the data rate to 10 Mbytes/sec, but still over an 8-bit data path. All light and rosey? No, this is SCSI, remember! Fast-SCSI had two possible signalling methods: one, called single-ended, was cheap but could be prone to errors. It worked by sending binary data along a wire with a second wire as a reference ground wire. Differential signalling uses the second wire to carry an inverse of signal, providing far better immunity against noise, and so is less prone to errors. The downside is that differential signalling costs more to implement. However, the advantages are so great that almost all SCSI-2 controllers with Fast-SCSI use differential signalling. It is also true that to say that almost all new SCSI-2 controllers are capable of implementing Fast-SCSI.

The problems of Fast-SCSI are nothing compared to havoc that Wide-SCSI caused within the drive manufacturing industry. Wide-SCSI offers a wider data path over Fast-SCSI and improved data transfer rates of between 20 and 40 Mbytes/sec. Problems started when trying to define this wider data path. To begin with, the simplest method seemed to be to add a second cable that would carry a 32-bit data path. This 68-pin cable complemented the existing 50-pin cable. Did manufacturers like this idea? No. A compromise was reached that used just one 68-pin cable (doing away with the original 50-pin cable), but this was only capable of carrying a 16-bit data path. The promise of 40 Mbyte/sec transfers with a combination of Fast- and Wide-SCSI was never achieved and 20 Mbytes/sec is the common practical maximum transfer rate. Needless to say, Wide-SCSI has not been a success. This single 68-pin cable has been incorporated into the SCSI-3 definition and, as long as it has not changed again, should prove more popular.

This all paints a gloomy picture of SCSI. True, it has had far more than its fair share of problems, but it has a lot of advantages. The only rival, and I use this word cautiously, to SCSI is IDE which is simpler, but less suitable for power PCs where a lot of data is flying around. The major difference is that a SCSI controller is an intelligent unit with a processor of its own. The PC's processor sends the SCSI controller instructions to fetch data, and the controller then manages the drive and retrieves the data. This frees the PC's processor from a lot of wasted cycle time. It also means that a SCSI controller can work as a bus-master (on EISA or MCA-bus PCs), helping throughput further and increasing performance by lessening the load on the PC's main processor. An IDE controller, in comparison, cannot bus-master and needs more attention from the PC's processor.

The current hot topic in the controller market is speculation over the SCSI-3 specification, which is being managed by the X3T9.2 committee at ANSI. So far, only a few parts of the full spec have been finalized, so only some manufacturers are currently claiming SCSI-3 compatibility. Some features that will be included have been mentioned—such as better command queuing feedback (also called tagging) and the single 68-pin cable carrying a 16-bit data path. Another new feature will be support for adapter redundancy: you should be able to plug one drive into two adapters; if one controller fails, the second will take over. AutoDisconnect will also be featured, allowing drives to connect and disconnect from a SCSI bus without affecting the host operation (ideal for RAID systems). However, the big development for a parallel I/O interface like SCSI is that serial versions are being worked on and are generally seen as the future of SCSI. Some advantages of a serial interface are immediate: simpler, cheaper, lighter cabling; an interface better suited to driving plotter and scanner peripherals. There are three possible serial transmission methods currently being investigated: fibre-optic, serial storage architecture (SSA), supported by IBM; and what is called a high-performance serial link (T1394), supported by Apple.

Whichever wins, each is better for a particular application. T1394, for example, was devised to help multimedia applications; ironic since multimedia is the one area that has provided the main impetus to keep SCSI alive over the last few years and is now expanding the market. Multimedia applications and the huge demand for CD-ROM drives has forced the industry to try and standardize. The main problem was the interface to control the SCSI card itself. Previously, each card had its own often proprietary method with unique device drivers required. This has now been almost eliminated with the general adoption of ASPI (Advanced SCSI Programming Interface).

SCSI-2 is dominant as a controller in multimedia and many peripheral controller markets. It might transmute, under SCSI-3, to a high-speed serial link—still using the SCSI command set, but without the parallel data path. However, users can be assured that SCSI-2, with Fast-SCSI, is the current norm, is a settled standard, and is—finally—an accepted standard. Plug any current SCSI device into any SCSI controller and it is almost certain to work—something you could not have been at all sure of just a couple of years ago.

The IDE interface standard

Network servers and high-performance workstations appreciate the benefits of SCSI, as do users with scanners or CD-ROM drives. However, the dominant standard in the general desktop market is IDE (integrated drive electronics). IDE took over from the late ST506 standard as the interface for desktops. It differs in many ways from SCSI. A SCSI drive needs a controller that sits in an expansion slot and interprets the commands sent from the PC's main processor before passing these onto the drive itself. IDE, in contrast, moves almost all of the control electronics onto the disk drive itself. IDE drives do not need a separate controller that takes up an expansion slot, instead there is a simple feed from the main bus. IDE drives do not work as bus-masters and rely on the main CPU to control data flow. Even so, the data transfer rate can be a respectable 4 Mbytes/sec. In some drives, such as Quantum's ProDrive range, the on-board IDE controller can talk directly to a local-bus equipped PC, pushing data transfer rates even ahead of SCSI-2, to a mean 11 Mbytes/sec when connected to a PCI or VL-bus local bus.

IDE has had a far less colourful past than SCSI; it has also got a less interesting future. The one point that is of note concerns drive capacity. SCSI currently wins hands down with availability of 2 Gbyte drives. IDE hangs back with a current maximum supported drive of around 520–540 Mbytes. This limited capacity is being attacked by Compaq and IBM, with work going towards the development of a new BIOS that will break the 540 Mbyte barrier. Unfortunately, neither party is keen to discuss progress.

IDE is perfect as an inexpensive controller for small desktop systems, but it cannot compete with SCSI in high-performance transfer rates, or multitasking. Both these are now generally required features of RAID systems within high-performance servers. Since it lacks both, IDE will stay on the desktop—and do well there with a low price borne from being a relatively unsophisticated interface.

Choosing an Operating System for Your Desktop

One choice that will make most difference to your users is the operating system that you install on the workstation. MS-DOS is the predominant operating system for standard desktops; OS/2, Windows NT, and Unix are better suited to power workstation configurations (they are also covered in detail in Chapter 8). MS-DOS works away as the foundation for both Windows and Microsoft's newer Windows for Workgroups 3.11 graphical operating systems. There is a basic choice for DOS—either Microsoft's MS-DOS or Digital Research's DR-DOS. Both current versions offer similar functionality, and both MS-DOS 6 and Novell DOS 7 (the new name for DR-DOS) include disk compression to effectively double the capacity of your hard disk. Both also provide a useful virus diagnosis utility and a program to transfer data between a desktop and laptop.

Running on top of DOS, whichever variety, is Microsoft Windows. The current version, 3.1, will soon be replaced by 4.0, which will include more security and connectivity features as standard. Windows 3.1 is network aware and provides several useful functions for a networked user. Network printer support is good and persistent connection will re-establish drive mappings when you next log in. To provide these functions, you need to configure Windows for the particular network operating system software that you are using—and often the particular version of network shell that is installed. You can download the most recent copies of the shell software from on-line services such as CompuServe or CIX.

Windows for Workgroups 3.11 is really a peer-to-peer network operating system but it is often pre-installed onto stand-alone desktop machines. It provides similar connectivity to the main network system software—including Novell NetWare and Windows NT/AS. For a user, Windows for Workgroups has a number of benefits: it includes a version of Microsoft Mail and a group scheduler. The latest version includes built-in support for fax cards and better connectivity to third-party network operating systems. Whichever version of Windows you install, you will come across problems. Should you install one copy on the server to be shared by all users, or get better performance and install it onto each workstation? These are covered in the next section.

Running Windows on a Network

Microsoft Windows has given users a simple, intuitive front-end in which to work. The applications, such as Word for Windows, Ami Pro, or Excel, are powerful and graphical. To get the best out of Windows, you can network Windows workstations. This immediately presents a number of problems. A lot of administrators tried to install MS-Windows 3.0 on a LAN and ended up cursing. It would repeatedly crash with splendid error messages and soon most administrators gave up. Now, Windows 3.1 has a host of extra features that make it easy to install and manage on a LAN. Windows 3.1 has features built in to help the LAN supervisor manage users and workstations and includes utilities to make networking easier for users.

When installing Windows on a LAN, you can minimize the number of calls to the support department by forcing the users into accepting a fixed configuration. Normally, users can add groups to their Windows installation, move icons around the screen, and disrupt a setup. They can also run applications, games, and the Control Panel—none of which helps the support department maintain an orderly network. For example, with Windows 3.1 you should create shared groups containing the common applications that users cannot edit. You should also restrict how much access the users have to the Windows configuration utilities.

Creating a shared group has the added bonus that you can now add new applications to each user's workspace without having to touch their workstations. If you create a program group in a directory that users have only read rights to, you can be sure they can all share without being able to edit it or move icons around. The previous version of Windows, 3.0, produced error messages whenever a user tried to move an icon out of a group—now Windows 3.1 blocks this altogether.

To setup a shared group, create the group within a common shared directory on the server using the File/New selection. Move all the application icons into the group and flag the group and application files as read-only. You can now add this to everyone's workspace by editing the shared copy of PROGMAN.INI to include the line with your new group.

This degree of control will help cut the number of calls from users who have accidentally deleted an icon, reconfigured a program, or moved the icons around. However, as a manager you really want more control over the users and what they can (and more importantly, cannot) do. Previously, Windows 3.0 allowed users to run any extra programs not in the workspace by pulling down the File/Run menu option. Windows 3.1 lets you limit this.

Within PROGMAN.INI is a section labelled [Restrictions] that lets a supervisor limit the potentially dangerous uses of the Windows Program Manager (Fig. 5.1). There are a dozen entries within the [Restrictions] section that you can set depending on the control you want over your users.

1 NoRun set to '1' will disable the File/Run menu command, preventing users running any applications that are not already on their desktop. Setting this to '0' or leaving it blank will enable the Run option.
2 NoClose set to '1' will disable the Exit option from the File menu. This effectively stops any user from exiting Windows and having a free romp around the DOS system. It will also prevent you exiting by disabling the Alt-F4 action and double-clicking on the top-lefthand corner of Program Manager.
3 NoSaveSettings set to '1' will prevent a user from saving their desktop settings—any of their rearranged icon or group placings—on exiting Windows.

If you want to keep your Windows screens looking the same on startup, set this option to '1'.

4 NoFileMenu set to '1' will completely disable the options within the File menu. Remember, even with this set a user can still exit using Alt-F4 unless NoClose is set.

5 EditLevel defines the level of control users have over their desktops. A quick summary of the five levels is: Level '0' imposes no restrictions. Setting this option to '1' prevents a user from deleting, creating, or changing parameters of groups. Level '2' adds to level 1 by preventing the creation, editing, or deletion of items within a group. Level '3' adds to level 2 by disabling the Properties dialog box. Level '4' prevents users changing anything except moving icons around the screen.

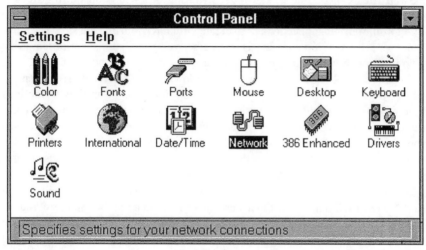

Figure 5.1 Network settings can be accessed from the Control Panel in Windows

A combination of carefully setting up shared read-only group files and using the [Restrictions] section of PROGMAN.INI should cut out a lot of calls to your help desk from self-inflected wounds. These two measures will also prevent users from wandering around your system as they please.

One point that is often missed by larger companies is to do with the Windows wallpaper. It might look great to have your company logo displayed. If you have networked Windows, a quick tip to minimize network traffic is to get rid of the logo: as a bitmap for wallpaper on each workstation it can take up over 200K of RAM. Give them all a plain background and see increased performance.

Another simple idea for increasing security with Windows workstations is to use the built-in screen-saver. One of the most inviting opportunities arises when a user nips out to lunch or make a coffee—they leave their workstation logged in and open to anyone passing. This is very inconvenient, forcing users to log out, then log back in—so why not use one of Windows' built-in features. There are solutions that will log you out during a DOS session, but they cost. Why not use the bundled Windows screen-saver? Start it from the desktop icon in the Control Panel—you can add a password, which stays encrypted within WIN.INI—and it will cut down casual hacking.

How to Install Windows on a LAN

The argument rages around user groups, supervisors are divided, and Microsoft has little to say on the matter. What are we talking about? Swap files and servers. Windows stores data in a number of temporary swap files—especially if you are running several applications at the same time—and there are pros and cons as to the type of swap file to setup and where it should be located.

Swap files can be one of the most irritating and time-consuming areas of Windows to get right on your LAN. The file is used by Windows as a temporary store for minimized applications or to create virtual RAM using the slow hard disk. Windows 3.1 gives you a choice as to whether you use a permanent or temporary swap file. For network managers, it is this choice that needs explaining.

If you are installing a shared copy of Windows on the NetWare drive, then you will have to setup the swap files. First, try and direct the swap files to the local drive on the workstation. If you save the swap files to the server, it will cause heavy traffic that will soon slow your network. In addition, NetWare 2.1x users who direct swap files to the server will come up against additional problems as NetWare's security fills the file with zeros before allowing access. Because of this, NetWare 2.x users will find Windows slows very dramatically.

To setup your swap files, and direct them to the correct drive, you will need to edit SYSTEM.INI and define the general drive letter that will be used by Windows for its swap files. By including the line PAGINGDRIVE=C in the [386enh] section of SYSTEM.INI, Windows running in enhanced mode will now be forced to swap onto the user's local drive.

Forget to do this and your LAN would collapse in a puff of overload—the traffic incurred if Windows used its default setting and swapped megabytes of data to a network drive would be colossal. What is really annoying for supervisors who like everything to be neat and tidy is that Windows uses two swap files. The first is for the shell itself, the second is used for applications. Since you are running Windows over a network it is best to setup a permanent swap file that is directed to the local drive. If you do not do this Windows could decide to swap to a remote drive and your LAN will be flooded with traffic.

A temporary swap file is deleted after you quit out of Windows; a permanent swap file remains intact. To set up a permanent swap file, Windows needs to be shown a patch of contiguous hard disk space. You might need to run a defragmenter program on your local disk first (do not even try to run a defragmenter on your networked drives—most should detect this, but some might just go ahead and corrupt your NetWare volume). A better, and faster, solution is to use a RAM disk (set this up with SMARTDRV.SYS included in the Windows directory). To tell Windows that you want it to use a permanent swap file, and to select the RAM disk as the destination, do the following. In WIN.INI, comment out the LOAD= parameter and run Windows in real mode ('WIN /R'). Run SWAPFILE using the RUN option of the FILE menu. Once complete, uncomment LOAD= statements in WIN.INI. The size of the swap file determines how many applications can be run concurrently. Just the action of setting up a permanent swap file will be enough for you to notice that Windows loads faster.

Even if you have expressly defined a permanent swap file, Windows still sneaks in a second, temporary SWP file. By adding the PAGINGDRIVE statement to SYSTEM.INI, you can control this too.

If you have to look after workstations running Windows on a LAN, you should invest in a copy of Microsoft's Windows Resource Kit. The cost is around £25 and provides an excellent source-book for problems, queries, and information on installing Windows over a LAN. Best of all, you get a diskful of utilities including WinLogin. This utility lets you keep a central database of user's configuration files. You can implement changes and updates to the configuration of a user's Windows setup without walking around each workstation.

6
Network Printers

Ultimate hell for any LAN administrator is every user having their own personal printer sitting on their desk. Faced with this, an administrator would have to have a colossal budget, the patience of a saint to cope with the setup and help calls, and a large store-room to keep all the consumables.

Contrast this with the calm, relaxed administrator who has got just one large printer servicing all the users on the network. Just one point of failure, one set of consumables, and one configuration for all the users. You can feel your worries melt away. Of course, this is exaggerating the problems and benefits of each, but the decision to install a networked printer can prove a boon for users and administrators.

The first and biggest hurdle will be the resistance of the users. A user's ideal is very different from that of the supervisor. Users would like their own, personal printers on their desks. If he has a dot-matrix, he wants a laser printer. If she has to share a printer via a manual printer-sharer box with a couple of other users, she would prefer her own. It can be very difficult to convince senior users senior within your company that they should share a central printer. Accounts departments are notorious for requiring their own printers—for security, of course. In some cases, however, the reasons are justified; accounts often require a dot-matrix to print on multi-part stationery and the financial director probably does need his own private printer.

Instead of providing a single large printer to service the entire company, compromise and split up the load into workgroups—typically with a dozen or fewer users per printer. When choosing a printer for this number of users, you can still look at high-end personal printers rather than departmental printers. Sticking with well-known personal printers means that there is more of a chance your software will directly support the printer, rather than relying on the printer manufacturer to provide drivers.

But how does your network operating system route print jobs from a workstation to the correct printer? Novell's NetWare 2.x and 3.x use a program that runs on the server called PSERVER. This VAP or NLM, depending on the version of NetWare, looks after routing print jobs from various queues to various printers. The basic methodology is this: define a number of queues for your particular workgroups, e.g. ACCOUNTS and SALES. You can then use the local NetWare command,

CAPTURE, to redirect output from a workstation to a particular queue (Windows recognizes NetWare queues directly, so there is no need to use CAPTURE). At the console, start PSERVER. You can then attach queues to the print-server. The print-server will control one or more local printers. If you have a remote print-server device (either a hardware adapter described below, or a PC running RPRINTER) you must specify this in the print-server's definition (Fig. 6.1).

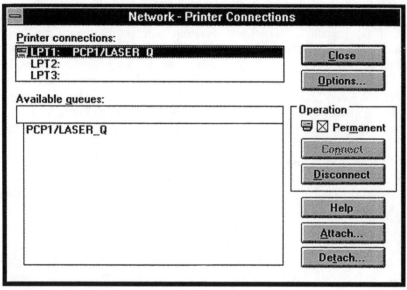

Figure 6.1 Connecting to a remote printer through the printers' icon in the Control Panel in Windows

NETWORKING A PRINTER

Connecting a printer to a network is not a difficult job. High-end personal printers and departmental printers will either have a network interface card already fitted, or have an option for an internal card. For example, QMS and DataProducts both sell departmental printers with output speed up to 32 pages per minute (ppm). Both manufacturers provide a choice of an internal Ethernet, 10Base-T, or Token Ring interface.

If you want to connect a personal printer, or one of your existing printers, to a LAN, you can do so using a network printer adapter. These are similar in size to a pocket network adapter; one end plugs into the printer's parallel port and the other to a choice of network cabling system. Typically, these adapters operate as a stand-alone print-server and can work as a print-server with a NetWare 2.x, 3.x or Windows NT/AS server. Portable print-server adapters have a lot of advantages; you can make better use of your resources by connecting your existing printers into the main network and providing an easy way for users to share them. The adapters are very quick and simple to install and, best of all, your user's existing software does not have to be reconfigured.

Portable print-servers are available from some of the major printer manufacturers, such as Hewlett-Packard and IBM/Lexmark and are also available from adapter manufacturers such as Intel and Xircom. Intel's NetPort Express for an Ethernet cabling system costs £599, compared to a typical internal Ethernet adapter from HP (the JetDirect card) which fits into a LaserJet 4, costing £400.

There is an even simpler way of connecting a printer to the network—plug it into one of the parallel or serial ports on your server. Initially, this might seem to have a couple of big pluses. It is cheap: you need nothing more than a printer cable. It is compatible: all network operating systems will drive a local printer from the server. But it also has several major disadvantages. The main problem is a conflict of interest over access. You should ideally lock your server away from inquisitive or malicious users, but if a printer is sited in the server room, you need to give users easy access to their printouts. You could snake a long printer cable into an adjoining room, but this is a clumsy solution and often impractical. Lastly, driving a local printer will use some system time and CPU cycles through parallel port interrupts and could degrade server performance slightly.

By connecting a printer directly to the network cabling system, data is transferred far faster than over a parallel cable: with little other traffic on a normal 10 Mbps Ethernet cable, a print job will be downloaded to the printer around 10–15 times faster than over a parallel printer connection. This does not mean it will print fast—it still has to pass from the print-server's buffer to the printer via a parallel connection—but it is not using workstation or server time.

Remote print-servers are almost as straightforward to setup as a local printer. Under NetWare, the portable print-server will start to identify itself to the main server once it is switched on. Attach a predefined queue to the server and you are ready to go. You should make sure that it is easy to configure the remote print-server. Some products, such as the Xircom adapter and Intel's NetPort, have utility software that runs on any workstation and provides remote management and setup of the print-server unit. Others have a fixed print-server name or make it difficult to change the name. In a small network, it might not matter that the print-server is called 'PRINT-SERVER', but in a large multisite or multiserver network, this is not helpful for management or identification.

Installing a remote print-server adapter may be straightforward on a standard NetWare LAN running IPX, but if you have an OS/2 or Unix network make sure that the print-server has drivers for NetBIOS or TCP/IP. Many print-server adapters limit you to a choice of Ethernet or Token Ring and only have drivers for NetWare and NT/AS; if you want Mac or Unix connectivity, check that drivers are available.

Novell's RPRINTER

If you are running Novell's NetWare 3.12 or 4.0, you have, hidden among all the utilities, a program called RPRINTER. This is a small resident program that runs on a PC workstation and turns this workstation into a remote print-server. Attach a local printer to this PC and it is accessible to any other user on the network (once you have assigned a queue to it at the server console).

If you are upgrading a lot of your current PCs, why not keep one old PC/XT aside and use it as a dedicated print-server? This way, you do not need to buy a remote print-server adapter. Of course, any PC on your network can run RPRINTER without being dedicated to the job. RPRINTER is a resident utility, so it does take up RAM on the PC. Worse, if a lot of other users are printing, anyone using the PC will find it slows to a crawl because RPRINTER takes all the CPU's time.

CHOOSING A PRINTER

When selecting a printer that is going to be shared between a number of users with different needs, you have to look at specific features. The most flexible and popular type of printer are laser or LED printers. These page printers are quiet, fast, and provide high-quality output. Cheaper personal printers tend to employ Hewlett-Packard's PCL page-description language standard. The current version, PCL-5, is used in HP's LaserJet 4 range and offers almost the same font and graphics capabilities as its rival, PostScript. If a printer tries to clone the PostScript interpreter, you can sometimes get error-messages when downloading new fonts or attempting to print complex graphics. Printers that use the 'official' interpreter licensed from Adobe print a message to this effect on start-up—they also cost more.

Older applications for PCs may not recognize PostScript, instead they will output using PCL (which is used by all HP LaserJet-compatible printers and is downwards compatible). If your LAN uses Macintoshes, you will find that they normally stick to PostScript. Ideally, you should pick a laser printer that can handle both, and many such as the DataProducts LZR2080, HP LaserJet 4, QMS PS1700, and Compaq PageMarq range do. If you have a mix of users with applications that use PCL and PostScript, you must make sure your printer has automatic sensing to switch between the two page-description languages or you will end up with hundreds of pages of PostScript code rather than a single page of graphics. Emulation that has to be manually switched is no good if the printer is shared.

One way around this problem is used by DataProducts in its LZR range of 16–20 ppm laser printers. With these printers you can dedicate a particular port to a particular emulation. For example, if you have a mixed network of PCs and Macs, you could dedicate the LocalTalk interface to expect PostScript data, and the parallel port dedicated to PCL jobs.

Many of the high-end laser printers, such as the HP LaserJet 4 and DataProducts' LZR2080, provide extra high-resolution output. Instead of the usual 300 dots per inch (dpi) of personal printers, these offer the ability to print at up to 600 or 800 dpi. There can be some problems with this that might trap the unwary supervisor. Firstly, some printers require a special driver before they will work at the higher resolution: this means reconfiguring all your workstations. Others need to be manually set from the printer's console. You might be tempted to leave it switched to 600 dpi, but this slows printing.

Which brings us neatly to speed. It is not too important if a personal printer on your desktop is rated at 8 instead of 10 ppm. For a shared printer, the speed determines how capable it will be. As a guideline, for a network of 8–10 users sharing a single printer, you should choose a model that can print at 20 ppm otherwise your users will have to wait for print output. Departmental networks with tens or hundreds of users need several large, fast printers. QMS has a range that will go up to 32 ppm.

The advantage of buying a faster printer is that it has been designed for a continuous, stressful life and should prove more reliable than pushing a desktop personal printer to its limits. It should also be designed for a role as a shared printer; this includes a high-capacity paper tray and multiple paper trays. A printer running at 30 ppm will empty a 200-sheet feed-bin in around six minutes. You should also choose a printer with multiple paper trays: with plain A4, headed notepaper, and perhaps A3. The DataProducts LZR2080 and Compaq PageMarq can both handle paper sizes up to A3. You should also consider the cost per sheet in terms of consumables. As an example, the HP LaserJet IVsi has a cost per page of 1.8p (manufacturer's supplied price).

One of the eventualities of life is that you will at some point have a paper jam. It is then that you are grateful for easy access to the entire paper path. The DataProducts range of printers has access from the top, front, and sides to the paper rollers, making it very easy to remove a crumpled sheet. It also has a useful feature that will reprint the page that jammed—this way you do not wreck a long print job.

If your users have particular font requirements, perhaps the 10 000 Japanese characters, or a complex logo that is always downloaded, you can help reduce the print time by fitting an external hard disk to the printer. High-end printers often have an internal SCSI hard disk to hold fonts and print routines. Check if there is an external SCSI connector to allow you to boost the printer's storage capacity to hold extra fonts or images and cut download times for fonts by around one-third compared to sending data down the wire.

Finally, you should look at the reliability and sturdiness of the printer. A good indicator to this is the printer's rated duty cycle. This tells you how many pages per month it can print without stressing it or affecting its reliability. A personal printer is normally rated between 3000 and 6000 pages per month. A high-end laser printer designed for a role as a shared printer should manage a duty cycle of around 30 000–50 000 pages per month. One tip: beware some manufacturers that quote duty cycles in pages per year.

If you do decide to buy a central network printer, make sure that you choose one that is easy to hook up, easy to manage, and easy to service. Do not forget when justifying the cost that you can split it between several users. For your users' sake, site it somewhere convenient—if it is too much bother to walk to it, you will soon get requests for personal printers.

PRINTING FOR SMALL WORKGROUPS

Typical of a small, cheap desktop laser printer is the HP LaserJet 4L. Although designed for lightweight duties as a personal printer, you can share one among a small group with occasional printing needs. The LaserJet 4L does not accept an internal adapter, but you can use an external adapter, such as HP's JetDirect external Ethernet adapter (£400 from HP), or by using a third-party print-server, such as the Intel NetPort Express XL (599 from Intel).

At 2.3p per page, running costs for the LaserJet 4L are higher than a network laser printer, but can be reduced to 1.1p by switching the 4L into Economode (a draft mode).

PRINTING FOR LARGE WORKGROUPS

The DataProducts LZR2080 is designed to work as a print-server on a network. It has a high-speed engine that is rated at 20 ppm; it will also print at a maximum resolution of 800 dpi. A choice of internal network adapters are available, including Ethernet, 10Base-T, LocalTalk, and Token Ring. Drivers are available for NetWare, NT/AS, Unix, and Macintosh connections. Setup and management is via a dedicated serial link and no remote management over the LAN is possible. Although the LZR supports both PCL and PostScript, it cannot automatically switch between the two, though you can dedicate a different emulation to each port. Lastly, if you use a large font library, you can attach a SCSI hard disk to boost local storage.

7
Improving Performance

INTRODUCTION

If your users are beginning to complain that the network is slow, it is likely that you have a bottleneck somewhere. If you have unlimited funds, then you could simply upgrade across the board: new cable, new server, and new adapter cards. If you want to make sure that you are spending the right amount of money in the right places, this chapter will take you through the possible problem areas and explain how to improve your LAN's performance.

There are three main areas where an upgrade would improve performance: the server, the workstation, and the signalling method used to link the two. I am assuming that you do not want to swap out your installed Ethernet system for an FDDI solution, instead I will concentrate on optimizing the server and the workstation.

You might think that adding extra memory will boost performance, but which sort of memory and should you add it to the server or the workstations? Similarly with hard disks; if users are complaining that they are running out of disk space, what can you do to help them out, improve performance, and keep within a budget?

TUNING YOUR SERVER

In a LAN with a dedicated server, it seems natural that you should try and boost its performance. All the network's traffic passes through the server and its performance directly influences its response time to a user.

If you want to supercharge your server you will have to consider how your server is being used and, ideally, use a network monitoring tool to help you spot your LAN's weak points. Chapter 5 details how to select the right server for your needs; in this section I will work through the best add-ons to get the most from your server.

High-performance Network Adapters

Network adapters turn data arriving in serial form over the network into words of parallel bits which it moves into system RAM using the PC's main bus. The cheapest network adapters have an 8-bit interface to the PC's bus. If your PC's central processor is only an 8088 or 8086, then an 8-bit adapter matches the 8-bit data path of these processors. If your PC is powered by a 16-bit 80286, its bus will be 16 bit. A bottleneck is formed around the adapter which can only transfer 8-bit words across the 16-bit bus. Similarly, 32-bit processors like the 80386 or 80486 can accept data 32 bits at a time across a 32-bit EISA or MCA bus (ISA is limited to 16 bits maximum).

To cut any possible bottleneck between the adapter and the processor, the two should be matched. This becomes vital in a server, with its very high volume of data, but is less critical in a normal user's workstation. If your server uses an 80386 or an 80486 processor and has an EISA or MCA bus, you will find overall network response time is cut and performance improves if you fit 32-bit adapters. For better performance still, bus-mastering adapter cards will remove any load from the central processor by looking after the data transfer into system RAM (see Chapter 3 for more explanation of adapter cards). Most workstations will operate at near peak performance using just a 16-bit adapter card. It is only worth upgrading a workstation's adapter to a 32-bit card if the workstation is a heavy CAD or database user and if you have already upgraded the server.

Double Your Data Rate

All networks have a maximum data bandwidth. If you add too many users, or the users start to transfer more data—perhaps they have just moved to Microsoft Windows with its higher data overhead—your network will soon suffer. Ethernet transmits data at 10 Mbps and has an effective throughput of only 4–5 Mbps. It would be great if you could just double your network's data-carrying capacity. You can, by fitting extra network adapters in your server.

If your server is a fast EISA or MCA-bus PC, then it has bandwidth to spare on its bus. One Ethernet adapter card has a bandwidth of around 5 Mbps; split your network into two and drive each from a separate adapter fitted in the server. Each half of the network will work exactly as before; only the network operating system and your wiring diagram need know. Before you buy another card, make sure your software can support multiple adapters—Novell's NetWare 2.2 and 3.12 operating systems support up to four adapters. With NetWare 3.12 on an EISA PC, the process would be to fit the new adapters, then run the EISA setup utility to specify the location and I/O address of the new cards. Finally, start NetWare, load multiple copies of the same adapter driver from the command line, and modify the AUTOEXEC file so that it will load the drivers automatically when next booted up.

If you have not yet fitted bus-mastering cards into your server (assuming your server is either an EISA or MCA-bus PC), then you could save money and improve on performance by adding a second adapter. For example, if you are using an NE2000 (a 16-bit ISA Ethernet card), replacing it with an NE32000 (32-bit bus master card) would cost £1300 and offer around a 20–40 per cent gain in performance. Adding a second NE2000, which can be bought for £300, will increase performance by 70–80 per cent by effectively almost doubling your network's bandwidth.

By fitting multiple adapters into your server, you are turning it into a bridge. If you need to bridge two different types of network, e.g. Token Ring to Ethernet, use this technique to save you the cost of an additional, external, bridge. By loading the ROUTER NLM utility onto your NetWare 3.12 server, you can also turn a server into a router (see Chapter 12 for further details on routers). Using this method, you can create an internal router that will handle traffic in the standard IPX protocol as well as routing TCP/IP and AppleTalk protocols.

Making Best Use of RAM

One of the most difficult jobs for any supervisor used to be tuning a Novell NetWare server. With the arrival of version 3.0, and the current 3.12, memory management and tweaking the AUTOEXEC parameters has gone—NetWare will dynamically tune itself, making the best use of the available RAM. There are, however, still a number of points you should check on your server if you want to make the best use of your RAM. This means careful attention to the SET parameters within your server's AUTOEXEC file. Before you start tweaking your server's settings, you should monitor the sort of files stored and the load it experiences over a typical week.

In Chapter 4 the question of how much RAM a server needs is discussed. The answer, in the case of NetWare, is as much as possible. NetWare 3.12 will dynamically allocate cache RAM and system RAM by itself. If it runs low of cache RAM, system performance will suffer dramatically. The full equations are described in Chapter 4, but as a guideline, a NetWare server running with less than 8 Mbytes will provide very poor performance and 16 Mbytes is recommended for more than 10 users.

On the question of upgrade, it is better to provide a NetWare 3.12 server with as much system memory as possible. If you are using a drive controller card that can be fitted with cache RAM, you will find better performance by fitting system RAM rather than controller cache RAM. In fact, NetWare can be slowed down by a cacheing disk controller.

Increasing Disk Capacity

The simplest way to increase your server's storage capacity is to fit a second hard disk. If you are using an ESDI or SCSI controller, this poses no problem—the new hard disk can be added, daisy-chain fashion, after the existing drive. For servers running with an IDE controller, the expansion is down to your particular controller card. Many IDE cards will control two drives, but if not, you will either have to fit a second IDE controller with considerable implications of reconfiguring the system's interrupts, or fit a new, higher-capacity drive.

If you can, take this opportunity to upgrade to a SCSI hard drive subsystem in your server. SCSI-2, the latest standard, is now supported by most controllers, and will work with existing SCSI and SCSI-2 drives. With a SCSI controller in place, you can daisy-chain up to seven drives (including backup drives, CD-ROMs, or

WORMs) managed by one controller.

Avoid fitting a cacheing disk controller into a NetWare 3.12 server. NetWare uses its own, very efficient, software cacheing system that can actually be slowed down if it has to pass through a second cacheing system.

TUNING YOUR WORKSTATION

All workstations need to run a redirector and a protocol stack before they can connect to a LAN. The redirector makes sure that any references to shared drives are sent across the cable rather than handled by the local operating system. The protocol stack ensures that the data transmitted conforms to the protocol standard used across the rest of the network. Both need to be loaded into local system RAM. In some cases, they can take up a considerable amount of memory.

Users will not thank you if networking their PCs means losing a large chunk of their usable memory. However, there are several tricks to minimize the impact of networking.

NetWare requires two files to be loaded as TSRs (terminate and stay resident): IPX, the default protocol stack for NetWare, and the redirector, NETx. A typical NetWare scenario will require around 64K of workstation RAM: IPX taking up 20K, 4K to the driver for your network adapter, and 40K to NETx. To check how memory is being used in each workstation, run DOS's MEM command with the '/c' switch (this will only work in MS-DOS version 5 or higher).

If your workstations are fitted with more than 640K of basic memory, you can configure the RAM above 640K as EMS using the DOS HIMEM.SYS driver in your CONFIG.SYS file. MS-DOS 5 (or higher) allows you to load the network files into EMS rather than into standard RAM, which means your users' DOS applications will gain an extra 64K.

If your workstations are using MS-DOS 5 or 6 and have a 80386 or higher CPU, you can make use of the processor's memory-handling functions. MS-DOS 5 and 6 have commands that will load resident programs and device drivers into high memory, i.e. memory above the 640K base area. If you load your network drivers and redirectors into high memory, you could save up to 100K of conventional RAM that is better used for DOS applications. Running MS-DOS 6's MEMAKER utility will identify the type of memory you have installed, and the utility will try and conserve as much as possible. Next, edit your network batch file and use the LOADHIGH command to move IPX and the network card driver into high memory. NETx can also be moved high, but there is a special version, called EMSNETx, that is specially written to take advantage of high memory.

Software vs Hardware Cacheing

When you buy a new copy of DOS or Windows you will get a bundled copy of the software cacheing utility SMARTDRV. It installs in a minute, often automatically, and makes most applications run faster. Installing a cacheing disk controller yourself takes between 10 minutes and a couple of hours, and costs between £250 and £850. However, a good controller can improve disk throughput considerably.

The algorithms described in Chapter 5 in the section on cache algorithms can require significant processor power and time; SMARTDRV uses the PC's processor for this, reducing the time it can spend with applications. A hardware controller has its own on-board processor dedicated to this one purpose, freeing the PC's CPU to get on with the next task.

SMARTDRV also consumes memory that could be used by your application, and few people have enough memory in their systems for that not to be a consideration. SMARTDRV is, however, intelligent enough to surrender memory to the system if it is needed, but it takes processor time to make this decision. If you want to see how effective SMARTDRV is on a particular workstation, add the command-line switch '/s' and it will display the number of cache hits.

In addition to this basic cacheing, a good controller will try to order requests using elevator seek. These calculations could be done by the operating system but would consume so much of the processors' time as not to be viable for software cacheing systems.

An advantage that a software cache, such as SMARTDRV, has over hardware methods is that it is easier for the operating system to communicate tips as to the type of file activity that is happening. These could indicate if it is carrying out directory manipulation, swapping, and to some extent what sort of file is being accessed. Program files are accessed in a different way to data files while, if you are using the XCOPY command to transfer files from one part of the disk to another, swamping the cache, the cacheing software may take the view that the source files are unlikely to be accessed immediately and not cache the data.

Software caches are just as vulnerable to system crashes as hardware caches. Because DOS's and Windows' own data areas are not fully protected from stray pointers in defective applications, software cacheing runs a slightly higher risk of corruption. In a multitasking system such as OS/2 or even Windows, you will have a very different balance of processor, disk, and memory usage than under DOS alone.

While a DOS application is waiting for the disk, there is little it can do, as it needs the data to proceed, whereas if there are other tasks on the system they can make use of the processor. Having multiple tasks active also requires more system memory than does a single one, plus the overhead of the operating system managing them. In deciding the best approach for your PC you have to work out the cost-to-benefit ratio.

Depending on your PC and supplier, RAM costs between £23 and £210 per Mbyte (some manufacturers are somewhat predatory when it comes to pricing strategy). It will often be better, for instance in heavy graphics applications, to spend the money on more RAM than a cacheing controller.

For most people a faster disk is of marginal importance, especially so in the case of DOS character-based spreadsheets or wordprocessing. Users running Windows will get more immediate benefit from added system RAM, with a fast hard disk coming a close second. Unlike network servers, where a cacheing controller can actually slow down the performance, DOS has no built-in software cacheing, so a hardware cacheing controller will always boost performance. The question is, how much do you want to spend for this performance? Most users will have adequate performance from a standard configuration of a 80386 with 4 Mbytes of RAM, a standard IDE drive, and Windows' SMARTDRV installed as the only cacheing system.

8
System Software

INTRODUCTION

Creating a physical network is a straightforward business: install network adapter cards into each PC or Macintosh, link together using your chosen cabling, and switch on. There are definite reasons why you should choose one type of adapter card over another, and one style of cabling over its rival.

Once you have linked the workstations, you still need software to create a useful network. The popular operating systems running on a PC know nothing about networking—you have to install special network software. It is not so bad with a Mac, which has a degree of built-in support, but for advanced features, you will still need additional software. Enter the network operating system (NOS). I have already described the two main types of network: peer-to-peer and server-based. However, if all you want to do is share a printer between a few users, or copy an occasional file from one workstation to another, then you should use other options such as multi-user operating systems.

This chapter looks at NOS software. In a peer-to-peer network, this runs on each PC and provides utilities to share another PC's disk drive, and send your print jobs to a particular printer, as well as a degree of security using passwords. In a server-based network, the main NOS runs on the central server. Each PC connects to the central server and stores files in private or shared regions of its hard disk. The NOS makes sure that a particular user can access his or her files, and manages printers, shared modems, and links to other servers.

WHAT DOES AN OPERATING SYSTEM DO?

Working hard at the heart of any LAN is the NOS. This ensures that references to remote drives are redirected and shared resources are available. There are three main jobs that such an operating system must carry out: (i) provide file sharing, (ii) allow communications devices to be shared, and (iii) allow a printer or other peripheral to be shared. These three tasks sound simple, but how they are tackled can make or break a system for you, the manager, and the users.

86

In some operating systems, these three tasks are integrated into one operating system running on a single, dedicated PC. In other systems, the load is spread among the workstations that form the network, doing away with the need for a central, dedicated PC. Peer-to-peer network operating systems, such as Artisoft's LANtastic, Novell's NetWare Lite, or SPI's InvisibleNet, all run as background tasks on each of the workstations in the network. Each workstation takes a share of the load—although it is typical for one PC to be given the job of e-mail server or, by virtue of an attached peripheral, printer-server. However, the philosophy remains the same; the NOS sits on top of the standard, local workstation operating system (such as DOS or OS/2), and shares the load of storing files and managing peripherals between the workstations.

The other extreme in network design is adopted by the heavyweight operating system vendors, such as Novell's NetWare 3.12, Banyan VINES, Microsoft's Windows NT/AS, or IBM's LAN Server. They all recommend (although LAN Manager and LAN Server do not, strictly, require) a powerful dedicated PC running the NOS software. Each workstation then runs a small redirector that sends any network instructions or resource requests over the LAN to the central server, where the command is dealt with by the operating system running on the central server.

This central server is normally the store of all shared files, and can also manage shared printers and peripherals. In addition to dealing with the demands of, perhaps, hundreds of users, these operating systems can also run specially written applications on the server's processor. For example, Novell calls these extra applications NLMs (NetWare loadable modules), and they can be database managers, e-mail applications, or custom-written data-handling programs. The NOS is still running in parallel and channels any requests between the NLMs to the user. More often, the central server is used as a file-server to store data or application files which are used by a local workstation's processor.

So far, you will know how the differences between operating systems affect the theoretical design of a LAN, but they can also appear very differently to a user. Novell's NetWare, for example, is controlled by either command-line instructions or menu-driven utilities. It looks similar to DOS, and its command-line instructions are extensions to standard DOS commands (such as NDIR to display the extended directory information contained in a NetWare drive rather than the DOS DIR command). It can be very intimidating for a new user or someone unused to setting up or controlling a network. In contrast, many of the peer-to-peer LAN operating systems, such as Artisoft's LANtastic, go to considerable lengths to make a new user or raw administrator feel comfortable and right at home. LANtastic for Windows provides Windows-based tools and icon-driven applications to let you log on to the LAN, connect to printers, and send mail. Contrast this with NetWare or Windows NT/AS's complex combination of command-line instructions and menu-driven utilities that you would require to do the same.

These usability aspects will help to get a LAN accepted by new users, but in the long run, it is the network manager who will be controlling the LAN and using the utilities more than anyone else. A great-looking user front-end is good news in the short term, but make sure that it is backed up with usable and powerful tools to manage and setup the network.

Usability is very important when learning how to use a new LAN. However, in the longer term, one of the biggest differentiators between network operating systems is the ability to control external peripherals and communicate with other systems. Most peer-to-peer LAN operating systems fall short of the abilities of the heavyweight, central server-based products in their connectivity with other systems. A good example is your company's expansion. If, in a few month's time, some of your users might want to log in to the network from home, can your LAN support this feature? (In actual fact, this function can be achieved on any LAN using third-party software such as PC Anywhere or Carbon Copy.) When linking LANs, the functionality of the system software and its limitations becomes even more important. Novell's NetWare has built-in support to allow it to link to other LANs, including its main rival, Microsoft's NT/AS. Some peer-to-peer networks can do this, but it is not a common function. When demands become greater, e.g. when setting up a WAN, the ability of your network software to talk with other LANs via routers, modems, or internetwork links is vital.

There are two further types of operating systems that fall into part of each of the categories mentioned, namely Unix and multi-user versions of standard operating systems. Both are normally left out of network books, but could be the ideal solution for your installation if they match your requirements. Unix is generally considered to be one of the least logical operating systems for a user to get to grips with, but provides excellent connectivity options, especially for WANs.

Custom-written multi-user versions of DOS, such as Digital Research's Multiuser DOS or IGC's VM386, allow standard, cheap dumb terminals attached to a central PC using standard serial cable, to run DOS applications. There is little sophistication for connectivity to WANs or control of bridges and routers, but it is the cheapest way to allow up to a dozen users to run DOS applications.

In this chapter, the various flavours and architectures of NOSs are covered. If you are considering installing a new LAN or considering upgrading, read carefully the hardware requirements and capabilities that each of the major players offers. You will find that in high-end systems where cost is secondary, it is best to pick the operating system software that can do what you want of it, then select the hardware to run it. For lower-cost solutions, particularly peer-to-peer LANs, it is best to look at the hardware you already have and want to keep, then pick the software that will run on this and fulfil your requirements.

MULTI-USER OPERATING SYSTEMS

Until recently, plain vanilla DOS contained little that could make it even remotely network or multi-user capable. MS-DOS 6 has changed this to a certain degree by including basic support for serial connections (used to transfer data from a desktop to a laptop) and some limited network utilities. DOS can support network drives, as long as a special network redirector is loaded (this arrives with your NOS). DOS certainly cannot execute more than one program at once, so its role as a central server is very limited. OS/2 has better support, is multitasking, and has better file-handling routines. Windows, running on top of DOS, can also multitask, and, with Microsoft's Windows for Workgroups 3.11, can support file sharing and resource sharing.

For small installations, where money is tight and no one wants to spend their time looking after a network, there are alternatives that push DOS to its limits. The cheapest is called $25-Network. It costs $25—surprise—and offers basic file and resource sharing using standard serial ports instead of network adapters. The performance is poor, thanks to the limited speed of serial ports (115 Kbps compared to a Ethernet's 10 Mbps), but it is very cheap and quick to setup.

Also using serial ports are multi-user versions of DOS, such as Digital Research's Multiuser DOS. Running on a central PC, this allows several dumb terminals to appear to run DOS programs. It works by rerouting keyboard input and screen output via serial ports. If you have a number of existing dumb terminals, and want to network cheaply, while still using DOS applications (text-based rather than graphics-based applications), Multiuser DOS offers one of the few solutions.

PEER-TO-PEER NETWORK OPERATING SYSTEMS

Peer-to-peer networks are ideal for small groups of users—a dozen or fewer—that need to share a printer, files, and perhaps a modem. Peer-to-peer network software runs on each PC and you will need to repeat the installation process for each workstation. Installing this type of simple network software is no worse than any other application. In fact, because networks always worry users, even more of an effort has been put into making them simple to install and setup.

Peer-to-peer means that all the network tasks are spread out, a little responsibility on each PC. You can still carry on working, running your normal applications on each PC just as before. Some software, such as Artisoft's LANtastic, will happily cope with over 100 PCs connected together. However, realistically, if you are thinking of connecting this many PCs you should consider a server-based network.

In a peer-to-peer network, the software relies on DOS to manage storing files onto the local hard disk. Unfortunately, DOS is not very good at this and cannot cope well when lots of different users all want to open the same file. In a central server-based network, the NOS has been written to optimize hundreds of users accessing different files at the same time. It is far more efficient at reading and writing data onto the hard disk and so is normally faster than peer-to-peer network software. To be blunt, it does not have to rely on DOS, which is a hindrance when it comes to lots of users and networks.

Each PC has DOS installed as normal. The network software is actually a small program that sits resident in memory. It makes sure that any calls to a remote device are sent across the network. For example: if you access drive A:, your PC's floppy drive, the network software does nothing. However, if you access drive E:, the network software realizes that drive E: is actually on a different PC on the network and so sends this command across the network to the right PC. Same with a printer. You can have a shared printer that is somewhere on the network and a local printer plugged into your printer port. The network software will seem invisible if you print to the local printer, but will reroute the data across the network if you select the shared printer. The software does all this invisibly, but to do it the software has to be setup—which is more complex.

You can mix makes of adapter card within a network but not standards. As discussed in Chapter 3, there are a number of standards and types of network adapter. Most peer-to-peer systems arrive in a starter kit, with software, network adapters, and cabling. If you do not buy a kit with hardware and software, you will have to make sure that the network software supports the particular make of adapter that you have chosen. Avoid unknown makes and, for the simplest choice, pick an adapter that says it is NE1000 or NE2000 compatible—all the software here will support these types of adapter.

Some vendors cut prices by supplying proprietary network adapter hardware. It works very well, but is not standard and is not compatible with cards such as the NE1000. The software, too, will only work with this particular brand of hardware. In short, if you ever want to expand your network, you will have to buy network hardware from the peer-to-peer software publisher, rather than shopping around for a cheaper, standard adapter. Artisoft, Sage, and SPI all have cheaper starter kits that tie you into their own type of hardware. If you think you might expand, you would do well to pay an initial premium and choose the software option from these publishers that runs on any type of network adapter.

Using the Software

Peer-to-peer network software tries hard to be user-friendly. To control the network, e.g. map a drive letter to connect to another user's drive, or connect to a shared printer, you will need to use the network's commands. Once setup, your users should not need to run any of the network utilities or commands unless they want to change their setup. All peer-to-peer networks can be controlled using commands typed in at the DOS prompt followed with a long string of parameters. This is fine when you want to include setup within a batch file, but is cumbersome when using the network every day. For general use, all network software also has menu-driven utilities. Instead of typing a complex command to map to a remote drive, you see a list of available drives listed and use the cursor keys to pick the one you want. Going one step further, most software also has a special version that runs under Windows. Some products, like Microsoft's Windows for Workgroups 3.11, will only run under Windows; others, like Artisoft's LANtastic, includes both Windows and DOS programs in the same box.

Sage MainLAN 4.0

Sage's MainLAN 4.0 is a straightforward, no-frills network that provides reasonable performance. There is good, basic documentation for new users. Network cards are included in the starter pack and a proprietary hardware option is available. The interrupt and memory address of each network card is setup using jumpers (Fig. 8.1).

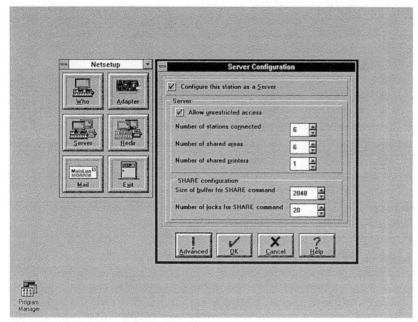

Figure 8.1 Screenshot of MainLAN

Installation of the software is easy, helped because MainLAN 4.0 does not support user's accounts—it uses shared level security (see Chapter 10 for more information). Security is limited to the directories on each PC or to shared resources such as a printer. You do not create security settings for individual users nor can files be individually protected. In a normal small office, this does not matter, but if you have a lot of temporary workers using your network, or want to control, say, the delete right for a particularly inept user, MainLAN 4.0 will not let you configure this setup.

MainLAN 4.0, in common with all the other software reviewed here (except for Windows for Workgroups), provides Ctrl-Alt-Del trapping. This means that if you try and reset your PC when connected to the network, you will see a warning message and be asked to confirm your actions. This is a useful feature and ensures that the disk cacheing software used by the network program has a chance to make sure all data held in memory is safely stored on disk.

The network adapter cards supplied with MainLAN 4.0 use a slight variation on the common Ethernet standard. The software will also work with most standard Ethernet cards, but you cannot mix Sage cards with other Ethernet cards on the same network. You must make the choice before you buy whether to be tied to Sage for your hardware if you ever want to add PCs to the network.

The MainLAN control software that lets you connect to printers or share files runs under Windows and DOS and is simple to use. One criticism is that there is no on-line help, so if you get stuck, you will need to look in the manual. Luckily, the functions are all obvious and the menus easy to navigate. You can share up to six printers on a MainLAN network, and share a modem between users, but not a CD-ROM player. All the other software provided hooks to share a CD-ROM player or other SCSI storage device.

One nice feature of MainLAN is that messaging and simple e-mail functions are included. These are not as sophisticated as Windows for Workgroups, but are one up on NetWare Lite. For small networks, MainLAN 4.0 is simple to install and use. Performance is reasonable but the number of features pales compared to Windows for Workgroups and the security is poor compared to NetWare Lite.

D-Link LANsmart

D-Link's LANsmart has evolved into a neat, simple network system that is very easy to use and setup. Like Sage's MainLAN it does not operate a user-level security. That is to say, you can setup security levels for resources, such as a printer, or directories, but not on an individual user-by-user level. Performance is good and the software can cope with a theoretical 128 simultaneous users.

Operating the software under DOS is simple and relies on menus to configure printers, share directories, or send messages. Once you have stepped through the menus necessary to attach a drive letter to a remote drive, you can save the configuration. If you are comfortable working at the DOS command line, you can do this using LANsmart's command-line utilities (typically, you would put these commands into your AUTOEXEC.BAT file to log in and configure your PC as it powers on).

A PC running LANsmart can operate either as a workstation (i.e. sharing resources or files on PCs), or as a server (allowing other PCs to share local resources). The amount of RAM taken up by the LANsmart resident software depends on the task. A workstation loses just under 50K, which compares well with LANtastic's requirements for just under 100K. One small point is that if your PC has more than 640K of RAM (and most new PCs do), LANsmart will not automatically detect this high memory or try and load the drivers high—you have to edit the CONFIG.SYS file after installation.

Unlike MainLAN, LANsmart will allow a CD-ROM player to be shared over the network, and supports a wide range of standard network adapter cards. D-Link is better known as a maker of network adapter cards, so the choice of hardware in the kit is good and includes D-Link's pocket adapters that plug into your PC's printer port.

SPI Invisible LAN

SPI's Invisible LAN product is normally sold as a complete package with network adapters included. You can choose from a wide range of cards—from a proprietary standard to a normal Ethernet-standard card with several options between. The basic differences in each card are mainly accounted for in a price-to-performance difference. Watch out if you pick the proprietary card, like Sage although this is cheaper to start with, you will be stuck to one supplier for any future plans.

The software, called Net-30, is a flexible NOS that straddles the gap between peer-to-peer and server-based—if you have a lot of PCs connected, you can setup Net-30 on a dedicated PC to gain extra performance. However, most users are likely just to stick to the basic configuration. Net-30 proved very easy to install and configure and was only let down by a big appetite for memory—the resident software took up 130K of RAM, leaving little for other applications. If you have high memory this is reduced by around half, but is still a large overhead to carry.

The Net-30 software provides better security measures than Sage or D-Link. Users can be defined to have particular security rights together with passwords. Net-30 also provides the concept of groups to which users can belong and allows you to specify the read or write access to particular directories or disks—not quite as comprehensive as NetWare Lite, but a big improvement on MainLAN and LANsmart.

Once safely logged in, you can connect to remote disk drives or resources either using the command-line MAP instruction or through a simple menu-driven utility (Fig. 8.2). One limitation is that only three printers can be setup, although this is unlikely to be a real problem and can be overcome by setting up a second PC as a print-server. Performance of Invisible LAN is good—helped by a good software cache utility that speeds up disk access.

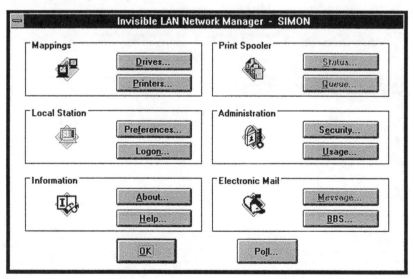

Figure 8.2   Invisible LAN

Novell's NetWare Lite/Personal NetWare

Novell is best known for its high-end products such as NetWare 3.11 and 4.0, which can support hundreds of users on a server-based setup. Novell's only peer-to-peer product, NetWare Lite, will soon be incorporated in Personal NetWare that will include DR-DOS, a compatible version of MS-DOS. The software is simple to install, supports a very wide range of network adapter hardware, and provides good performance.

Lite shares many common commands and a similar style of menu-driven utility with Novell's high-end products. The basic functions of connecting to another drive or sharing a printer can be either carried out from the command line or using menu-driven utilities. NetWare Lite uses a similar form of security to its big brothers—and it is very comprehensive. The security is based around users and groups. You can define the rights a user has to particular files, directories, or disks—you can limit who can change a file or who can read a file. It is also possible to limit the times at which a user can log in (Fig. 8.3).

NetWare Lite has a separate disk containing utilities for Windows. These are grouped under a central control application and are usable, but not terribly friendly for a timid user. There is no e-mail and only a very basic way of sending one-line messages to other users. NetWare Lite has one big advantage over all the competition: because it is similar in operation to the rest of the NetWare family, it is supported by a very wide range of applications. There is also a huge mass of reference on NetWare—online via the NetWire conferences on CIX or CompuServe, and in books.

NetWare Lite is sold in single-user packs, so rather than buy a 10-user licence for just six users, you can buy just as many licences as you need. Unfortunately, this also means that you need six key licence disks, one for each PC.

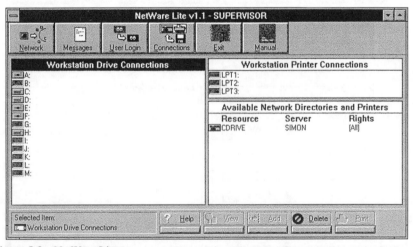

Figure 8.3   NetWare Lite

Microsoft Windows for Workgroups 3.11

Microsoft Windows for Workgroups (WfWG) is an odd-ball. The software is an enhanced version of standard Windows that lets you share files and resources with other PCs and comes bundled with some of the best add-on utilities around. Microsoft is currently selling WfWG with network adapter cards made by Intel—

so the pedigree is impeccable. Installation of Intel's Ethernet card is very simple and all configuration is carried out through a software utility rather than fiddling with jumpers on the board (Fig. 8.4).

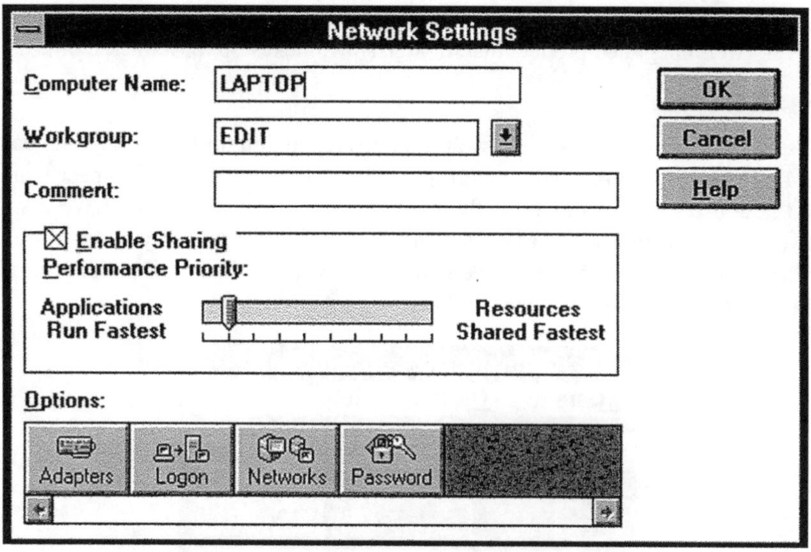

Figure 8.4 Access to adapter, network, and workgroup settings from Windows for Workgroup' Control Panel

The software installs as a direct replacement for Windows and supports a good range of network adapter cards other than the Intel model, so you are not limited to one manufacturer. If you already have Windows installed on your PC, the setup utility will give you the option of just adding the new networking applications, keeping your existing Windows setup intact.

Once installed, there are just a few small details that differentiate it from standard Windows. The first are two utilities that allow you to see how your network is performing and track down any problems. The second are two network applications—Mail and Schedule+. Mail is a cut-down version of Microsoft Mail and offers an excellent e-mail package that should satisfy almost everyone. You can attach files to messages; unlike the e-mail programs in the other network products reviewed, Mail is a full-blown, professional application that will link in to almost any existing e-mail system in your office. It's great—almost as good as Schedule+, which is a very powerful diary. Schedule+ integrates well with Mail to automatically send messages requesting meetings with other users.

Most of the functionality of WfWG is already in Windows. To connect to a shared printer you use the normal printer setup icon in the Control Panel. Print Manager has been enhanced and now shows more detail about the type of shared printer you are using. Linking to shared drives is done through a new utility that uses names to identify drives—it also allows you to name your local drives. You can then view the list of available resources and their names (the names are useful and can be meaningful, e.g. 'Simon's drive').

Windows for Workgroups is aimed almost solely at sharing resources for Windows applications. DOS applications only get access to the network resources when run as a DOS window. If you and the rest of your office just use Windows, this is a very well integrated product that, though slow, makes up for it in ease of use.

Artisoft LANtastic

Artisoft's LANtastic has earned a well deserved reputation for bringing all the power and functionality of high-end network products to the low-end peer-to-peer market. As a new user, you can skip all the powerful security features and have a small network installed in just a couple of hours (Fig. 8.5). However, if you are a stickler for detail or an experienced networker, you will find LANtastic full to the brim with features—the five manuals alone will keep you busy.

Figure 8.5   The Windows interface to all functions offered by Artisoft's LANtastic

Unlike many of the other products, LANtastic includes a lot of features that are not for the user; they are for the administrator who has to make sure the network runs smoothly and at optimum performance. Security is very detailed and gives you control over file read, write, create, or delete for any user in any directory. Like NetWare Lite, you can specify times of day when a user cannot log in. In addition, LANtastic knows what to do if a UPS is connected to your PC. If the UPS signals that the mains power has been cut, LANtastic will trigger an e-mail message to the supervisor to warn her. Utilities are provided to let the administrator see how much traffic is being generated by each PC; she can then decide which PCs might need to be upgraded.

The e-mail system within LANtastic is basic but add a couple of Artisoft's sound cards and you have got a great internal phone system. The sound cards come complete with a telephone handset and allow you to 'dial' another user's PC and have a phone conversation.

Artisoft supplies various versions of LANtastic for different types of network adapter hardware. If you want full independence, choose LANtastic/AI which will work with a wide range of adapter cards. Otherwise, you are limited to Artisoft's own brand of Ethernet hardware.

The software is very easy to use and get used to. Installation can be quick if you are a novice, or complex if you are an old hand at networks. The additional management features are excellent and help the administrator keep the network running smoothly. LANtastic competes head on with NetWare Lite: it is just as easy to use, just as powerful, and has excellent security. It does not match NetWare Lite for performance and does not have the upgrade path Novell provides.

Conclusions

Peer-to-peer network software is easy to install and normally very easy to use. Buying a starter kit is a great way into networking, but watch out you do not get trapped into proprietary standards if you want to expand. Peer-to-peer networks offer good performance and features on a par with price—the more you pay, the more features you get. Top of the list are LANtastic, Windows for Workgroups, and Personal NetWare. These operate with similar features to high-end server-based software costing thousands of pounds. The one great advantage of Windows for Workgroups is that it is now often bundled free with new PCs instead of vanilla Windows.

UNIX

A basis in academia and an original minicomputer platform have done little to enhance Unix's unfriendly image. Unix is a multi-user operating system that normally allows dumb terminals to be connected to a central server computer over sluggish serial links operating at up to 115 Kbps.

The latest versions of Unix challenge these preconceptions and compete well with network operating systems. The most popular is SCO's Unix 386 System V which runs a generic version of Microsoft's NT/AS to provide networking capabilities to a network of PCs and Macintoshes.

One of Unix's strongest claims is that a version is available for nearly every hardware platform on the market. For the PC, enhancements have steered its features towards those sported by rival LAN operating systems such as NetWare. Some implementations support standard network interface cards rather than the original serial links.

The beauty of Unix for those holding the purse-strings is the price. If you have no hardware investment to support, then the low price of buying one PC for the server and a clutch of dumb terminals that Unix can drive makes it a cheap solution for a complete installation. DOS applications can be run using software emulators, but at a memory and processor premium that far outweighs any advantages. There is a wealth of Unix applications available and the C programming language (which all versions of Unix support) makes it ideal as a platform for custom-written applications.

LAN Manager for Unix

Unix has the largest user-base of any operating system and there are more Unix applications than DOS applications. SCO Corporation ships more copies of its version of Unix for the PC than any other company. Its version of Microsoft's LAN Manager for Unix (LMX) brings networking to Unix together with the more normal LAN Manager concepts of domains, groups, and user-accounts over and above the usual resource-sharing functions of Unix.

LMX was developed from its original OS/2 platform. It provides a good bridge between the two operating systems—applications written for OS/2 can be easily ported to Unix running LAN Manager. LMX is a rare breed among network operating system software in that it can support either intelligent terminals such as PCs or Apple Macintoshes and dumb terminals over a standard serial link. It is the LMX shell loaded over Unix on the server that provides support for standard network interface cards and multiple protocols such as NetBEUI, TCP/IP, and FTAM (an OSI protocol developed to help interoperability). There is no support for Novell's IPX, so you cannot have a mixed network. Novell, in contrast, supports FTAM as well as its own IPX protocols.

Supervisors come off worst in the change of LAN Manager from OS/2 to Unix. The OS/2 server software provides an menu-driven front-end to install new users, change passwords, allocate resources, and manage the network. LMX on the server has not yet got this utility, so supervisors have to resort to using the NET command at the command-line prompt.

LMX supports both user-level and share-level security, which means flexibility when planning a network. It is less flexible about supporting some network adapters; although LMX uses the NDIS interface, so should drive most network adapters, it has problems with some 32-bit cards, such as the NE3200. It is also currently limited to driving a single network adapter in the server. NetWare and LAN Manager for OS/2 can both support up to four network cards, which spreads the load and gives better throughput on busy networks.

SCO Unix has one major benefit over the other NOSs. It has full support for computers with multiple processors. NetWare cannot currently support more than one processor, and LAN Manager for OS/2 can support two in some situations. Unix can support as many as fitted to the multiprocessor server and distribute workload accordingly.

LAN Manager for Unix provides a good connectivity tool if you want to include DOS- or OS/2-based workstations into a primarily Unix-based network.

HIGH-END NETWORK OPERATING SYSTEMS

High-end NOSs run on a dedicated server PC that acts as the central store for share files and resources. Workstations (PCs or Macs) connect to the server and share its resources, rather than sharing their own—as is the case with peer-to-peer networks. The NOS looks after file storage to disk, coping with hundreds of requests from different users to access different files at the same time. The software must also manage printers and support print queues. It must also manage security—maintaining user accounts, passwords, and audit records of file accesses. Lastly, it must also be able to manage communications channels with other servers in the network or with dedicated servers, such as a database-server or print-server.

The front runner in this field for PC-based servers is Novell with over 60 per cent of the market. It currently has three products: NetWare 2.2, NetWare 3.12, and NetWare 4.0. Other strong players include Microsoft's Windows NT/AS (which provides full LAN Manager compatibility with a Windows NT front-end), IBM's LAN Server (which has similar working methods to NT/AS), DEC's Pathworks, and Banyan's VINES. All of these products are designed to support hundreds of users in one building or across countries. They can work together with other servers running the same NOS, or integrate (with varying success) with other operating systems. They can also provide links to a company's central mainframe computer, giving desktop information processing power to the huge data-storage facilities of a mainframe.

If you want to install a network that is expandable, offers connectivity, and conforms with standards, you need one of these high-end NOSs. Peer-to-peer software does not compare in the range of options nor in the capabilities to handle multisite networks with hundreds of users. These software systems can, and best of all do so on a standard PC server.

Microsoft Windows NT

Microsoft's Windows NT has been developed to take over from Windows as the power-user's operating system. Its 32-bit engine also forms the backbone for the new version of Microsoft's LAN Manager. There are two versions of the product: NT and NT Advanced Server (NT/AS)—NT is designed for a power workstation or basic server installation, and NT/AS as a central domain server.

There are a lot of advantages of switching to NT, especially if you have a mixed workstation installation. Most publicity has been focused on NT's 32-bit engine, and its ability to run 32-bit applications, which is ideal for CAD users. With this 32-bit engine, NT can access 4 Gbytes of RAM, compared to the Windows 3.1 limit of 32 Mbytes.

If you have been using a mix of OS/2, DOS, Windows, and even Unix workstations, NT could dramatically simplify your job. An NT workstation will run applications from all these operating systems (although this is limited to character-mode OS/2 and POSIX applications). However, it is when using NT in a network that you will see a lot of benefits over Windows 3.1. But first, before we get carried away, the problems. The main problem for anyone who wants to connect an NT workstation to a NetWare server is that Novell has not yet delivered a full NT-compliant shell. NT does ship with a version of IPX/SPX, together with Microsoft's standard NetBIOS and NetBeui, Services for Macintosh, and TCP/IP.

At present, then, you will see the main benefits of NT if you are using it within a Microsoft network. Both versions of NT can work as a LAN Manager server and recognize the LAN Manager concept of domains, but only NT/AS, with its additional functions, can operate as a domain controller. NT/AS also supports RAID out of the box and, in common with vanilla NT, provides support to monitor a UPS.

Do not fall into the trap of thinking that NT is only suitable for workstations—it is a full server operating system, but without the extra functionality of NT/AS; NT knows about users, groups, and domains. If you are trying to supervise remote sites, or have remote users who want to access local data, NT includes a utility, called RAS, that can support incoming calls via a modem link (NT supports one remote link, NT/AS supports 32).

Microsoft has included a couple of server-specific utilities that allow supervisors to monitor the access and relative performance of various components of the server—displayed graphically in real time. This links to the second utility that allows a supervisor to set limits on particular components, perhaps when the traffic reaches a certain point, and so trigger an alarm. These events are all logged within a central database and can monitor hardware functions to file or directory access. Lastly, NT and NT/AS integrate into a Windows for Workgroup solution providing an alternative to the combination of NetWare 3.1 or 4.0 and NetWare Lite.

Novell NetWare 4.0

Novell's NetWare 4.0 is aimed squarely at a customer that wants to link LANs. Most corporate customers that currently have small, individual LANs scattered around various buildings will want to integrate into a larger WAN (wide area network). A typical setup would include a dozen linked servers and hundreds of users.

NetWare 4.0 is not an upgrade for Novell's previous high-end network system, NetWare 3.12 (which will take its turn and be replaced by NetWare 3.2 later this year). Instead it embodies a completely redesigned core structure and methodology. All the previous versions of NetWare (with the exception of the peer-to-peer system) had a very similar base architecture that made it easy for system managers to upgrade and still understand the principles. NetWare 4.0 takes a very different turn and, for the first few hours, will leave you wondering what has hit you.

The most fundamental change incorporated into NetWare 4.0 is the way it stores information. Previously, all user and resource information for a LAN was stored in one big file—called the bindery—on the server. This could be interrogated by NetWare itself or any NetWare-aware applications to check a user's rights and permissions. But there is a problem with this method of a central database on each server. If two servers are connected, user information must be checked in both binderies.

With NetWare 4.0, Novell has scrapped the bindery and replaced it with NDS

(NetWare Directory Services). This is a naming system designed for multiserver installations. Each linked server will continuously update each other with any changes to any user or resource, so maintaining a single, logical, shared database rather than multiple, individual databases as previously used.

For example, it is now possible for a user to log in away from his normal home server, because every server on the WAN knows that this user is registered and will route his requests back to his home server transparently. This user can still log in with his normal password and all his normal shared resources are still available. This is ideal for e-mail-dependent companies because every user now has a unique, globally recognized identity, so sending messages to distant colleagues is easy. The snag at the moment is that there are currently no e-mail packages that support NDS. Several companies are working towards support for NDS, but there is nothing available. The messaging standard, MHS 2.0, does not support NDS and will not until its next release later this year. If you are using an MHS-compatible e-mail system, then you will either have to wait or to manage two global directories—one NDS, one MHS.

If you have been following the developments in open systems architecture then NDS may sound very familiar. It should be: NetWare 4.0's NDS is very similar to the X.500 international directory standard and should be able to support software written to the X.500 directory standard.

NDS will initially attract most of the attention of new users—and it has been trumpeted loudly by Novell. In fact, the system is neither new or unique: Banyan's VINES introduced a version of NDS, called global naming services, several years ago.

This should not detract from NDS. It is, though initially complex, a very structured method of ordering shared objects around a distributed WAN. For any system manager, especially those looking to downsize from a mainframe, linking a dozen servers, NetWare 4.0 provides an excellent means of managing all the resources. To ensure that the clocks on each server are all synchronized (a major problem in distributed WANs), you can set up a central time-server which all other servers will lock onto. The means that your e-mail and distributed applications will stay in sync.

But hang on. NDS is completely different to the old bindery system of storing network information and most third-party applications used the bindery to some extent—even if it was just to query permissions. Novell realized this and gave NetWare 4.0 two modes: full NDS and NetWare 3.12 bindery emulation. By default, it starts in bindery emulation mode so that existing NLMs applications still work.

The directory services is the impressive part of NetWare 4.0, but it has also been redesigned throughout the rest of the core architecture. One major complaint that was repeatedly thrown at Novell was its non-existent memory protection. A NetWare 3.12 server had no more memory protection than DOS. In a multitasking environment this could spell disaster: without memory protection all server-based applications (called NLMs—NetWare Loadable Modules) run in one big pool of RAM, called Ring 0. Every application can allocate any memory it wants, reconfigure resources, and generally cause havoc. Worse, if one application crashed, then the whole collapses in a heap and your server stops running. In practice, this rarely happened because Novell laid down strict guidelines to developers and took the job of certifying new products. If you wanted to be sure you were not buying a rogue product, make sure it had a certified sticker on it. This did not help sites with custom-written products but it did minimize the risk.

With the release of version 4.0, NetWare now has a standard memory protection architecture. You should remember that OS/2—the basis for NetWare's main competitor, LAN Manager—has had full memory and resource protection measures since it was launched. In NetWare 4.0, the system manager is given the choice of where to run his software. Ring 0 is fastest and unprotected. In this ring runs the operating system itself, together with various NetWare libraries. The cautious can start by running new or suspect applications or drivers in Ring 3, which offers full memory protection. They can then move the software into Ring 0 when they are convinced that they will not crash. These two rings are called domains and are easily setup. To protect a suspect NLM, load DOMAIN.NLM, set a domain name for the suspect NLM, then load the NLM itself. This can be repeated for other suspect applications. The applications can talk to the operating system and the system libraries in Ring 0 (the OS Domain) but not to other quarantined NLMs in different parts of the Ring 3 memory protection area (called the OSP Domain).

The third main area of change within NetWare 4.0 is how it manages data storage on the server hard drives. NetWare, like any other operating system, stores data in blocks of a fixed size. Previously, you could change the size of the block at setup but you were then stuck with it. This meant you either gambled better performance against wasted disk space or, more usually, simply stuck to the default block size. For large database servers it would be wise to increase the block size since most requests will be to big files: a larger block will thus speed up disk reads. Unfortunately, even a small config file would take up a whole block so you could lose out depending on the mix between database and normal use.

NetWare 4.0 adds a new feature called sub allocation that helps get around this problem. It is very simple—instead of, say, an 8K block being used for even the smallest file, you can now set, say, a 512-byte sub allocation block. So a 1K file will now take two sub allocation blocks rather than one 8K block. This option is turned on and configured during volume setup and cannot be reversed.

The second option available is data compression. There are a whole stack of options giving you control over NetWare's use of data compression. The space conscious can set on-the-fly compression of all files—but performance will suffer. Alternatively, you could tell NetWare to compress files of a certain age (there would be a decompression delay when they are next accessed) or compress all files overnight. The data compression is still linked with TTS (transaction tracking system) and with other integrity checks that try and guarantee data protection.

In addition to the standard features of TTS and various other verify checks, the one big development in data integrity is SFT III (system fault tolerance level III). The bad news is that it is not ready, but is due out soon. NetWare 4.0 with SFT III will guarantee that your server and the data it holds will not go down.

If your main server drive is clogged up with rarely used files, then NetWare's

Data Migration Services could help. These automatically move data from a normal NetWare volume onto a backup media, but to the user it looks as though the files are still on the volume. The file name is still there, but this actually points to the secondary storage device. All a user will notice is more disk space and a slight delay when accessing archived data files. For the supervisor, the method of data migration can be very sophisticated and based on time, age, or more complex rules.

Lastly, as you would expect from an operating system that spans multiple sites and servers, the security has been beefed up. There is now provision for an independent auditor, totally separate of the normal supervisor, that can monitor logins, file accesses, and data updates. This helps provide the integrity of the security system, but does not actually change the security system used. To boost security, NetWare includes a key-exchange crypto-system based on the RSA technique. This uses 'keys' to decrypt the secure data. It is generally considered the most secure system available (although this depends on the size and choice of keys).

NetWare 4.0 can support up to 1000 users per server. Installation is simple, however, since it arrives on a single CD-ROM. This means that your server has to have a CD-ROM player or you cannot install the software, but it also means that all the manuals are now in electronic form on the CD-ROM, and so are easier to search.

At the heart of a NetWare 3.12 workstation there beats a combination of two resident programs: IPX and NETx. These older NetWare 3.12 shells can still be used to connect to NetWare 4.0 servers—although you should start to phase in the new shell software as soon as possible. The new shell is distributed as a VLM (virtual loadable module) to support the naming services rather than the old NETx, which does not support NDS. However, VLM can emulate NETx so a new workstation can still recognize 3.12 or 2.2 servers as well as support 4.0 servers.

The changes provided by the new workstation shell now mean that a workstation can support links with up to 54 000 servers (NetWare 3.12 allows you to attach to just eight). The resident part of the shell also takes up slightly less RAM—6K less than the 3.12 shell, at a modest 52.5K. The new shell now uses ODI drivers to interface to the network adapter—unless you are using a particularly non-standard adapter in which case Microsoft's NDIS standard is used as the interface.

It should be clear by now that it is the administrators who will notice the most differences from 3.12. Gone is the old SYSCON utility that provided most functions for everyday management of the 3.12 server. Now, NWADMIN, a Windows or OS/2 PM graphical application, is the mainstay. It allows a supervisor to manage the objects (users, resources, or workstations under NDS) on the LAN. Gone too is the old Novell menu system—now replaced by a cut-down version of the popular third-party Saber menu software.

Another big difference for the supervisor is the lack of manuals. All documentation is in electronic form on the CD-ROM and can be easily searched using the browse utility, which makes it easier for a supervisor to check the 'manual' while away from her desk. Lastly, a supervisor can now, finally, backup users' DOS, Windows, or OS/2 workstations from her console. NetWare 4.0 achieves this using TSAs (target service agents) that allow backups to be made of almost any client or NetWare server.

Novell NetWare 3.12

NetWare 3.12 has now been surpassed by NetWare 4.0 as the ultimate version of NetWare. However, it still has a useful role for large companies that want a solid, flexible, and powerful NOS. NetWare 4.0 is proving to be complex to setup and there is not as much support for it from third-party software publishers. It is still easier to buy a database server application to run on NetWare 3.12 than most other NOSs.

Unlike LAN Manager or VINES, which tend towards internationally agreed open protocol standards, Novell's Internetwork Packet Exchange (IPX) and Sequenced Packet Exchange (SPX) protocols represent one of the most perfect examples of a *de facto* standard. This sums up much of NetWare's operating system's features. Stubbornly proprietary, IPX and SPX have nevertheless proved themselves so thoroughly and so repeatedly that no sensible manufacturer would seriously launch an alternative without some kind of link to NetWare. Novell has now modified its approach slightly, by including full support for the internationally agreed open standards, but by default all NetWare products use its proprietary IPX protocol. They no longer load them as separate object files, but instead have adopted ODI stacks which, like Microsoft's NDIS, allows several protocols to be loaded at one time.

With IPX and SPX, NetWare 3.12 is able to run typical PC applications more efficiently than other protocols by requesting smaller blocks of data at a time. The downside of this is slightly less efficient LAN-to-LAN communication than, say, VINES or LAN Manager.

File management utilities give the supervisor a very high level of control in terms of file access and file characteristic reporting. Files and programs can be designated shareable or restricted to one read/write user at a time. Shareable files get around the read/write problem by including a default record-locking capability that allows several users to operate in read/write mode simultaneously, as long as only one user is writing to a specific record at a time.

Directory creation is straightforward and access is made simple by NetWare's mapping capability, which presents users with single keystroke access to files scattered around different network directories and volumes. The FILER utility lets users display and change key information about the directories and files under their control, although the supervisor can also use FILER to preset access rights for specific files.

One of the system's more important file management upgrades is the NetWare Naming Service, which gets round the fiddly task of logging on individually to multiple servers when resources are widely distributed. The Naming Service relies on the concept of 'domains' whereby servers are grouped into logical units. Logging onto multiple servers can now be done as a single entry to a domain. Although not as flexible as VINES' directory naming service, and adhering to open standards such as X.500, it improves WAN communications for Novell. Novell has now changed this in NetWare 4.0 to embrace what is called NetWare

Directory Services (NDS) that offer flexible, powerful, but complex naming of every user and resource on a WAN.

Print management within 3.12 is undoubtedly an improvement on 2.2. For a start, the print-server is a NetWare Loadable Module (NLM), of which more later, and supports a maximum of 16 printers per server. PCONSOLE controls all network printing, allowing supervisor and workgroup-manager status users to examine print queues, add and delete print jobs, alter priorities, and check server and queue information. Print devices and modes can be defined in a step-by-step procedure using PRINTDEF. More detailed parameters are available under NPRINT and PRINTCON.

NetWare does not incorporate a full-blown messaging system, although there are plenty of add-on packages available. These attach to Novell's Message Handling System (MHS) e-mail interface standard which resides on a single PC and facilitates communication between a wide range of third-party e-mail systems. Novell's SEND utility offers a crude system of communication whereby one-liners can be broadcast to one user, a user group, or all users.

These messages flash up on the screen of an active terminal, locking all activity in the process, and cannot be stored, replied to, or saved. To resume work the recipient(s) must remove them from the screen by hitting Control Return, which is a trivial matter if you are there in front of your workstation. If you are not, because you are running a major processing job, you might find the broadcast locks up your PC. It is possible to configure your workstation so it does not receive any messages at all.

User setup is easy and it is a simple matter to allocate detailed rights to individual users. Login times, number and location of terminals where a user can login, and session durations are easily controlled and provide tight security as well as good management (Fig. 8.6).

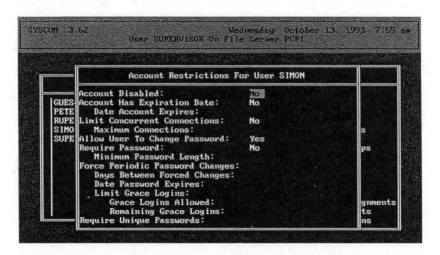

Figure 8.6   Using the SYSCON utility in NetWare to set up security for each user's account

It is possible to force users to change passwords or restrict them to passwords of specified lengths. Within SYSCON, the system configuration utility, an accounting facility allows users to control the degree of network access granted to users and the costs of operating the network. The system manager can charge users for their disk storage and processing time, and can even apply higher rates at peak computing time to discourage unnecessary file transfer and report printing.

NetWare users who have taken advantage of the information-rich FCONSOLE panel in version 2.2 may be disappointed with 3.12's RCONSOLE. Although 3.12 still has FCONSOLE, it no longer displays the detailed performance figures present in 2.2. These, supposedly, are accessible via the more powerful RCONSOLE, but for system monitoring purposes, clues are sparse. The argument goes that NetWare 3.12 no longer needs that kind of close monitoring, but if you are used to anticipating problems before they arise, the loss of 2.2's FCONSOLE could be a little unsettling.

The basic security procedures within NetWare 3.12 are the same as those of 2.2. Hardly surprising, given that even the earliest version of NetWare contained excellent user-level-based security structures out of which much of its reputation emerged. The added complexity of 3.12 may even be a drawback. Because you boot to DOS on the server before entering NetWare, it is theoretically possible to drop back into DOS and tamper with NetWare files via Norton Utilities. This is a small but subtle loophole, and is best overcome by locking your server in a separate room. (OS/2, the basis for LAN Manager, also allows similar loopholes, since a user can start a second process on the server and tamper with system files.)

NetWare Loadable Modules (NLMs) make the biggest difference to NetWare 3.12 in relation to 2.2. They succeed VAPs as the means of integrating third-party applications into NetWare, but greatly exceed VAPs in terms of functionality. Loadable applications range from Micro Channel card drivers, print drivers, and SNA gateways to sophisticated network management and workgroup productivity products, all of which become integral components of NetWare once loaded.

The modular approach of NLMs allows a supervisor to load and unload them while the server is still running. The downside is that existing VAPs for NetWare 2.x will have to be rewritten to work in this mode, and like TSRs in DOS, a crashed NLM could easily mean a crashed file-server.

Novell's philosophy of openness ensures that NetWare is on speaking terms with all other major NOSs as well as mainframe computers. LAN-to-LAN communication is made possible through a dedicated workstation holding interface cards for both networks, as well as Novell's bridge software, offering a highly tolerant link. To chat to mainframes, Novell has the option of its own SNA Gateway with five different hardware options.

Novell NetWare 2.2

Novell still dominates the PC LAN market and top in sales is NetWare 2.2. It is cheaper than its bigger brothers, 3.12 and 4.0, it will run on a cheaper 80286 server, and yet its utilities look the same and offer nearly all the same functions.

Without the hardware requirements of NetWare 3.12, version 2.2 is a good way into high-performance networking for many small workgroups. Aimed at the smaller networks, 2.2 supports up to 100 users. NetWare 2.2 is straightforward to install, although this does not mean that it is easy. NetWare 3.12 assumes a fairly extensive knowledge of Novell's philosophy and technology, and though you do not need quite the same amount of experience to tackle 2.2, it certainly helps. If you planned your network properly to begin with, the installation is simple. There are plenty of Novell-qualified dealers who can take this off your hands, and a lot of short courses to show you how to do it yourself.

NetWare 2.2's file management has much in common with past versions, suggesting that Novell feels it has gone a long way towards definitive file-management procedures. From a supervisor's view, the system is easily controlled, while user-configurable mappings give individuals sufficient control over their own environments to support personal preferences without compromising flexibility.

Print management capabilities are comprehensive, although less polished in execution than the utilities for file management. Despite extensive print queue management facilities, NetWare 2.2's print spooling software takes the edge off overall performance, lacking the ease-of-use and speed of the other print utilities. Novell admits that third-party intervention is generally advisable here, in the form of programs written to NetWare 2.2's programming interface: such VAPs run on the server and are the best way of adding to NetWare 2.2's functionality.

NetWare's reputation grew in part out of its excellent security procedures and version 2.2 follows in its predecessors' footsteps. At login, the system can be configured to request username, password, and server, and will wait for all three before confirming or denying access. The supervisor is able to specify time periods during which the password is recognized by the system (between 7.00 a.m. and 7.00 p.m., for example) and also the length of time for which a password is valid and the workstations at which a user may login (Fig. 8.7).

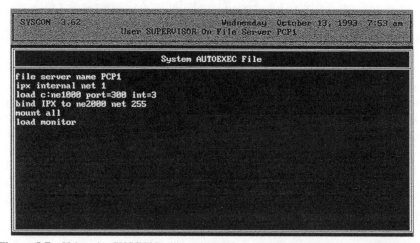

Figure 8.7 Using the SYSCON utility of NetWare to edit the file-server's AUTOEXEC file

On logging in, two script files are executed. A general login script, created by the supervisor, sets application mappings and welcome messages. Users also have their own personal login scripts which can be amended by users without the intervention of the supervisor.

NetWare 2.2 permissions and rights are assigned with user-level security, rather than share-level. Users can be assigned rights individually as part of a group of users. User-level rights and the concept of groups are of benefit to large organizations with several departments and workgroups. With more than one server, it is foreseeable that the need to create and update data identifying groups, rights, and users could become a full-time job.

NetWare 2.2 is unusual in its ability to run on a PC with an 80286 processor (LAN Manager running on OS/2 1.2 can do the same). Not that this is recommended, since performance figures would kick their heels in disgust, but it can also work on 80386-based PCs. This upgrade path gives wary customers a cheap way in, both in terms of hardware and software. Installation of the server is simple, workstations can prove more difficult, and connectivity features to the outside world and other LANs are thin on the ground. It is the most popular PC LAN on the market, and rightly so.

Microsoft LAN Manager/Windows NT/AS

Microsoft's LAN Manager has now been integrated almost totally into its Windows NT/AS product. This offers a 32-bit engine with all the benefits of a Windows front-end. From the start, Microsoft has stuck to open standards and the software resources that it had already developed. LAN Manager originally used OS/2 1.3 as a base, a multitasking desktop operating system. It has now swapped OS/2 for Windows NT, its current 32-bit multitasking operating system. Since both OS/2 and Windows NT are multitasking operating systems, you could run other applications concurrently. It is certainly possible to use your server as another workstation, but this is not advisable for security. Its most practical use is to debug and setup your server *in situ*: allowing you to change config and protocol description files in one window while observing the effects in another.

Where LAN Manager benefits greatly is with NT and OS/2's disk filing system. Unlike DOS's sluggish method of storing files on disk (using a File Allocation Table, FAT), NT turns up the octane with HPFS (High Performance Filing System). Since a LAN concentrates its activities around the disk, cutting access times boosts performance of an HPFS system over a similar FAT-formatted disk by up to 30 per cent.

OS/2 (in its older version 1.3 rather than the newer version 2) can also be run on an 80286 processor, and so the HPFS drivers do not make the most of a typically 386-driven server. LAN Manager, if it detects a 386 during installation, will use its own HPFS386 drivers—with slightly better performance.

Novell imposed its proprietary protocols, IPX and SPX, on the world by market presence—they have since become the *de facto*; Microsoft, in comparison, has stuck with open standards. Unfortunately, it has paid the price of performance and

IPX is well proven to be faster than LAN Manager's native NetBEUI (an enhanced version of NetBIOS) protocol for typical PC applications.

The interface LAN Manager uses between software and the network adapters is NDIS. For the server, multiple NETBEUI protocol stacks can sit on the generic NDIS hardware drivers talking to multiple adapter cards—it happily accommodated our four 32-bit NE3200 Ethernet cards and supports up to 12. Adding further protocol stacks is a simple option from the menu-driven installation program. Installing the main server software uses the same friendly program and the whole process of breathing life into your server takes around half an hour.

The workstations use similar setup programs and proved to be very simple to install. The redirector software can be tailored to offer either basic or enhanced services. The basic redirector offers the simplest level of functionality, little better than sharing files and printers, while the enhanced redirector includes access to administrator's functions with a greater overhead in memory.

DOS workstation efficiency is improved by the inclusion of support for SMB (Server Message Block). This architecture was designed as a group effort by Intel, IBM, and Microsoft to improve a DOS workstation's sluggish efforts when connected to a LAN. It encodes network disk requests into a simpler format and bundles data and requests into larger 64K blocks, which are more economical to transmit (with less wastage from addressing and error-checking data overheads). OS/2 workstations are also well supported using Named Pipes—similar, but faster, to NetBIOS and easier for programmers to implement.

All LAN Manager actions stem from the NET command. User control and upkeep is carried out from the server with the NET ADMIN utility, or from the command line at a workstation. Controlling user's rights and carrying out system maintenance from a workstation has always been possible with NetWare, but previously only with OS/2 workstations under LAN Manager. The ADMIN program uses pull-down menus to give an administrator-level user access to system statistics, including cache usage, mean response time, and node information. From the same menus, LAN information such as the server's role in the DOMAIN and the security system used, either share-level or user-level, can be assigned. Additionally, a local server password can be assigned to lockout inquisitive passers by.

User groups, security rights, and account restrictions are setup from the same NET ADMIN utility as are shared resources. A historical log, including an error log, is invaluable and is within another menu option from this one administration program. NetWare, in comparison, uses a suite of utility programs, each carrying out a different set of tasks. All the ADMIN commands available from the menus are also accessible from the command line. It is this route that LAN Manager for Unix, from SCO, travels, unfortunately losing the excellent front-end.

A LAN through Microsoft's eyes can be split into domains. These are groups of servers of which one holds the central information base covering users, resources, and account data, while the others help it out with their resources and processing. As with the other NOSs we reviewed, each server holds its own user database. This causes problems when multiple servers are connected. Global naming is the solution, keeping a record of every server's resources and users. This is vital for efficient maintenance of large LANs or WANs.

LAN Manager gets around this to an extent with domains. The role of each server is initially stand-alone. If two or more run within the same LAN, one can be designated domain controller and will look after all resource management. The role each server plays can be easily changed, and together with the security level defines how a user participates with the resources.

Two security levels are available: share-level allocates passwords to resources rather than users, while user-level allocates passwords to users who are then granted rights to resources. In most installations, user-level security offers greater flexibility and ease of user management for the administrator, but is more complex to setup. LAN Manager and its generic forms are the only NOSs to offer a choice.

LAN Manager is able to take advantage of PCs with multiple processors. LAN Manager, together with VINES, are the only two NOSs that can begin to use this. LAN Manager shares specific tasks between the two processors. This is not true distributed processing, as is VINES, since it will off-load a complete process, such as an SQL-server, onto the second processor while it manages the LAN on the other. The result, if you rarely use the SQL-server, is one idle processor. VINES spreads according to need. NetWare is available for multiprocessing platforms such as NetFRAME, but it relies on OEM versions to accomplish this.

LAN Manager has good security and reliability features. It offers good disk duplexing and mirroring functions, and an automated file replication backup that copies a file to another server at a specific time. This together with comprehensive UPS support rival NetWare's functionality.

Microsoft appears to be fighting Novell with bear-hug tactics—LAN Manager goes out of its way to embrace NetWare. Included is the ability of both workstations and servers to connect with NetWare servers. For mixed network systems, this is an excellent implementation of cross-operating system support. A client can now view and access both LAN Manager and NetWare servers and their associated resources. Perhaps more importantly, the two types of server now recognize and talk to each other.

LAN Manager users get the benefit of persistent connections; a record of each user's connections to resources is kept and next time you login, they are re-established. From a system manager's view, LAN Manager has error reporting to an IBM NetView master. The installation of clients can now be carried out over the network for both Windows and DOS workstations. Client support includes OS/2 2.0, Windows 3.1, and Macintosh support.

LAN Manager has, as mentioned, now been incorporated into Microsoft's latest version of Windows NT—called NT/AS (advanced services). A Windows NT workstation can carry out many LAN Manager functions, and can recognize users and domains—but you need a PC running NT/AS to work as a central domain controller. Windows NT improves on OS/2, keeping a similar high-performance disk filing system and adding a true 32-bit engine.

Banyan VINES

Designed over six years ago, VINES has from the start aimed itself at 1000-user global network installations. It is for this reason that Banyan was the first NOS vendor to introduce global naming services as part of the package. This has been so successful that the service, StreetTalk, is as well known as the VINES product itself. Novell, with NetWare 4.0, has now produced its own version of a global naming service, NDS.

StreetTalk works in a very simple way, more design concept that product, but for widespread WANs, it is very useful. It treats every resource within a network similarly and assigns each a unique name. Every user, printer, group, shared directory, or even file can be given a name. Each StreetTalk address is made up of three components: the item name, the group name, and a company name. This makes organization-wide networking simple as each group or small division can be easily distinguished.

The complexity of global naming becomes apparent when several servers begin to talk. The problem other vendors have had is how to make sure every server knows the users and resources of every other. VINES and its protocol get around this by exchanging StreetTalk address updates with each communication. This leads to what can be significant traffic overhead, but for sites with multiple servers it improves productivity and makes system management considerably easier.

To a user, StreetTalk appears at first to be a step back. Users must login with their full address, up to 63 characters long. However, Banyan allows nicknames which are short user names replaced by VINES with the full address.

Users benefit from global naming in their ability to talk to other users. To send mail to a person means entering the complete three-part address, but an entire group or division can be addressed by using a wild-card for item name. Similarly with resources—a user can immediately access any resource on any server, be it a file, directory, or printer, by typing the correct address.

Managing these addresses within a 1000-server system, each server with tens of resources, and remembering the correct address could be hell. VINES supplies an electronic Yellow Pages, allowing users to search for any resource, user, or nickname on any server. Much of this technology will become redundant when global naming standards from the ISO are ratified, but until that happens, Banyan's solution remains one of the few available for PC-based WANs.

Workstation support is also good. Banyan has worked with Microsoft over the years to ensure client workstations can use SMB for DOS, and Named Pipes and LAN Manager APIs for OS/2 clients over its native NetBIOS protocol stack.

Specific hardware-level support is also well in evidence, far more so than with any other NOS. Multiprocessor support is included with the top-end version of VINES, VINES/SMP, which will take advantage of Compaq SystemPro and ALR machines, both of which can sport two 386 or 486 processors. Microsoft's LAN Manager can also spread its load, but not as efficiently and neatly as can the VINES product.

VINES also directly supports the SystemPro's IDA (Intelligent Drive Array) controller, which includes disk duplexing and data guarding within hardware. NetWare, particularly, uses software to ensure data integrity with its Transaction Tracking System (TTS) which records every data transaction enabling rebuilds but cannot directly control an IDA card and the performance boost it carries with it.

Strangely lacking from the base product is local printer sharing. Printers connected to any server can be accessed by any user with the correct rights, but declaring your personal printer to be available to any other user on the network can only be achieved with third-party add-on software. NetWare and LAN Manager already support this extremely useful feature, saving money by sharing printers without the security risk of having your users wandering into the server room to pick up printouts.

The user interface for VINES is basic, but acceptable. There is no colourful NET program, as in LAN Manager, instead a menu-driven front-end allows a user to select printers, search for StreetTalk names, and attach and share resources. Banyan has also included usability with Microsoft's Windows 3 environment and StreetTalk names can be accessed from within specific enquiry windows. Similarly with printing, Windows enhancements make this rather easier for a user than NetWare.

Accessing other users is particularly easy with the VINES utilities and this facility is its main claim to increasing productivity. Currently VINES runs on top of a modified version of AT&T's Unix operating system. It should soon be switching to SCO's Unix. To the user and administrator little will change since VINES hides Unix almost completely. In hiding Unix, it might be depriving itself of cross-platform base for users who might now go for SCO's LAN Manager. Banyan is well placed for the immediate future as large companies look to WANs to solve problems.

For multiple servers with a tens of users on each, where communication is important, Banyan offers the ideal solution. For companies requiring both connectivity and performance, third-party products for NetWare could achieve a similar effect for the user. This method would take a little longer to setup, cost more, and be harder to manage.

DEC Pathworks for OS/2 1.1

Pathworks is Digital Equipment Corporation's software bonding product. It is available in a number of versions for different hardware platforms and each can happily talk to any other. Its platform base is, not unnaturally, centred upon the Digital range of minicomputer hardware. Because of this diversity of server platforms and code, DEC has taken up an unusual pricing strategy for Pathworks. The server software is normally free (but there is a charge for the PC version), and it is the client software, running under DOS, OS/2, Unix, or VMS that costs. The implications of this are that it is much easier to tailor a system and, importantly, spend no more than is needed.

The software is supplied in two parts. The server runs Pathworks for OS/2, which can also operate as an OS/2 client. The server software sits on Microsoft's

OS/2 and LAN Manager and uses this combination with the DECnet protocol rather than LAN Manager's native NetBEUI.

Network adapters are driven using the generic NDIS driver option or directly if supported by DEC. The newest version will now run multiple adapter cards in the server; adding multiple cards into a server can effectively increase your available bandwidth—a great help on busy networks.

Client workstations use the DECnet protocol as a preferred default, but can also communicate effectively with Novell NetWare systems. DEC supplies a software layer that sits between LAN Manager's NDIS layer and a Novell IPX stack. TCP/IP is also supported from the workstation using another supplied protocol stack. As a part of the code installed onto your workstation, several VAX workstation emulators for Microsoft Windows are included, together with a full X-Window server, again for Microsoft Windows.

Server security can be based either on user accounts or on share-level in which resources are available if the user has its password. Once connected, both Pathworks and LAN Manager commands can be executed. The price for this is that 210K of memory disappears to a hungry redirector. If you have any memory above 640K, this can be used effectively by the built-in memory manager. As a last resort, sections of the redirector can be unloaded from RAM.

One of the most useful and well-integrated parts of Pathworks is its mail application. During installation, each node within a DECnet network is assigned both a name and a unique node address. By coordinating your network strategy across not just desks but buildings and countries the power inherent within the DECnet protocol is released. DECnet started deep within laboratories as a protocol for WANs. Because of this incidental piece of history, enterprise-wide connectivity and the usefulness of the supplied, otherwise standard, e-mail utility is vastly increased. This does not make it as flexible or as easily changed or managed as NetWare 4.0's NDS, but it works well.

Attach a modem to the server of each site and you immediately have a WAN. Other NOSs can offer this level of productivity, but not bundled and not with such ease—mainly due to their need to implement DECnet's node naming standard with additional code, either using third-party products or gateways.

Managing such a widely spread system could prove very difficult, so DEC has produced NCP, DEC's proprietary network management tool. With it, nodes can be quizzed and their local address, setup, and working characteristics displayed at the server. This level of interrogation can, thanks to the interoperability of the platforms, work for VAX minicomputers or any DECnet node.

If yours is a company based mainly around minicomputers with a mass of heterogeneous desktop computers—workstations, PCs, Macintoshes—then few other NOSs rival Pathworks with its ability to simplify and coordinate complex systems.

9
Electronic Mail

INTRODUCTION

Electronic mail boosts productivity, improves communications, and cuts costs—
and that is just for starters. Once you have got a network up and running in your
office, you should start thinking about electronic mail. Over the last five years, the
popularity of e-mail has rocketed; in the United States—land of communications—
the benefits have been as welcome as a shower in the desert. With e-mail, you do
not have to hold in a telephone queue, or face an electronic voice-mail box; e-mail
is more reliable than the postal service and you know exactly when your message
was read.

Defining an electronic mail package is the first problem. Some people could
argue that terminal-emulation software connecting you to CompuServe or CIX
gives you access to e-mail—it does. However, in this chapter, we are sticking to
software that can provide electronic mail functionality over a LAN. Of course, it
need not stop at the boundaries of your LAN; all the products we reviewed can
send mail on, via gateways, to large commercial e-mail carriers such as
CompuServe, MCI, or CIX.

An electronic mail program has one simple job definition—it lets you send
information to another user on the network. So far, so boring. You could telephone
your colleague and give them the message. An e-mail program will also let you
add attachments to your mail message—literally adding any file or group of files to
the message. With this, e-mail becomes a useful way of distributing data. Under
Windows, you can make it a little neater and drag files into the body text of your
message. Drag an Excel file into your message and an icon appears; when the
recipient double-clicks on the icon, Excel starts and loads the file. You can even
add voice annotations this way by including WAV objects in your mail.

So far e-mail is a great way of distributing data, but this is why you bought your
LAN in the first place—e-mail just makes it more convenient. E-mail is very good
at giving you feedback. You can ask for a receipt of delivery: when the recipient
actually opens the mail message you sent, a message is automatically sent back to
you giving details of the time and date at which the message was read (invaluable
for cutting office politics).

If your company has sales reps on the move, or has offices or workers abroad, it is often inconvenient and costly to keep up to date with a telephone call. With e-mail, attach a modem to your server and let your remote users call in whenever it is convenient for them. Any messages composed off-line are transferred with a short call. If you want to cut phone bills to a minimum, you can prevent attachments being sent to remote users.

Even for a small company, e-mail is more efficient: you can send a note about a telephone call or meeting to a user rather than write out a PostIt. Integrating mail into everyday life is one of the goals of Microsoft, and you will soon see its new applications sporting a Mail menu; this will give you access to the mail system from within your application.

Of course, e-mail will never get going in your company unless everyone uses it and checks their mailbox regularly (although most software will popup a message if you have received new mail). To get the ball rolling quickly, it is best to send your users on a short mail-appreciation course. The problem that many large companies soon run into is that e-mail becomes too popular and the traffic swamps the LAN's bandwidth. In many cases, supervisors have had to install a separate server just for mail. But watch out. The extreme of e-mail has already happened— Beyond has the most sophisticated system, but Lotus and Microsoft have joined in and added intelligence to their e-mail programs. Users in big companies receive so many junk mail messages that they want software that reads their incoming mail for them, deletes any junk mail replies to simple requests, and just leaves them with the important messages from the boss.

CONNECTING TO THE OUTSIDE WORLD

It is great having a closed electronic mail system running over your LAN. But what happens if you want to send a mail message to someone who is not on your LAN? Maybe you want to reach a field-engineer who has only got a pager or a new customer has just given you a telex number. To give your e-mail program extra power, you can connect to the outside world using a software gateway. All the e-mail software reviewed provides optional gateways that cover everything from driving a fax card to signalling a pager.

At its most basic, each of the products includes a simple gateway that lets your LAN-based e-mail system cope with a remote user with a modem. The cut-down remote e-mail software is installed on the user's laptop and the gateway software on the LAN server setup to recognize data from a modem. Whenever the remote user wants to send mail, the delivery system passes it to the gateway which dials out to the server. To cut costs, you can set the gateway to dial out at the end of each day to deliver all the mail and pickup any new mail. If you want to provide links to a commercial mail system such as CompuServe or MCI, you will need to buy a gateway for your e-mail package.

Problems occur if you want to link different types of e-mail system. Your group may run cc:Mail, but the rest of the company still uses PROFS on a mainframe. In this case, you will need to buy a software gateway to reformat and address messages to PROFS users, together with hardware to connect to your mainframe (which could be an asynchronous link or simply a LAN connection via an existing LAN gateway).

ELECTRONIC MAIL PRODUCTS

Finansa WinMail

WinMail is designed as an e-mail product for Novell NetWare networks (Fig. 9.1). If you are connected to LAN Manager, NT/AS, or VINES network, it will not work. The other main products in the market cater for a variety of network platforms, but Finansa sticks with Novell. The result is that WinMail is very easy to install, and users are easy to setup—the software works in close partnership with the NetWare kernel.

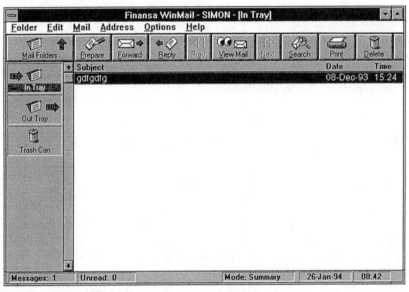

Figure 9.1   Finansa WinMail

Unusually, WinMail has been written as a DLL. This might seem an oddity, since all other programs are stand-alone EXE files, but it gives the administrator and user considerable flexibility. You can run the application straight or call it from any other Windows program. Finansa includes macros to add a Mail option to Word. In addition, for a totally custom-written installation Finansa includes sample code in Visual BASIC and C to show how to call the WinMail DLL.

The first version of WinMail was only available as a Windows application. This combined with its requirement for a NetWare server made it seem very limiting. Finansa has now developed a DOS client program that is included with version 1.5. The DOS client has been well written and provides total mouse and keystroke compatibility with the Windows client application—there is no difficulty switching between the two.

One of the big problems with many electronic mail systems is that they are a real pain to install. WinMail is different and very easy to install. It arrives on a single disk and does a fair bit of detective work as it installs. WinMail will, unlike Microsoft's Mail, automatically scan the NetWare user bindery (the database in which user names and rights are stored) and create a basic user list. WinMail runs happily out of the box on small LANs, but if you want to add gateways, connect LANs, or support hundreds of users, then you will need to buy Novell's MHS system. If this is already present, WinMail will install itself as an MHS-managed application and automatically provide MHS with its user-list. In short, installation is easy.

Users can take a lot of persuading before they eventually take to an e-mail system. Finansa has tried to make its client front-end as user-friendly as possible. Running along the top of the window are big friendly buttons that let you create a message, send it, view it, print it, or delete it. Click on the far left down button and a panel of buttons is displayed running down the lefthand side of the screen—each button represents one of your folders (folders are like directories in DOS and let you store relevant messages together). With this button bar it is easy to manage your mail and folders.

Another nice addition is WinMail's viewer capabilities. If you have received an attachment created in an application you do not have, you are stuck. WinMail has a file viewer built-in that lets you view graphics and fax files as well as Word files.

WinMail has some rules capability. These are nowhere near as powerful as those in BeyondMail, but adequate for a unsophisticated user to create simple rules for message housekeeping. Like Lotus's cc:Mail, WinMail does not yet support OLE within messages—as does Microsoft Mail. You have to send files as attachments.

WinMail offers a very flexible system for any PC-based office. It can only cope with Windows and DOS clients, but does so with a friendly and easy-to-use front-end. Administration and setup is equally easy and a joy compared to the high-end, complex systems. If you have got a Novell NetWare-based network on one site, WinMail is an excellent choice. If you want multiplatform support or e-mail for hundreds of users, it pales.

Beyond BeyondMail 2.0

BeyondMail broke all the rules in its first version. It included what everyone needed, but had not realized—intelligent, programmable rules. Rules are similar to macros and allow you to program BeyondMail to read and reply intelligently to the mail to receive. If you go on holiday, BeyondMail can send a note back to anyone that mails you to this effect. It can store all the boring or junk mail in a special folder, while routing any messages that contain the words 'pay increase' over gateways to your hotel's fax. Of course, with such a good idea, everyone else started doing the same. Lotus's cc:Mail 2.0 now provides good rule-based intelligence, WinMail offers a basic macro language, and only Microsoft Mail does not include the facility for user-defined rules.

One new feature of 2.0 is the inclusion of House Rules. These let an administrator define a company-wide set of basic rules that will apply to all users. As he changes these rules, so the changes are passed on to each user—a good way of managing rules.

BeyondMail 2.0 arrives with both a Windows and DOS client applications. BeyondMail took the opposite route to Finansa and started as a DOS program, then launched the Windows client. No support for Macintoshes or Unix is available, so multiplatform installations will have to rule BeyondMail out for the moment, although both Mac and Unix clients are being developed.

BeyondMail, like WinMail, will run with most NOSs including NetWare and LAN Manager. It prefers NetWare and offers better integration and smoother installation for this NOS. It goes one step further than WinMail and is one of the first applications that provides direct support for many of NetWare 4.0's features—in line with its claim to be an ideal solution for enterprise-wide mail systems. BeyondMail can use Novell's new NetWare Global MHS delivery system (NGMHS) and ties in directly with NetWare 4.0's NDS (NetWare directory services—a global naming system).

BeyondMail has always offered the flexibility and power to be used as an enterprise-wide workgroup and workflow system. Previously, you had to understand how to create rules to carry this out. With this new version comes a feature called the SRS (Serial Routing Slip) which makes workflow a reality for all users. If you want to send a file, say a report, to various people in your company, you can attach an SRS and set when you want each person to receive the data. The SRS keeps you informed, letting you track when each user has read the file. To create an SRS, you turn to BeyondMail's forms functionality: fill in a standard form and mail it. BeyondMail lets you interrogate existing dBase, Paradox, or SQL database files through the forms and the SRS feature keeps a track on where the form has passed through the company. You can create your own forms using the built-in forms designer, or use the stock of predesigned forms.

BeyondMail itself is a complex and large application. Installation should be left to a network supervisor and the options are so numerous that they tend to overwhelm you. The manual, too, has to cope with several different delivery systems, and user naming lists (NDS, BeyondMail itself, and MHS) and can get confusing. BeyondMail does take a lot of the drudgery out of the installation by scanning NetWare's bindery for users and automatically synchronizing name lists with NDS or MHS.

Once installed, the client screens are easy to navigate and use. There are unusual terms for many of the functions, e.g. AutoTickle is actually an intelligent alarm that can be added to a message prompting you to do something at some time in the future.

BeyondMail has always been very good at tying in with other workgroup software; it has got better in version 2.0. If your company uses Lotus Notes, you can use BeyondMail as a front-end to the mail functions. In addition, BeyondMail 2.0 is currently being bundled with Watermark; this is an OLE-based utility that lets users embed images into their messages—the recipient can view, edit, or annotate the image and send it back.

BeyondMail 2.0 offers the most comprehensive range of workflow tools into a total workgroup environment. It builds on the basic e-mail system with its excellent intelligent rules, and adds forms capabilities and a tracking system. The server program can interface to a wide range of platforms and gateways and BeyondMail is one of the very few applications that uses the enterprise-wide NDS naming system of NetWare 4.0. In total, a powerful and flexible application for anyone who wants to create an integrated workflow environment. When Mac and Unix support arrive, it will be unbeatable.

Microsoft Mail 3.2

Microsoft Mail has, with Lotus's cc:Mail, long filled one of the top two slots as the power-user's mail program. In its latest version 3.2, MS-Mail adds several new features that the administrator will find useful, but there are few noticeable changes to the client shell (Fig. 9.2).

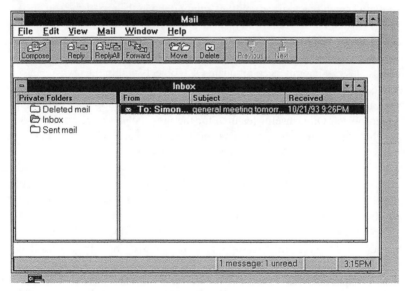

Figure 9.2 Microsoft Mail

Microsoft, like Lotus's cc:Mail offers excellent support for most common client and server platforms. Any MSMail installation needs at least one post office. When you buy the starter pack, this includes the post office and a 10-user licence together with all the client programs. Support for DOS, Windows, OS/2, and Macintosh

Macintosh clients is included as standard. The rival cc:Mail installation is a little more complex in that you need to buy separate user packs for each client platform.

You can tell MS Mail 3.0 is meant for power-users who like to fight with their network because the main installation program is a DOS utility. Everyone has friendly Windows-based front-ends, but not Microsoft (only when installing client software does the installation utility become a Windows application). MS Mail manuals were clearly laid out, but had too many references to installation on a LAN Manager network rather than the more popular Novell NetWare (LAN Manager, now incorporated into Windows NT is Microsoft's rival to the NetWare NOS).

Once the basic software is installed, you turn to installing your users. This used to be a nightmare in MS Mail, since it was not able to read the user list from a NetWare bindery or similar LAN Manager database. Now, thankfully, Microsoft has included a utility that helps. It is still not as smooth or automatic as, say, Finansa's WinMail; the utility queries the NetWare bindery, and produces a text file containing the user names which must then be redirected into MS Mail.

The user front-end is straightforward and simple to use. There is no rules feature so your users cannot get into a muddle with complex rules, nor can they gain the advantages of an intelligent post box. Although MS Mail is one of the very few e-mail packages without rules, it would have a tough time bettering the excellent add-on, WinRules from Beyond.

The main screen has a row of buttons running along the top of the screen. To the left is the structure of your folders in a display reminiscent of Windows' File Manager; to the right is a listing of messages in the selected folder. Creating a message pops up the main editing window; unlike many other e-mail programs, MS Mail messages can happily accommodate OLE objects within the text, e.g. a spoken comment as a WAV file or an Excel spreadsheet. You can also add attachments to a message in case the recipient does not have the relevant application to view the embedded object. Other useful features for the user include a receipt function that tracks who read your message and when. One drawback of Mail is that, unlike cc:Mail's SmartIcons, it is difficult to customize Mail for a particular user.

However, it is the administrator who is spoilt with MS Mail. Sure, the installation is difficult and entering the users is a chore. But the gateway, platform, and multiserver support in Mail is very good. If you want to connect several LANs each with a Mail server, no problem: the MS Mail post offices will each exchange data automatically—cc:Mail needs an extra utility to do this. Connectivity via LAN, modem, or X.25 links is supported, but cc:Mail betters MS Mail in this department by adding TCP/IP.

Gateway support is very good. If you want to route your messages via a central MHS delivery system, via X.400, MCI, or PROFS, then MS Mail can do so simply and efficiently.

One bonus that is often overlooked is that Windows for Workgroups, now bundled free on many PCs, includes an MS Mail client built in. Microsoft Mail 3.2 improves the administrator's job by speeding up user setup. Downsides include that the user interface is not easily customized, nor does it include rules support. However, Mail offers a powerful system which can happily link multiple, different platforms via a wide range of media and is ideal for large, enterprise-wide installations where there is a need to connect different computing platforms.

Lotus cc:Mail 2.0

Lotus has come up with a straightforward, segmented way of installing cc:Mail (Fig. 9.3). First pick your platform pack which implements the post office within your network. Each platform pack supports a different type of client: DOS, Windows, OS/2, or Macintosh. Next, buy user-licence packs for your platform. This method works well and keeps costs down if you want to equip an office of PCs running Windows. However, if you have a few users on Macs, a few on DOSs but most running Windows, then you will need three different platform packs and the necessary licence upgrades.

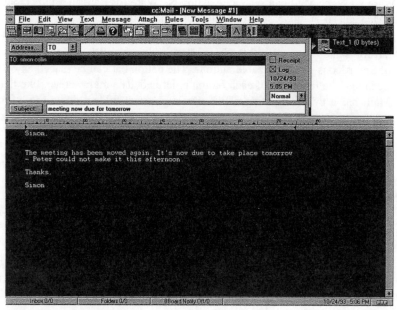

Figure 9.3 Lotus cc:Mail

To expand cc:Mail, Lotus uses a similar vertical tree pattern. To install the good group scheduling application, Network Scheduler II, requires a basic DOS pack followed by a Windows upgrade to run under Windows, and user-expansion packs for extra licences. It is a policy that means that you do not pay for anything you do not want, and is very flexible and can be tailored for any installation - but you do end up having to order a lot of different packs just for one product. Microsoft Mail, in comparison, bundles all client shells, routing, and some gateways into the main pack. However, this is secondary to the product itself.

Lotus has put a lot of effort into producing the ultimate e-mail program and has, by and large, succeeded. The software is about the most flexible on offer and will run on almost any type of LAN, with support for DOS, Windows, OS/2, or Mac clients. The installation is straightforward, but the manuals tend on occasions to be a little confusing with the mass of choices.

The administrator in a cc:Mail setup is spoilt for choice of connectivity products. cc:Mail has the widest range of gateways, including X.400, PROFs, MCI, and fax. If you want to connect two networks each with an existing post office, you will need an extra utility, Router, but this supports TCP/IP, X.25, IBM APPC, and normal dial-up modem links (MS Mail includes the functionality of Router in the base price, but it has fewer connectivity options). Connecting remote clients via a modem dial-up link is considerably easier than connecting two servers, and the software is bundled in with cc:Mail Platform Pack.

The administrator is given a helping hand during installation: MS Mail needs a rather protracted, two-stage process to import a user list from the bindery of a NetWare LAN. cc:Mail can scan an existing NetWare (or Banyan VINES, but not LAN Manager) user database and create a user-list automatically.

Users get a varied front-end, depending on their platform. The most flexible is cc:Mail for Windows version 2.0. This, in common with all Lotus products, has a row of SmartIcons—customizable buttons. The button bar can be placed anywhere on screen and the functions of each button redefined. The main screen, like that of MS Mail, has a tree-like listing of the user's personal folders down the lefthand side of the window with a list of messages on the right. Lotus has added rules functionality to cc:Mail, bringing it into line with the other 'intelligent' products and ahead of MS Mail—its rules are similar to those of BeyondMail and give you the control to filter your incoming mail. Lastly, cc:Mail can, like MS Mail, cope with OLE objects, but they can only be sent as attachments rather than be embedded in the text of a message as in MS Mail.

Lotus's cc:Mail 2.0 is still, just, the most flexible e-mail software on the market, and can manage a wide range of platforms and gateways. The user's software can be easily customized and includes rule-based intelligence, which is one up on MS Mail. However, the price is higher than other products and the mass of different products that you have to buy for an installation is a little off-putting. In short, if you have a complex, enterprise-wide installation where money is no object, but different platforms are, cc:Mail just tops the rest.

daVinci 1.8

daVinci has always sat in the shadow of the two main players in the e-mail market: Microsoft and Lotus. There is no good reason why this should be so, it is a friendly, easy-to-use product with good connectivity options. The basic product, like BeyondMail, uses Novell's MHS delivery system. Since MHS is the *de facto* standard for e-mail, it is supported by almost all e-mail products, and so, by association, is daVinci. With MHS installed (you have to buy MHS separately from Novell), the installation of daVinci is straightforward. Support for a range of client platforms is good, and includes DOS, Windows, and OS/2 users—but there is no Macintosh support yet. The server software runs most effectively on a NetWare LAN, but via MHS can run on most network server platforms.

The administrator will like daVinci—setup is very simple on a NetWare LAN. daVinci will scan the bindery and automatically add users to its own database, unlike MS Mail which needs a special utility to do the same. daVinci for Windows lets you control it to a good degree from within other applications using a DDE link. It is not as powerful or flexible a method as a DLL (used by Finansa's WinMail), but it is easy to write a macro in, say, Word, and from within Word, send a document using daVinci.

Connectivity to other systems from within daVinci is good. It supports gateways to commercial carriers such as MCI and CompuServe, as well as links to a fax or telex, X.400, or SMTP links. When you do send a message, daVinci keeps a log of who was sent what and any cc's. This is a useful backup tracking system in case you have deleted the original message or want to make sure you did send it.

Lotus Notes

Lotus Notes is often mentioned under the heading of e-mail because it can send mail, but it does far more than this. In its most clinical description, Notes is an information store that allows groups of users to share information. Notes is rather difficult to describe, since it depends on each setup, but at its core it is rather like a large, organized bulletin board—users can define topics and create threads of messages (Fig. 9.4). A lot of Notes' power comes from the flexibility of its forms. Like a database, you can create a form which is used as a basis for data entry in a particular topic. If the topic is e-mail, the form has check-boxes for urgent, receipt, and carbon-copy, together with a list-box for available users and a text-entry panel.

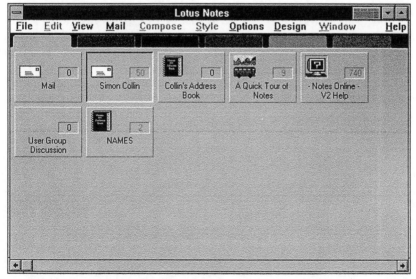

Figure 9.4   Lotus Notes user interface showing sample Notes applications

The client-tracking topic would have a different form design with details of address, potential spend, and telephone number.

The front-end to Notes runs under Windows on the PC, and a Macintosh version is also available. The user sees a stack of indexed cards as a main display; each card can hold large icons which give access to particular topics. For example, under the office card could be a topic listing the internal phone directory, another for a department's diary, and another for e-mail. Each of these topics is just a specialized Notes form design and you can modify the forms if you want to provide your users with an extra function.

The front-end of Notes often gets a lot of criticism. The e-mail and diary form designs are poor compared to dedicated software, the e-mail is slow, and so on. This is more a criticism of the form design rather than Notes itself—given the time, you can create virtually any groupware application using the Notes form design tools. However, where Notes stands alone is in its back-end power. Notes is designed for multiple server installations. It is ideal as an information backbone for large, multinational companies. In order that everyone has the same information, Notes replicates its databases. At a supervisor-defined interval (often at night), Notes will update all the other Notes servers it is connected to and swap new data.

The Notes back-end will normally run on a dedicated OS/2 server. With the release of Notes 3.0, Lotus provided a version that ran under Windows on a PC, making this an ideal version for supervisors to try out. However, for any site with more than a half-dozen users, you will need a dedicated server to cope with the traffic. Lotus is due to release a version of Notes that will run as an NLM on a Novell NetWare server. This will make for a more efficiently integrated network setup, but requires sizeable resources on the NetWare server.

With Notes, Lotus has one of the few information management systems that works efficiently in a large PC network. Notes has been instrumental in seeing some companies downsize from a mainframe to a PC-based LAN. It is resource hungry, sometimes temperamental, and ideally requires its own server. However, it is the only system that can provide a complete environment for many information-based companies.

ELECTRONIC MAIL STANDARDS

Electronic mail is a simple concept; making it work is not always quite so straightforward. The major problem is when distant e-mail systems want to exchange messages. The idea of a global message network might sound great, but with proprietary standards still defining the way most messages addressed, connectivity is a problem.

There are two major considerations. First the e-mail system must be able to identify the intended recipient of a message. Next it must be able to locate the receiver and find a route along which the message can be transported and delivered intact. There are reckoned to be some 400 different 'standard' methods of addressing, routing, and commanding a system to perform enhanced message-handling functions.

Among the contenders for survival, one of the favourites is the group of companies that have opted to pool their resources and applications program interface specifications to produce a standard they have dubbed VIM for Vendor Independent Messaging interface. The VIM consortium includes Apple, Borland, Lotus, and Novell. This group planned to have VIM ready for early 1992, but that date has slipped by.

Others tipped to win through include Microsoft with its Messaging API (MAPI) e-mail interface. Sheer weight of numbers should make MAPI a viable standard, say the tipsters. They also believe that Macintosh application developers will write to Apple's Open Collaboration Environment (OCE) since that is likely to form a foundation for a uniform address directory, security, and services for 'collaborative' applications.

In the meantime, though, the leader is hailed as Novell whose Message Handling System (MHS) standard is claimed, by Novell at least, to have emerged as the most widely used e-mail standard and API over LANs. Many see Novell as the dominant partner in the VIM group, along with Apple. And as a result, they say that the Open Messaging Interface (OMI) announced by Lotus with Apple and IBM will be remembered only as a catalyst to VIM.

In the MAPI–VIM race, Microsoft's MAPI was first off the blocks with a developers' kit and recommendations. It will form the basic communications method used by Microsoft's mail-enabled applications. These are future versions of Excel, Word, and similar that carry an extra menu option titled 'Mail'. The idea is that e-mail should become such a standard feature that everyone will use it and so productivity will improve. VIM has lagged behind the MAPI developments and as yet no concrete developers' kit has been launched.

The real winner of the moment is Novell's MHS. This is the only standard that is here now, works, and is almost universally accepted by e-mail vendors. Its only drawback is that it was not designed to work with mail-enabled applications.

The Current Standard—Novell's MHS

Among all the confusion surrounding future standards and directions, there is one standard that has stood firm over the last few years and is the *de facto* for transport of messages between LANs in different offices and countries. Novell's NetWare MHS is the one standard that any e-mail package should include within its specification list to guarantee a good degree of interoperability.

MHS uses a store-and-forward communications architecture. Store and forward does exactly what it says—it accepts a message, stores it temporarily, and then when the time is right, passes it on to another location until it eventually fetches up with its intended recipient.

MHS comes in two versions: one for personal users with stand-alone computers, and one for use on network client terminals which log onto on network server. Both perform similar functions in receiving, delivering, and transferring messages;

recovering from errors and disconnections; issuing reports on the status of the system and particular messages; and collecting and making available statistical information such as the duration of connections.

MHS has three components: a directory manager, a connectivity manager, and a transport manager. The first is described as an administrative tool that defines its internal database and manages applications software that overlays it. The database comprises a directory structure contains tables that associate addresses with the routes to users, hosts, and workgroups. It is used by the system supervisor to set up and configure the host; manipulate the database by adding, amending, and deleting usernames; and to define the routes to take between user workgroups, hosts, and gateways to other networks, and to define the names of affiliated workgroups.

The connectivity manager actually carries out the routing of messages between hosts. It runs only when needed to connect to a remote host or gateway or when an application requires it to carry out a 'local' delivery on its behalf. Periodically, a connectivity manager installed on a host will search proactively for incoming messages. If it finds one, it will read the address of the recipient, look up the route to that address in the routing table, and either pass it to the transport manager for transmission to the next host or arrange for its storage or delivery into a local mailbox. The connectivity manager may run on a dedicated workstation, but not necessarily.

The transport managers can be configured as either primary or secondary transport-servers. In the former case it transmits and receives massages either through telecommunications lines or through internetworks. As a secondary server it collaborates with other host systems. Four virtual communications channels are available to each transport manager, of which one, designated Line 0, is dedicated for use in the primary server mode. Message transfer can use an asynchronous connection using a modem and telephone line, over an internet connection, or through a gateway.

When a message is composed and addressed by a user, it is wrapped in an electronic envelope which contains at a minimum both destination and return addresses. With that there may be other message headers containing any special instructions and descriptions, followed by the ASCII text of the message and up to 64 attached files.

Attached files may be of any type containing a variety of data such as text, graphics, database or spreadsheet information, or executable program code. Messages are routed in a format known as SMF or Standard Message Format. This contains keywords that identify sender, recipient, the subject, and the names of attached files.

Addresses must be in a standard format. It must consist of at least two parts: a recipient username and a target workgroup or host name; these are separated by the @ symbol. In addition, the first part of the address header can have added the name of the application that the recipient intends to use to action the message. The optional application name is separated from the address by a dot.

The beauty of MHS is that it is supported by almost all e-mail vendors. Your e-mail package can concentrate its efforts on the front-end, safe in the knowledge that the delivery is being taken care of by MHS. The one disadvantage of MHS is that it is not terribly efficient on a PC-based LAN. Because of this, vendors introduced their own proprietary delivery systems, which led to the incompatibility in the first place. If you are running e-mail over a single site, with perhaps just a fax gateway, then you are unlikely to benefit from MHS. If you are connecting multiple sites with links to different gateways and users running several different e-mail packages, your life will be considerably easier with MHS installed.

Tying It Together with X.400

If you want to send a message from your PC to a user on mainframe in another country, you are going to come up against a number of problems. The first is that two different computer systems, each running a different e-mail program, want to talk. To solve the problem of data exchange there are a number of proprietary solutions. To bring standards to the issue, the International Consultative Committee for Telegraphs and Telecommunications (CCITT) published a set of recommendations, called X.400. Simply put, X.400 is intended to define how dissimilar computer messaging systems can exchange information. It has many parts, X.400 to X.435 inclusive, and runs to more than 600 pages of documentation. It is now in its second iteration, the first draft appearing in 1984, the second and most current in 1988.

This standard sets out not only to cover the basic workings of an electronic store-and-forward message system but also to anticipate the future. For example, its definition of the 'Body Part' or main contents of a message specifies a score of different types of information that it can carry, including dynamic and still video and audio messages, though some of these are there merely as 'place holders' at this time.

The recommendation derives directly from the idea of an Open Systems Interface (OSI) conceived by the International Standards Organization (ISO) in the early 1980s, and the seven-layer computer model. Within the seven-layer model, the X.400 specifications apply to what goes on in the seventh or topmost layer, the Application Layer. This provides for standardization of the services offered by an application to a user. What it does not do, however, is to define how those services are presented to the user. So although an X.400 compliant application will be able to pass data down the seven-layer stack, across a communications link, and back up the seven layers on a possibly dissimilar machine, the users at either end of the link will not necessarily be using the same application to view and operate the results of the message transfer.

The problem is that as the message passes down through the seven layers, additional data is added as each layer encapsulates the information received from a higher layer with its own protocol data. This is stripped away layer by layer at the receiving end, but it does mean that a very simple message of a few tens of bytes of text can have grown into a hulk measured in kilobytes by the time it gets to travel the physical link.

There are two main parts to the specification. At the centre is the Message Transfer Service (MTS). This is a generic message switching network, similar in concept to a packet switch except that rather than regular sized packets of data, the MTS switches whole messages, where a message is anything created and submitted to it in a manner defined by X.400. Within the MTS network, individual nodes are known as Message Transfer Agents (MTA).

The second major definition describes the Inter Personal Messaging Service (IMPTS). This describes the electronic mail facilities that should be offered to various types of user, and how messages are passed to the MTS for delivery. It covers such services as mailing lists, alternate receiving addresses, automatic forwarding, deferred delivery, priority, receipt notifications, and so on. These services are presented to users via a User Agent (UA).

A UA represents a single user; an MTA can support many UAs and interfaces to an intermediate service for delivery of the message in another, possibly non-electronic form, to its final destination. These intermediate services are provided by an Access Unit (AU) which offers what the CCITT calls 'Telematic' services such as telex or facsimile or good old-fashioned paper post. A message store (MS) can also be introduced between a UA or AU and the MTS. An MS allows the network operator to hold messages if the recipient is unable to take delivery immediately. Finally, the specifications call for a special highly secure service for Electronic Data Interchange (EDI) for financial transactions.

That, briefly, is how X.400 defines the electronic architecture. In the same way that telephones can be connected to the public network or to a PABX, so an X.400 network can be either public or private. These are defined as Management Domains and are known respectively as Administrative Management Domains (ADMD) or Private Management Domains (PRMD). Although a message originating in one private domain but destined for a recipient in another would normally pass through an ADMD, it is practical where the volume of traffic justifies the cost of leased circuits for two or more PRMDS to establish direct connections between them.

This seems complex, but X.400 was intended to be a global messaging standard allowing messages to be passed directly from any terminal to any other anywhere in the world. So each user of an X.400 compliant service must be able to construct a unique name.

The X.400 address is known as an Originate/Recipient (O/R) address, which in its fully expanded form contains not only the names of the individual users but also the paths by which they may be found. Generally, the bulk of the path information would be stored in a local directory and added automatically by the system.

A typical O/R address lists the users' country; a code for appropriate ADMD—in the UK at present there are just a few of these; next comes the code for the PRMD as appropriate, followed by the full name of the organization. The individual's location on the globe can be further pinpointed with provision for up to four 'Organization Unit' locations. Finally, is the user's 'Common Name'.

This complex address structure has led to a need for a very sophisticated directory capability. That problem is currently being addressed by the CCITT, which is preparing a new set of recommendations, X.500, to define directories. Yet a third set of definitions are embodied in the X.700 series, which set out recommendations for common specifications for the physical management of large networks.

Finally it should be noted that the CCITT does not write standards, but simply issues recommended specifications that have been agreed by its members. This raises at least two issues so far as X.400 is concerned. First, other standards bodies, both national and international, are free to interpret the recommendations as it suits them either in agreement with others or unilaterally. For example, the CCITT states simply that a recipient's name is comprised of a number of printable characters. Now other standards bodies have agreed that that number should be a maximum of 40 characters.

All this means that some implementations of X.400 may not be the same as all the others. Nevertheless, X.400-based e-mail products offer the most reliable standard available for meeting the integrated electronic messaging needs of the corporate environment.

10
Security

INTRODUCTION

Installing a network makes it easy to share information. In the long term, this can help productivity in an office. Networks also bring with them a question of security. Many users will be reluctant to trust their important letters and documents to the server if they feel everyone else can access them.

The job of a network supervisor is to make sure that the network's security prevents unauthorized users gaining access to company-sensitive information. She must also make sure users are confident enough in the security of a network to trust their data to it—this without intruding into their normal use.

Security in a LAN should be tackled in the three risk areas: the workstation, the server, and the transmission medium. Data security in these three areas of the network can be applied using hardware controls, using software techniques, or using the facilities provided by the network operating system. In this chapter, we will look at all three risk areas and see how to increase security in each case.

HARDWARE SECURITY

Workstation Security

Workstations can pose a problem for supervisors: they have to be as easy to use as possible, with the network intruding little. Yet they must protect against unauthorized users gaining access to the data on the network.

You should consider the types of attack you are vulnerable to. Would it be disastrous if someone accessed your data and changed the data? Or would it be worse if someone copied your data without you realizing they had done so? Either case requires the intruder actually to log into the network, more specifically the file-server.

There is no one solution to effective security. You could implement all the suggestions given here and find that the overhead makes your LAN unusable to normal users. However, you should not ignore security altogether. Instead, try and strike a balance between the two extremes that best matches your worries and the tolerance of your users. We will move through the security options according to their complexity and difficulty in setting up. Let us start with the simplest measures.

Stopping access to a workstation

More often than not, security breaches are carried out by casual intruders. If you avoid presenting them with an easy opportunity, it might be enough to deter them from proceeding.

Do your PCs have the facility of a power-on password? Most current system BIOSs (although not in an XT-compatible PC) allow you to set a password that the user has to enter once the PC is switched on or after a hard reset has occurred. The PC will not continue with the boot-up process until the correct password is entered.

Setting up this feature could be enough to prevent a casual intruder switching on a PC and looking at the local data on the PC's hard disk or logging in. But power-on passwords are not foolproof; it is easy to get around them since all BIOS settings, including the password, are stored in battery-backed RAM. An intruder only has to open the PC's case and unplug the battery and the password defence is broken.

To prevent someone opening the PC's case and disconnecting the battery, you should make use of the locks that all PCs have fitted. Make sure that the PCs you buy have physical locks rather than just electrical locks. Physical locks will lock the system unit casing shut, whereas electrical locks will not—instead they normally prevent the keyboard being used or power being switched on. If your PCs have physical locks fitted, you can keep the keys without inconveniencing the user, but still keep total control.

An alternative is to buy a PC with active security built into the motherboard. Apricot Computers sell a range of workstation PCs that will only allow access if you have a coded infra-red 'key'. Point the tiny key at the PC, press its transmit button, and the PC will continue its boot-up process, requesting a password and only then loading DOS.

Server Security

Stopping access to the server

If a casual hacker wanders past a workstation and, because of poor security, can log into to network, he can do a lot of damage. Consider how much more damage he could do if he was let loose on the central file-server. There are three potential weak points that you should protect against:

- A casual user just switching off the server.
- Gaining access to the console prompt and changing system settings.
- Copying or installing 'rogue' or infected software.

The first problem is that someone will switch off the server computer—whether for a joke or to bring down the network. This will not do any lasting damage, but it could corrupt some users' data and, if the system administrator is not present, could shut down an office for a few hours. The simplest solution is to fit a power-switch lock and an uninterruptable power supply (UPS). (UPS are described in greater detail in Chapter 13.)

The power switch lock will prevent anyone being able to physically switch off the power with the server PC's power switch. Our hacker could still flip the switch on the mains electricity socket, but this is where a UPS comes in. A UPS monitors the mains supply and, if it drops, will provide mains electricity for a few hours from a bank of batteries. The network operating system can monitor the UPS and, if it switches in, will send an urgent mail message to the network administrator. Remember that to monitor a UPS under Novell's NetWare 3.12, you will have to load UPS.NLM first; type the following command at the console prompt: 'LOAD UPS'.

With luck, you will be alerted in enough time to switch on the server's mains power supply before users suffer any down time. Apricot Computers provides a range of PC-servers that include even stronger deterrents. If you switch off one of its servers, nothing happens; a built-in UPS inside the casing takes over. Next, an alarm sounds and, as before, the network operating system can mail the supervisor that something is wrong.

From the server, you can carry out all the maintenance and administration tasks; you have direct control of many of the network's resources. You must protect this power by ensuring you make it as difficult as possible for someone else to use the console commands.

Under NetWare, the main status screen and management utility is called MONITOR. It is an NLM so first you will have to load it by typing 'LOAD MONITOR' at the system prompt. From within MONITOR, you can force users off the network, reassign memory and resources, and control the basic working methods of the LAN. You can also lock the server from within MONITOR. From the 'Available Options' menu, choose the 'Lock File Server Console' option. You will be prompted to type in a password. Once you have entered the password, the server console is locked; NetWare will ignore any commands typed from the keyboard until you enter the correct password. Obviously, do not forget the password once you have locked the console.

Microsoft's LAN Manager runs under the OS/2 operating system. As a multitasking operating system, OS/2 lets you switch to the main program manager and start a new session or window. There is no way of preventing this, and indeed sometimes it can be a help when troubleshooting your LAN to have workstation and server software running on the same machine. LAN Manager does lock its areas of disk and requires a password before you can access its management utilities.

For network operating systems that offer a remote console utility, giving full control of the server from a workstation (like NetWare's Remote Console utility), you will need to ensure that security rights in its directory prevent anyone but the supervisor from running it.

Blocking server software access

If an intruder is more capable and persistent, she might want to try and load a disk with a virus or rogue utility onto the server. In practice, this is extremely unlikely. Viruses under NetWare or OS/2 are virtually unknown—DOS and its wider audience offer a virus creator a larger and easier target. For an intruder to load an NLM or VAP onto a NetWare server, they would have to be an experienced NetWare programmer—it is not a trivial job writing a NetWare application. With LAN Manager running under OS/2, it is easier to recompile a utility to run under OS/2, but if it tries to interfere in another processes memory or disk space, OS/2 will stop it.

A more likely scenario is that someone will load an untested NLM or utility onto the server in good faith. The utility then crashes and brings the server down with it. Under OS/2 it is very difficult for one process to interfere with another, so it is more robust in these situations than NetWare. Loading an untested or unapproved utility NLM or VAP onto a NetWare server could, easily, crash the entire server. The reason is because NetWare allows NLMs to run in Ring 0 of memory—an unprotected and unsupervisored mode that offers the highest performance but greatest risk. The solution is again to lock the server console using NetWare's MONITOR or fit disk drive locks. Apricot's servers, for example, include a motorized door that normally covers and prevents access to the server's floppy drives. You can only get it to slide down, revealing the drive bays, by using an infra-red 'key'.

NETWORK SECURITY

Network Intruder Prevention

User accounts and passwords

Network security has two important roles to play. The first is to make sure that your company's data is safe from intruders. The second is to provide a real sense of security to users so that they are not afraid to save their private or personal data onto the network server. These are the principal aims of network security. But there is also a secondary aim—to minimize the entire effort that is required from users and supervisors. If maintaining security becomes a drudge or a nuisance, it will be dropped and your LAN will be wide open to intruders or accidental damage (Fig. 10.1).

All network operating systems provide some form of data security, from basic password protection to data encryption and government-approved status. There are two basic types of network file security:

- Share-level security associates a password with a shared drive, directory, or single file. You can limit the read/write capabilities assigned to the password.

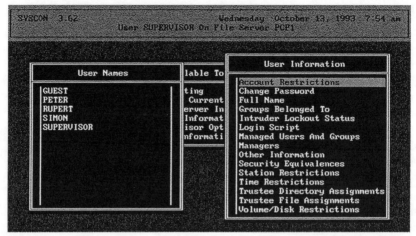

Figure 10.1   High-level user setup information can be configured using NetWare's SYSCON

This level of security is normally used by DOS-based LANs, making it easy to move the shared resources. The disadvantage is keeping track of all the passwords. It is easy for security to be breached, and security would be real headache since one password would be known to all the users of the drive, directory, or file. Simple peer-to-peer networks, e.g. Sage's MainLAN, use this level of security. Share-level security is cumbersome for large networks and not very flexible (it is hard to limit what a particular user can and cannot do). But it is quick and easy to setup and so ideal for small networks where security is not a big issue.

- User-level security moves the password protection to each user. A network administrator would setup groups that have rights to particular areas of a drive and individual users are assigned to groups. Each user logs in with their login name and a password. Once cleared, users have access to the LAN according to the security definitions in the groups they belong to. The supervisor can plan the network and ensure that security is not compromised by forcing regular changes of each user's password. Since they only have to remember one password, their own, security is tighter. User-level security is implemented in all high-end network operating systems like Novell's NetWare, Banyan's VINES, and Microsoft's LAN Manager (which also has an option to implement share-level security).

User-level security offers a supervisor the greatest control and power when designing a secure LAN. It is, initially, an effort to define the groups, hierachies, and user-levels, but you will be in control. Before you start to create users or define the rights of groups and managers, it is worth spending time drawing the hierachies and departmental divisions within your company. It will make it much easier to design a LAN that is usable and secure.

The users

Every person that uses your LAN is a user with an associated account. Every user has limited access to the system—only the supervisor has unrestricted access to the whole system. Each user has an account file that contains their rights for each drive, directory, and file within the system, together with other security information, such as limits to login times. In a NetWare server, these accounts are grouped together into the NetWare bindery—a large, encrypted file that is the core information source of all NetWare operations.

Users in a NetWare network are normally created using the SYSCON utility. If you are creating large groups of users, you will find it easier to use the MAKEUSER or USERDEF utilities. In LAN Manager, similarly, supervisors create users either through the NET menu-driven front-end or from the command line.

Every user's account carries information that will restrict access to the network in the following ways:

- *Login restrictions*—These define when are where a user can log into the network. This covers the times of login—for example, if you want to make sure no one can access the network in the middle of the night (Fig. 10.2). It also specifies which workstation the user can login from. Each workstation has its own unique ID number and, if your office has a fixed layout, and no one shares workstations, this provides a good way of blocking unauthorized network access. Supervisors can set the login restriction information on a single-user basis or for a group of users.
- *Directory rights*—With the exception of the LOGIN and PUBLIC directories, all users are blocked from using any other directories on the system until they are explicitly granted the rights to do so. NetWare supports extended rights flags

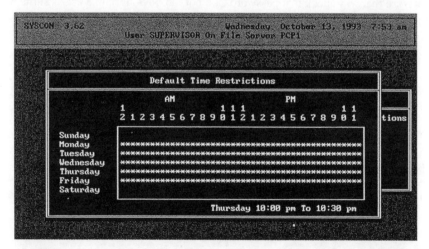

Figure 10.2 Improve the security of your network by limiting login times: in this example no weekend logins are allowed

that allow a supervisor to set whether a user can read, write, execute, delete, or create files within a directory. If a user creates a subdirectory, they inherit all the rights they were granted in the parent directory—unless a supervisor switches off this option.

- *File rights*—Individual files can be assigned special rights that will prevent users from editing, deleting, or copying them. These extended rights are particularly useful if you want to prevent application software theft or ensure that certain programs cannot be infected by a virus. Only supervisors can set an execute-only flag on EXE or COM files, and you should be careful only to do so on NetWare-approved software. Some applications can use complex swapping algorithms that may crash a PC if the execute flag is set.

In addition to these basic access rights, user accounts carry restrictions on passwords, disk use, and multiple connections. For example, a normal user would be setup with an account that required a password, to be changed every month, with no multiple logins (to prevent one user logging in a friend or an intruder logging in as another user). NetWare's SYSCON utility makes it easy to set each of these for any user.

Many network operating systems create a guest user as a default for limited access to the system. If you are concerned about security, it is worth deleting the guest user ID.

Passwords are a necessary part of logging into any network. To most office workers, they are also a nuisance. It is worth enforcing password protection since this is the single most effective deterrent against casual intruders. In NetWare, the supervisor can specify the minimum number of characters for a password and set a renewal date. Typically, it is worth setting a minimum password length of six characters and a renewal date once a month (Fig. 10.3). There are utilities for NetWare that will check that passwords are not too obvious, e.g. a user's surname. Remember that if you start to enforce password changes too often, users will get

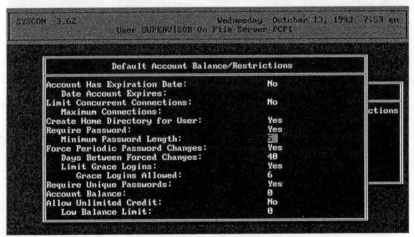

Figure 10.3   Increase the minimum password length to minimize security breaches

fed up and will jeopardize security with passwords like 'PASS1', followed next week by 'PASS2', and so on. One tip to deter users from telling each other their passwords or from writing them on the corner of the monitor is self-protection. Create a home directory for each user, to which only they have access. This will mean the users will start to save their personal data in this directory and will become sticklers for security to protect their own data.

• The NetWare command RIGHTS will display you access rights in a particular directory. For file access information, use NetWare's NDIR command to show the extended flag settings.

IMPROVING SECURITY

The access rights we have covered so far in this chapter go a long way to providing a secure LAN, but there are fundamental problems with most networks that they cannot address. The worst offender is that Ethernet, the most popular transmission method with over 60 per cent of the installed base, uses a bus-based topology in which every message goes to every workstation (see Chapter 4 for more details). The same problem exists with Token Ring and, normally, also with 10Base-T.

Every piece of confidential data you view on your PC's monitor, or type in, passes through every workstation's network adapter card. Normally, only the server and your workstation recognize the ID and read off the data. Any intruder with a network probe or monitor can view every packet of data that is carried over the cable. There is rarely any data encryption, so you can view exactly what is being sent around the network.

If you are worried about this threat, there are a number of solutions (Fig. 10.4). Passwords are not sent as plain text—they are encrypted before they are transmitted

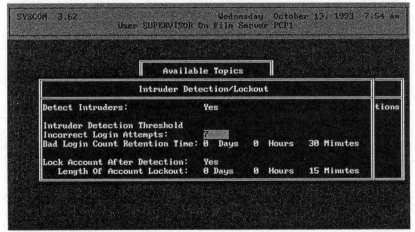

Figure 10.4 NetWare can be configured to inform the supervisor when multiple password attempts have failed

from the workstation to the server—but the rest of the traffic is not encrypted. LAN Manager and some other network operating systems have an option to encrypt all workstation traffic, which will provide a very secure LAN, but will slow down performance (admittedly, this performance drop is only by a few per cent and will not be noticed by most users).

An alternative option is open if your network is wired using a star topology with a hub in the centre. 3Com Corporation produce a range of secure hubs that will limit the traffic between the relevant workstations instead of a general transmission to all workstation.

The second problem that is often overlooked is the risk when a user walks away from their PC for a coffee or lunch break. Very few users can be bothered to log out for a short break. But then, the data on their local machine and a link to the network is open to any passing intruder. It is worth investing in software protection: if your users are running Microsoft's Windows, it comes bundled with a screen-saver that will clear the screen after a predefined period of inactivity. To continue using the PC, you have to enter a password. It is easy to get around this, for example, by leaving Windows, but it is a good deterrent against opportunists.

For DOS users, there is no bundled time-out utility, but a number of software houses have developed small utilities that will actually log out users after a certain number of minutes. Frye Utilities Corp. supply small TSR programs that take up just 3K of RAM and will log out a user after a defined number of minutes inactivity.

DISKLESS WORKSTATIONS

One threat to your data that you can easily forget is unauthorized copying. Your database of contacts will not be corrupted, but your business will suffer if a competitor gets hold of a copy of your data. This trail leads us to the workstation— it probably has a floppy disk drive and an internal hard disk. The floppy disk drive gives any user the opportunity to copy data from the network without trace. The first step is to remove the floppy drives from any workstations that do not need them (very few PCs need their floppy drive, unless they are installing software locally).

Removing the floppy drive still leaves the internal hard disk. Unfortunately, the hard disk is used to boot up DOS or OS/2 and has the network drivers stored on it. The answer is to remove the hard drive and fit a remote-boot ROM into your network adapter card. When you switch on the PC, the remote-boot ROM will send a request to the server, which then downloads a mirror image of a DOS boot into the PC's memory. To all intents and purposes, you now have a PC with a local drive (actually a RAM drive) that contains all the usual DOS files and network drivers. All high-end network operating systems, and the majority of DOS networks, support remote boot-ROMs. And this method will not only save money in PC costs, but will also increase security. If your PC users have low-end requirements, then a remote-boot ROM in a diskless workstation is an ideal answer. Added benefits are that the case is normally much more compact, saving space, and, with no moving parts, the PC is more reliable.

LICENCES

Once the foundation of your LAN is running, you can turn your attention to the applications. Unless they say otherwise, you can assume that almost all software packages have a single-user licence. This does not mean the software cannot be installed on a network, instead it normally means that only one person at a time can use the software. (Check the licence agreement that comes with the software to make sure of your licensing rights.)

Just because the software has a single-user licence, this does not mean you cannot install it on a LAN. Unless the software makes non-standard DOS or BIOS calls to the disk drive (e.g. some form of copy protection), any software will work when installed on a network drive instead of a local drive. This does not automatically mean that all users can run the non-network aware program. For example, during installation Windows applications tend to create a configuration or setup file, often with the extension .INI, in the WINDOWS directory of the local drive. To allow other users to run the program, you will need to trawl through the WINDOWS directory on the workstation originally used to install the software and copy any related files to other workstations.

A more serious problem with single-user licence versions of an application or programs that have no networking functionality built in becomes apparent when several users run the software concurrently. Unless the program itself implements some form of file locking, the last person to save their data could overwrite any earlier changes made by other users. This is one of the most basic functions built into software that is specifically designed for LANs.

If you are installing a custom-written application onto the LAN, there are a few basic rules. First, make sure that every user has the same drive mappings. Some workstations may have two floppy drives instead of one, and their login drive could be different from everyone else's. It will make problem-solving easier if you police the CONFIG.SYS and AUTOEXEC.BAT files of your user's workstations. Second, when installing the executable code onto a network drive, make sure that the EXE or COM file's shareable flag is set (using the FILER utility with Novell's NetWare operating system). Setting the executable file as shareable lets several users run the application at the same time. If your program uses any overlay files or database files, these too should be flagged shareable. To prevent attacks from viruses and prevent users copying software off the network to a local machine, set the program files' execute flag ON (again, using the FILER utility in NetWare). The execute flag will prevent users from copying, altering, or writing to the file.

If you currently have several copies of one application running on stand-alone PCs, you will need to get the networked version of the software. If there is no LAN version available, proceed with care and take into account the steps for custom software described above. When you upgrade from multiple single-user licences to a single multiple-user licence, check if the software house has an upgrade plan—many do offer low-cost licence upgrades for existing customers.

Licence Metering

Software piracy is not new. It is especially easy for a corrupt administrator to install a cheap single-user licence wordprocessor or spreadsheet application onto the network and allow everyone to use it. Software companies have tried various ways of countering this type of piracy, from counters that click up with every extra user, to applications that run on the server and can keep an eye on how many users have logged in and which applications they are running. In the end, these protection measures cause more work for one person—the network administrator—and she is unlikely to want to install protected software if this will increase her workload. Most software companies now supply applications on a per-server licensing agreement which is easier to enforce and yet does not cause constant bother for the administrator.

To get a better overall picture of how many users are running which program, or to keep an eye on licensing limits, you could install a software metering utility. These normally run either as an NLM from the server (taking up around 300–500K of server RAM) or as a small TSR on every workstation. Once the metering software starts monitoring an application (or rather the accesses to its EXE file), you can set concurrent user limits to stay within licence agreements. If too many users try and run the program, a warning message will be sent to them and a report generated for the administrator.

The software will generate a monthly or weekly report that lists how many users have been using which software and when. Although these licensing metering applications themselves cost between £500 and 800, they can help you keep within licence agreements, spot redundant software, and, best of all, help you make a case for a new software budget.

11
Detecting Problems—Using Network Management

INTRODUCTION

With the growing popularity of networks, more and more users are now relying on a network or shared resource to carry out their everyday job. If the LAN in an office goes down for an hour, it is likely that no one will be able to do any work, and the cost is in lost time that should be productive. In a bank or trading floor, downtime can begin to cost a considerable amount.

The most obvious option for a network supervisor is to ensure that the equipment is reliable and so will never go wrong. In a real world, this will rarely happen. A more realistic alternative is to provide enough insurance to minimize the downtime and, hopefully, give you enough advance warning to allow you to prevent a network crashing.

Network management provides the solution, allowing you to monitor any network node, or part of the network. A manager can sit in front of their management console and view the statistical information compiled about various parts of the network. This statistical information gathering includes details of performance, errors, loading, and usage. With effective network management, it becomes easy to spot if a device is being over- or under-used or if some part of the LAN might soon fall over due to excessive loading. In an ideal network, a database of all these statistics would be kept by the network management system and allow any manager to view the results, and provide early warnings, from anywhere within the network.

Network management includes two parts. The node that provides statistical information about itself or the network is called a managed agent or server. The firmware that runs on a dedicated processor within a hub or router to collect the statistical information is also sometimes called an agent. The management terminal that allows a supervisor to view the results and monitor these agents is called the management system.

These elements are collected within a management information base (MIB)—a database of all the nodes on a network that can be monitored or managed. These objects are monitored by a central suite of software that communicates with each object and collects the statistical information or controls the object. This software poses the greatest problem to anyone installing a network management system: which of the different protocols should be used?

THE OPTIONS FOR NETWORK MANAGEMENT

Network management systems fall into two camps: those that use proprietary protocols and messaging systems, and those that comply with a standard. The ISO body defines its management system within the Common Management Information Protocol (CMIP) system.

CMIP might be the official standard, but the *de facto* standard, with the greatest installed base, is the Simple Network Management Protocol (SNMP) suite that was defined by the developers of TCP/IP. Alternative proprietary systems, such as IBM's NetView, have a hold on certain market sectors. The future is simple, CMIP provides the most powerful and flexible system that most supervisors and vendors will eventually move towards. Currently, it is being restrained by high memory requirements in each monitored station, but it will, by the late 1990s, be the predominant management system.

The short message is that if you are responsible for a network, you begin to think about adding at least the option of network management. When you next buy a router or hub, make sure that it can also support management agents— conforming to an open standard such as SNMP or CMIP. If you do not have a network management system up and running now, you soon will and you should make sure that your equipment can be upgraded.

SNMP

SNMP was originally developed within the Unix environment and by the same body that developed TCP/IP and its suite of supporting protocols. As a result, it normally uses TCP/IP as its method of transmitting status packets around a network. It has now become the *de facto* standard for network management and is the most widely used, vendor-independent method of managing your LANs.

SNMP defines a basic set of commands that allows communications between managed objects and managed units. The manufacturers of a particular product are left with the choice of adding more features on top of the basic foundation. This means that even if multiple products are SNMP compatible, it may not be possible to manage them from a workstation running software from a different supplier.

One of the advantages of SNMP over other standards, such as CMIP, is its method of delivering messages. All SNMP messages are delivered as single-packets between the managed agents (the server) and the managing station (client). The advantage of using single-packet datagrams becomes more obvious when your network is congested or faulty—typically just when you need to use the network management software. A single-shot SNMP packet stands a better chance of getting through a congested network and across busy links than a connection-to-connection link with messages several packets long that is required by CMIP. A secondary advantage is that these single SNMP packets add very little overhead to the network load.

Detractors of SNMP usually cite its lack of security as its biggest weakness, together with the problems introduced with differing standards between different manufacturers.

An SNMP-managed network uses two main types of device: the managed agents (the servers) and a managing station (the client). The agents report back to the managing station and have just one basic function—to be able to gather statistics and store it in an MIB. The format of an MIB is standardized, though some manufacturers try and add extra information by using proprietary MIB extensions.

The agents within the network are the routers, bridges, hubs, file-servers, or any other type of LAN node that can benefit from management. Some nodes, such as routers and hubs, include a dedicated area of memory and processor to gather the statistical information and pass it back to the managing station.

The second half of the SNMP system is the management station. There is normally just one station, in the supervisor's office, but there are no restrictions. The station polls each agent and retrieves the statistical information it has gathered about its own performance. Normally, the management station presents the results graphically under a Unix/X-Window or DOS/Microsoft Windows graphical user interface front-end.

SNMP uses TCP/IP as a transmission protocol for its messages, but it can run over other LAN systems, such as Novell's NetWare. To do this, you must setup a PC that can interrogate the agents using IP.

How SNMP works

SNMP functionality can be split into two parts—the protocol and the MIB. The third possible element, the user interface, is down to the vendor and is not defined in any formal sense. Within the original specification of SNMP there are five message types defined:

- GET—this operator retrieves an object of information from the server MIB.
- GET NEXT—retrieves the next (in alphabetical order) object or group of objects from the server.
- MIBSET—this operator sets an object of information in the server MIB.
- GET RESPONSE—retrieves the response message from the server following one of the above instructions.
- TRAP—this operator is an event alarm message from the server to a manager.

CMIP has similar instructions, but misses out the GET NEXT operator. To retrieve a table of objects within SNMP, you simply ask repeatedly for the next object (using the GET NEXT operator). Within CMIP, retrieving a table of objects is a more complex operation and requires considerable processing overhead.

At its most basic level, a GET operation on a particular element MIB allows a management system to obtain raw data about the target end-system. The management system can then process the data it receives back. A SET operation allows the management system to take input from a user and set a variable within the end-system. Typically, this could be used to reset a statistic count variable.

As mentioned, the GET NEXT operator allows the management system software to step through the objects and can use SET to define the objects. The TRAP message is used by the server to alert the management system, normally to raise an alarm.

Management systems

How the management system software works and looks is not formally defined by anybody—it is left to the manufacturers to create a usable front-end. This is often based around a dedicated X-Window/MOTIF terminal or a PC running Windows or OS/2; one of the most popular devices is to use Sun workstations running Unix as an SNMP management terminal.

A simple interface would include a running display of an object's statistics. This would typically be produced using SNMP's GET operation. A user would select the object from a list within an MIB and the software would then quiz the object every few seconds using the GET command. In this way, a track of the object's statistics can be monitored. More sophisticated systems allow multiple objects to be monitored and trend analysis carried out. Some products, such as Spectrum from Cabletron, use artificial intelligence to predict and react to conditions in objects. This complexity of presentation and reaction within SNMP is still achieved using just five simple message types.

The future of SNMP

SNMP has built up a very strong installed base. The reason? It is here now, it works now, and it is relatively economic on processing requirements. Rival CMIP has the advantage of being based on an ISO standard, but has yet to be delivered in a fully working form. As CMIP is fine-tuned, so SNMP gains extra functions and a firmer foothold.

The consensus is that SNMP will give way to CMIP, but not until the late 1990s. Until then, some sites will move from SNMP to CMIP via the middle ground offered by CMOL (a derivative of CMIP that has smaller memory requirements), but SNMP is still a force to be reckoned with.

The ISO-standard CMIP

The ISO/OSI model for network management is CMIP. The commands used to perform the tasks are defined within a second standard, CMIS (Command Management Information Services).

CMIP is often given as the great rival to SNMP, but in fact most users agree that CMIP is the open standard to aim for. Take up of CMIP has been considerably slowed by the slow ISO approval that has meant that final definitions were only available late in 1990.

However, the biggest problem to the general acceptance of CMIP is its high system overhead. Because it requires the full OSI stack to be loaded, it can take up to 300K of RAM on a PC. Out of a normal maximum of 640K offered by DOS, this leaves little RAM for standard text applications and not enough to run large applications such as Microsoft Windows.

The CMIP definition

There are five areas within the CMIP definition covering all possible sectors of network management.

* Accounting allows a network manager to keep track of the network resources, who uses them, and how they are being used. CMIP management systems can use this information to generate a log of each user's activity and usage and so generate billings.
* Configuration management is used to provide names for each of the managed elements within the network. These can then be used to build up a network map of all elements and, in some user front-ends, display the map graphically.
* Fault management is used to detect when problems occur on the LAN and initiates actions that will try and solve them.
* Performance management concerns itself with statistical information such as packets transferred, disk accesses, and so on. Its main aim is to provide information to allow a supervisor to monitor the usage of the separate sections of a LAN and its elements.
* Security management controls access to particular areas of the network and protects sensitive sections of data. The lack of security offered by SNMP has always been criticized and OSI/ISO has taken steps to make sure that CMIP is secure.

CMOL

CMIP's biggest hurdle to general acceptance is its high memory requirements. To try and overcome this, a cut-down version of CMIP that runs over the logical layer of the OSI stack has been proposed by 3Com and IBM. Called CMOL (CMIP over logical-link layer), it is designed to offer the same basic functionality as CMIP, allowing statistical information to be gathered from LAN elements such as routers, bridges, and hubs. Many users who want to support CMIP, but without its high overhead, are using CMOL as a stepping stone between SNMP and full CMIP.

IBM NetView

IBM's NetView network management system uses dedicated PCs within a network to gather information. This information is then passed up to a mainframe to be analysed and monitored. The PCs run NetView/PC either under DOS or, in its latest version, under OS/2. The mainframe runs NetView—a not inconsiderable load on it.

When first announced in 1986, NetView was a proprietary system. IBM has announced that it will now move it into line with the CMIP standard, which will broaden its appeal. Unfortunately, NetView still remains the most expensive way of managing your network, both in terms of the cost of the software and the dedicated system resources required.

IBM announced, in mid-1992, that it would enhance NetView 2.0 to cover APPN (advanced peer-to-peer networking) resources. These enhancements will allow NetView to provide problem, topology, and accounting management functions. In theory, this will allow users to manage peer-to-peer networks as well as existing SNA networks.

Novell's Solution

Novell's NetWare 3.12 comes complete with a number of utility programs that can be used to monitor the status and performance of your LAN. In addition, add-on products allow an NetWare server to act as a NetView agent, an SNMP collection point or as a part of Novell's own network management strategy, NMS (NetWare management system).

NetWare 3.12 comes complete with support for an SNMP agent that runs on the server. The SNMP NLM acts as an agent for remote clients. It can access MIB objects that relate to TCP/IP and can generate the SNMP trap messages. This NLM does not yet support the full range of SNMP management tools. Instead, an NLM called SNMPLOG can be used to log trap events generated by other SNMP agents.

Novell has also provided support with NetWare 3.12 for IBM's NetView management system. An NLM, NVINSTAL, will forward NetView alerts to a NetView host across a Token Ring adapter fitted in the server. This NLM will also respond to requests from an IBM host for statistics about the server.

In addition to support for these two open standards, Novell announced its own management standard, NMS, in 1992. This specification is an open standard which provides an API to allow programmers to develop management programs. The NMS engine provides data about all servers, hubs, workstations, routers, and nodes. Any application running under DOS, Windows, or OS/2 can access this data using the specified API. The entire concept provides an open platform that should allow a supervisor to manage any part of a Novell LAN from her workstation. At the moment, software is still thin on the ground, but support from smaller utility vendors is growing.

Together with the built-in support for the NMS, SNMP, and NetView standards, NetWare 3.12 includes a number of stand-alone utilities that will help you to manage your server and network more effectively. MONITOR is an NLM that runs on the server and can be used by anyone with access to the server console (although it is wise to password protect the console using the MONITOR utility).

MONITOR allows you to view information about the server's utilization and overall activity, the status of the cache memory, how many connections are active, and their status and memory usage, together with information on drives, drivers, and NLMs. In short, MONITOR provides a lot of the data that a supervisor requires to ensure his server is running efficiently.

To run MONITOR, type LOAD MONITOR at the console. One of the most useful screens to check if your server is underspecified is to look at the Resource Utilisation option to view the server's memory statistics. The cache buffers available should be around 80 per cent. If it drops to below 60 per cent you should fit more RAM to your server to stop it thrashing and spending too much time swapping to disk.

MONITOR lets you easily check that disks, disk mirroring, and connections are all working correctly. If you suspect that your cabling might be causing faults, check using MONITOR to see if a workstation on the suspect cable is registered. If not, you should then use a cable tester or NetWare's COMCHECK utility to test the links to establish where in the cable the problem lies.

Remote NetWare management

NetWare's console command, MONITOR, provides vital information about the state of your server and network. But it is difficult for a supervisor to run to the server whenever he wants an update. To solve this problem, NetWare includes a remote management facility (RMF) that allows a supervisor to log in at any workstation and issue commands as if he were at the console. The RMF consists of three parts. Two NLMs, RCONSOLE and RSPX, must be loaded onto the server. The supervisor can now log in to any workstation connected to the server and, using the utility RCONSOLE.EXE, issue any console commands including MONITOR.

When RCONSOLE.EXE is first run, it displays a list of all available servers that can respond to remote management. The supervisor can then pick which server she wants to monitor. It is worth remembering that RCONSOLE can also operate through a serial link; if your server goes down, you can still manage it remotely using a pair of modems—one linked to the server's serial port. The only extra requirement before you can manage your server remotely over a dial-up link is that you must first load the RS232 NLM on the server.

INTELLIGENCE IN THE HARDWARE

Networks running a Token Ring or 10Base-T wiring topology have one major benefit over standard coaxial-based Thin Ethernet: both use a central wiring hub. Fit a processor into this hub and you suddenly have a means of viewing all the nodes and all the traffic on the LAN—all traffic must pass through the hub. If the hub is more sophisticated, it is also possible to control its functions through the same internal processor. For example, the processor could gather and send statistical information about nodes and traffic back to a monitoring station. In return, the monitoring station could also control nodes or shut down connections by sending instructions to the hub's processor.

Intelligent hubs from 3Com, David Systems, Proteon, Cabletron, and Synoptics all offer degrees of intelligence. In their most basic forms, the hubs require proprietary software to monitor and control the hubs, unless they are SNMP compliant. The advantage of being able to view the status of all your connections and entire wiring closet, remotely, on your PC is a considerable benefit to any supervisor, saving time and effort. If the monitoring software adds a little sophistication, it can provide views of load, errors, and workstation lock-ups. An alert message is displayed on your PC or an e-mail message sent. You can then service the downed user very quickly, in some cases restoring the connection automatically without having to leave your PC.

If you also want to view the traffic that is flowing through the hub, rather than the quantity, you will need to install a protocol analyser, which are discussed in Chapter 4.

CONCLUSIONS

All network supervisors must consider how to manage their network. A comprehensive network monitoring system is a must for any large or mission-critical network. However, even a small five-user LAN will benefit in performance if you use the basic tools provided with the network operating system.

Network monitoring tools and network management software can sometimes drown you in a tidal wave of statistical data. However, interpreting the data and spotting problems before they down a LAN can save you money, time, and effort.

12
Connecting Networks

INTRODUCTION

Your company sets up a new office in another town. They too have a LAN. Or perhaps your parent company is based in another country, or you just want teleworkers to keep in touch. Linking LANs together means sending data across wide-area links—such as the public telephone system. There are many options open to you if you want to expand your LAN into a WAN. This chapter shows you some of the options and gives their pros and cons.

REPEATERS

Repeaters are the cheapest and most basic method of connecting together two LANs. A repeater works at the physical layer in the ISO model and provides simple signal regeneration; as an electrical signal passes along any length of cable it is attenuated (the level goes down) and noise is introduced. A repeater takes the incoming signal and gets rid of the noise, regenerates the signal, and sends it on— they are often used to extend the length of a LAN segment which would otherwise reach the limits of the media (e.g. Ethernet over thin coaxial cable is limited to over 185 m, put a repeater at this distance and you can drive an extra 185 m).

Repeaters can also be used to link two identical networks, providing a simple and basic connection (Fig. 12.1). There is one big problem with repeaters: their sole function is to form a link between two LANs—everything that comes along is passed across. This immediately doubles the load on each LAN.

As shown in Fig. 12.1, the repeater allows the users on LAN 1 to gain access to the devices on LAN 2 and vice versa, but the load on each LAN has been increased. If each LAN was near its load limits, adding a repeater could easily kill performance in both LANs.

• Repeaters are a cheap and easily installed way of extending a LAN or connecting two small LANs.

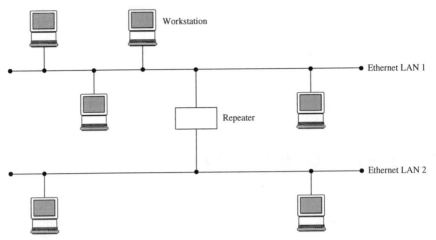

Figure 12.1   Using a repeater to join two Ethernet networks

BRIDGES

Bridges include a little more processing power than a simple repeater. Instead of just passing everything they receive over the link, a bridge reads the destination address contained in each packet's header data. It compares this to its internal address list and, based on this, either sends the packet across the link or keeps the packet local. Effectively, bridges work at the MAC level of the data-link layer within the ISO model and are often called MAC-layer bridges. All a user sees are the benefits of a newly extended network with remote resources now available. From a supervisor's point of view, bridges will not load either LAN unnecessarily.

A secondary benefit is that, unlike repeaters, bridges can link two different media types. You can link an Ethernet LAN to a Token Ring LAN using a

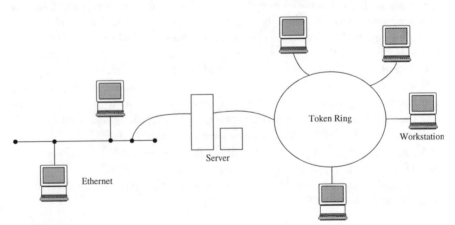

Figure 12.2   Using a central server with two types of network adapter as a bridge to connect two different LANs

bridge—as long as the transmission protocol used is the same on each side (e.g. Novell's IPX to IPX or NetBIOS to NetBIOS). Specialized bridges will link two totally different LANs, and can cope with different protocols at each end. They strip out the data packet from the incoming frame and insert it into an appropriate frame in a different protocol that is running over the second LAN (Fig. 12.2).

As we have mentioned, a bridge distinguishes between traffic that has to be passed over the bridge and local traffic. It does this by comparing the address header in each packet with an address table it has built up of every node. A bridge will send out a request to every node on each LAN it is connected to and, from the replies, can build up its table of node addresses and associate an appropriate LAN and segment with each address. Because of this, bridges also eliminate any badly addressed or corrupted packets, and errors are not propagated across the LANs.

Types and Uses of Bridges

There are three basic types of bridge: transparent, translating, and encapsulating.

- Transparent bridges provides a link between two LANs that use identical protocols at both the data link and physical layers. As far as any workstation on either LAN is concerned, every node appears to be on one large, single LAN. A transparent bridge is the least complicated of the bridge family, and cannot handle mixed protocol (e.g. it can link two Novell IPX LANs, but not an IPX LAN to one using NetBIOS).
- Translating bridges provide a link between two LANs that use different transmission methods, e.g. between a Token Ring network and an Ethernet system. Translating bridges cannot split up the packets from each LAN, it can merely readdress and reformat between LAN types (the difference between Ethernet, Token Ring, and FDDI packets are not that great).
- Encapsulating bridges differ yet again. They link identical LANs via a 'foreign' internetwork connection. For example, connecting three Ethernet LANs using an FDDI backbone is a typical job for an encapsulating bridge. It takes an Ethernet packet, repackages it for transmission over the FDDI backbone circuit to the appropriate bridge, which then strips out the Ethernet packet from the FDDI format and sends it on over its own LAN (Fig. 12.3).
- Source routing bridges were originally specified by IBM as a means of bridging Token Ring LANs. The difference between source routing bridges and the preceding three is that the message source must supply all the information to deliver the message across the link. Normally, this information is stored within the bridge, as in the other three types of bridge. The bridge decides whether to send a packet across the link based on the information in the packet header—it does not maintain address tables. Instead, a method called 'route discovery' is used to establish either the fastest or most direct route between the sender and the receiver. The sender node transmits an explorer packet that is then flooded around every other node of every linked LAN, and across all bridges. As it passes across each bridge, the bridge fills in its address to provide a route back. The

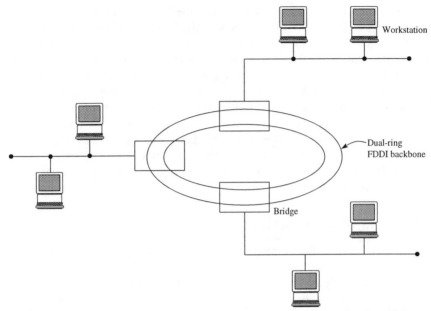

Figure 12.3   Using bridges to connect three separate Ethernet networks via a high-speed FDDI dual-ring backbone

specified receiver node recognizes the packet and transmits the explorer packet back to the original sender node. The sender now has a list of all the possible routes through the network to its intended recipient. It makes a decision as to which of the many routes it can use to transmit its data across the linked networks.

Conclusions

- Bridges are best suited to small networks within one building. They are cheap and provide one of the simplest ways of extending your LAN.
- If you are linking together LANs with different MAC-level hardware, use a router instead of a bridge.

ROUTERS

Routers work in a similar way to bridges—they effectively extend a network by linking together smaller LANs. However, they incorporate even more processing power than a bridge which allows them to pick the best route for a particular message. In a typical scenario, a router might have several delivery routes available—each with a different cost and speed of delivery. According to the size and urgency of the packet to be deliver, the router can select the best route for it. Routers provide connection service at the network layer of the ISO model (one layer higher than a bridge). This means a router can take more intelligent decisions than a bridge, but because of this tends to be slower. A router can connect LANs that use different protocols and transmission methods.

Routers are often used when connecting LANs over a long distance—either over a leased line, ISDN, X.25, or asynchronous modem link. The price of internetwork links like these is expensive, and routers make more efficient use of the link than a bridge. A router only reads the internetwork address, it strips off the MAC-level address which can, in small packets, be half the packet. In addition, it is often worth trying to buy routers with built-in compression algorithms—but only for slow or very busy links. It is not worth adding the overhead of on-the-fly compression when using high-speed links that transmit at over 64 Kbps; the overhead of compressing the data begins to slow down the transmission.

Novell NetWare Router

Novell NetWare 3.12 includes a number of utilities that allow a server or workstation to operate as a stand-alone router. All it needs is to have the IPX protocol running and either by using the ROUTEGEN utility or loading the ROUTER NLM onto the server, you can create an internal router driving up to four different network adapter cards.

NetWare exchanges address routing information in two ways. The first is using its SAP (Service Advertising Protocol) messages that servers send out to identify themselves to other servers. Every NetWare server and router sends out a SAP message once every 60 seconds.

In addition to this basic method of locating other servers and routers, the standard IPX protocol is used to carry routing information. NetWare 3.12 also includes the ability to route TCP/IP and AppleTalk packets as well as standard IPX traffic around the network, making NetWare's internal solution a flexible, powerful, and very cheap router option for smaller networks.

• If you can, use the built-in router provided as part of your NetWare, LAN Manager, and VINES network operating system software. They integrate well with existing software and are free.

Router Management

Routers are the links between complex segments of an internetwork. If a router fails or begins to go wrong, it can affect a lot of nodes, and so it is worth monitoring your routers with some form of network management protocol. Many routing vendors will try and sell their proprietary network management system, but for compatibility and flexibility, always stick to one of the industry standards, such as SNMP, NetView, CMIP, or Novell's NMS system (see Chapter 10 for a complete rundown of network management protocol standards and tools).

Routing Protocols

Routers have to obtain information about the rest of the network, and they do this by swapping information using a routing protocol. The routing protocol runs as a software suite on the router's processor. There are a number of established protocol standards:

- Routing information protocol (RIP) was developed for the XNS protocol and is still used with XNS, IPX, and TCP/IP networks. RIP uses the distance-vector routing method to determine how to send the packet on across the network. To do this, a RIP router reads the destination address and sends it on to the general logical direction using the path with the least number of 'hops' (steps across routers). RIP, like all distance-vector routers, is efficient on small internetworks but it becomes limited over large WANs. One big limitation is that RIP is limited to 16 hops—it cannot pass data to a router that is more than 16 hops (or other routers) away. RIP routers have an additional problem of high overhead. They distribute the address tables among themselves every 30 seconds—a load that can severely impact on low-bandwidth links. Although RIP is used within internal Novell NetWare routing, it is generally considered to be too old and limited for large networks, with too many overheads for small networks.

- Open shortest path first (OSPF) works with TCP/IP. It does not use distance-vector routing (as does RIP), but instead uses the link-state routing method of finding the best path between two points. OSPF routers need more processing power than RIP routers (and can be more expensive) to cope with the more complex best-route algorithms used in link-state routing. This takes into account the traffic load, throughput, costs, and priority of the circuit and packet. Unlike RIP routers, OSPF routers exchange address tables only when needed, rather than every 30 seconds. This is more efficient and considerably reduces the overhead. Typically, you would partition a large internetwork into smaller routing areas. Because OSPF does not broadcast the network address table (essentially, the network's topology), security is increased.

- Intermediate system to intermediate system (IS–IS) protocol works with the ISO's OSI-compliant networks. IS–IS routers work in a very similar way to OSPF, but can handle OSI systems rather than being TCP/IP-specific. Dual IS–IS is a derivative of the base product that will route both TCP/IP and OSI traffic.

- The last method is the routing table maintenance protocol (RTMP) and is used predominantly with Macintosh networks running the AppleTalk protocol.

Conclusions

- Routers are best used over enterprise-wide installations because they allow you to connect to several data links, support redundancy (if one route fails, another can be used), and support multiple network-layer protocols.

- Routers cannot work with protocols that have no network layer—for example, you cannot bridge a NetBIOS network or a LAN running DEC's LAT or LAVC protocols.

DO YOU BRIDGE OR ROUTE?

There are six key points to consider when trying to choose between a bridge and a router.

1 Is price important? Bridges are cheaper than routers. This is often offset against poor use of the link's bandwidth—which can mean installing a more expensive, higher speed link to get the same performance as a router.
2 Do you need fault tolerance? Most bridges are not tolerant of network failures—a failure can mean you lose or corrupt data packets. Routers are designed to work with multiple wide-area links and minimize the effects of one network failure by switching to another.
3 Efficiency. Bridges work most efficiently when both networks being bridged use identical packet sizes. Routers are more tolerant because they split packets then reassemble them during normal operation.
4 Is error detection critical? Bridges will carry out data link error checking that should stop bad packets crossing the link. Routers go one further and carry our error checking at the data link and network layers.
5 Is the delivery time critical? Bridges offer the shortest delivery delay because they carry out very little processing.
6 Capacity. Bridges can begin to form a bottleneck when serving LAN segments that carry more than 24 active nodes. In these cases, a router would normally work more efficiently.

BROUTERS

Brouters, as you can guess from their name, are a hybrid that combines the functions of a bridge and a router. Typically, a brouter would route one protocol and bridge all others. For example, if your company sent a lot of different protocol traffic along the same cable, a brouter could be useful to bridge the local NetBIOS packets and route the IPX traffic over a modem link to a remote Novell NetWare LAN.

REMOTE CONNECTIONS

When setting up a WAN, or one that stretches between two buildings, you will have to consider the options available for remote connections. This section is not just for power-administrators with hundreds of users to support; you might just want to setup a remote node from someone's home giving them full access to the network.

The subject of remote connections can be split into two. The first covers the hardware available: modems and transceivers. The second covers the transmission medium: satellite, microwave, telephone, or leased line.

If you have two LANs in neighbouring buildings, then the job of connecting them is relatively easy if they are similar LANs. A repeater can be used to boost the signal across the gap between the buildings. This will work fine for two identical networks (two Ethernet or Token Ring), but hits a problem if they are different. Some bridges, as described above, can be used to connect different transmission types, but normally need a similar protocol, such as IPX or NetBIOS, running on each.

The problems start when the distance to be spanned between the LANs increases. It becomes very expensive to try and provide a direct link between the two LANs at the speed of a transmission method such as Ethernet (10 Mbps). Expense dictates that you will normally have to try and find a low-cost, practical method of spanning the two networks.

If the sites are relatively close, within a couple of kilometres, it might still be practical to try and cross this using standard LAN transmission methods—notably by using a fibre-optic cable link. This is immune to electrical interference, offers good weather resistance and is capable of running to 100 km without a repeater. The cost of installing adapters at each end (at around £600 per adapter) is often prohibitive for standard workstations, but could be bearable in this situation. The main problem in this case is getting the permission to lay the fibre between the buildings.

For more remote sites, often the most logical method connection to a similar remote device is to use a modem. Remote bridges, routers, and gateways will connect to a modem and link, via the standard telephone network, to any other device around the world. Typically, you can expect data rates of 9600 bps, though current high-speed modems with carrier rates of 14 400 bps will transmit data at around 50 000 bps using advanced data-compression techniques.

13
Interoperability

THE JIGSAW

If your company uses one product and standard for all its LANs, you are in a minority. Most companies have seen their LANs grow within individual groups and departments. The heads of each group probably decided on NetWare or Windows NT/AS or VINES for their own reasons. Now, there is a whole gaggle of servers running different software and you have to get them talking. This is the problem; the answer is interoperability.

Each of the major operating systems uses its own preferred, and different, transport protocol. A LAN running under Unix would normally use TCP/IP as the protocol; Novell's NetWare uses IPX; LAN Manager and NT/AS use NetBEIU, a derivative of NetBIOS; Apple Macintoshes use AppleTalk. If you have to link LANs that use different protocols, there are several solutions open to you, depending on the protocols and your budget.

Broadly speaking, there are three ways to connect LANs running different protocols:

- The first is physically to link the LANs and run multiple protocol stacks on each workstation that needs access to the different servers. Each protocol stack gives the workstation access to the different servers.
- The second method is to move the burden of the multiple protocol stacks to the server. Each of the different workstations (Apple Mac, Unix, PC with DOS) is attached to a separate adapter card in the server according to the protocol the workstation uses. For example, the server might run TCP/IP and IPX on two adapter cards. The Unix stations would be attached to the adapter card running TCP/IP and the DOS-based PCs are attached to the adapters running IPX.
- The third method is to use a translator that will convert the different protocols.

THE PIECES IN THE JIGSAW

When tackling interoperability, you are likely to hit five major connectivity problems. They relate to the five most commonly used network operating systems and their preferred transport protocols. The first is connectivity to mainframes and minicomputers—dealt with later in this chapter.

The second is Novell's NetWare. Straight from the box, NetWare uses its own IPX (Inter Packet Exchange) protocol. This NOS has over 65 per cent of the installed PC LAN market, so you are likely to encounter NetWare at some stage. Fortunately, Novell has included in NetWare 3.12 a software router, which is discussed later in this chapter and in Chapter 12). NetWare is also extensible using NLMs, software modules that can be loaded into the operating system on the server. NLMs provide connectivity to TCP/IP and AppleTalk protocols.

Third in our list is TCP/IP. This transport protocol is used predominantly in Unix-based networks—be they PC, mini, or mainframe. TCP/IP normally runs over an Ethernet hardware media. The big advantage of TCP/IP is that software drivers are available for hundreds of different computers from IBM mainframes down. Most PC-based NOSs, such as NetWare and NT/AS, include options to handle TCP/IP traffic.

NetBIOS is the fourth in our list of protocols. It is now used, in various guises, by mostly DOS-based peer-to-peer NOSs such as Artisoft's LANtastic and by the server-based NOS, LAN Manager. Windows NT/AS uses an enhanced version of the basic NetBIOS protocol, called NetBEIU.

Apple Macintoshes provide the fifth protocol, AppleTalk. With the increasing importance of Apple Macs in offices, PC-based software vendors have tackled interoperability with the Mac in a different way. Instead of providing, for example, IPX redirectors that run on the Macintosh, Novell has added Macintosh protocol handling to the server in the form of a Macintosh NLM. Similar products are available for Microsoft's Windows NT/AS and Banyan's VINES. Because of this centralized solution, of changing the capability of the server rather than the workstation, it is actually easier to integrate Macs into a PC environment than many other computers. The Mac user still sees his normal Mac commands while the LAN supervisor can add them to the network by simply running one new utility on the server.

THE SOLUTIONS

Connecting Macintoshes

To connect a Mac to a NetWare server, there are a couple of solutions that depend on the release of NetWare you have installed. If you are running NetWare 3.12 or later, you need to buy Novell's Macintosh NLM, which loads onto the server. If you are using early versions of NetWare 386 you will need to setup a NetWare 286 server as a bridge using Novell's NetWare 286 Macintosh VAP. The Macintosh workstations need to have AppleShare running, which is supplied with System 6.0 or above.

Connecting OS/2 Platforms

Workstations running the OS/2 operating system can also connect to Novell NetWare servers using the NetWare requester for OS/2. This software runs on the server and on the workstation and can also be used to connect the workstation to both a NetWare server and an OS/2-based LAN Manager server, acting as a bridge. If you set up one PC as a bridge between the NetWare server and the OS/2 server, your NetWare users will gain full access to the OS/2 server. Typically, this would be used if an SQL server product, like those supplied by Sybase or Microsoft, is running on the OS/2 server.

Connecting PCs to Multiple LANs

Novell's strategy to connect PCs is the Open Data-link Interface (ODI) which adds support for multiple protocols and multiple adapters within a single PC. ODI was developed as a strategy to counter Microsoft's popular NDIS (Network Driver Interface Specification), which defines the software interface between driver and hardware.

ODI was first used by NetWare Lite—which can only use ODI-compliant hardware—and Novell is hoping that support from hardware vendors will build. The idea is simple: the network card manufacturer only has to provide one ODI driver and all NetWare software will work with it (rather similar to the idea behind Microsoft's rival NDIS). ODI works by creating a 'virtual' network board that multiple frame formats from different protocols can talk to. This virtual board is actually just one real network adapter. Using ODI, you can easily connect to different networks that use other protocols from NetWare's default IPX/SPX. Adding support for AppleTalk or TCP/IP is easy and you do not have to add multiple network adapters to the PC to do this. Because ODI is a fixed specification, any drivers that conform to the ODI requirements will work with any ODI workstation, and protocols can be added without rebooting the PC each time. It all makes good sense for busy network supervisors who want to provide multi-protocol support to their users.

There are three files that load in a PC configured as an ODI workstation. The first in the AUTOEXEC.BAT is LSL.COM (link support layer) that manages communications to multiple protocols. Next is the LAN adapter driver, e.g. NE2000.COM, which communicates directly with the hardware adapter. Third is the protocol stack used. For example, IPXODI.COM is the standard IPX/SPX protocol used by NetWare. There is also TCPIP.EXE for connections to TCP/IP protocol LANs.

The alternative to ODI, developed by Microsoft and 3Com, is the DPA (demand protocol architecture) specification. This is used in the current versions of LAN Manager and allows both IPX/SPX and a LAN Manager protocol stack (normally NetBEIU) to be loaded over the same network adapter.

TCP/IP—The Common Link

There is one common denominator within the world of interoperability—the TCP/IP protocol. This provides the means to allow almost any computer, from a PC to a mainframe, to exchange files and swap e-mail. TCP/IP (Transmision Control Protocol/Internet Protocol) was developed by the US Department of Defense to solve the problem of linking dozens of different types and makes of computer.

Typically, the group of dissimilar computers would be linked by Ethernet cabling; almost all computers have an option of an Ethernet port. However, with the increasing importance of Token Ring, it is also possible to run TCP/IP over Token Ring in order to connect LANs to a Token Ring-based mainframe. The TCP/IP protocol software on each computer strips away the Ethernet packet to leave the raw TCP/IP data. This software has to be tailor-written for each different computer platform, but presents the same standardized view to the network. Indeed, as long as the TCP/IP software is correctly written, the connecting medium can be a long-distance X.25 network or a local Ethernet.

In short, TCP/IP is the ideal protocol to use if you are connecting several different computer architectures together. If you want to connect a PC to a TCP/IP network, there are two ways of doing this. The first is to load TCP/IP driver software onto each PC, and the second is to use one PC as a gateway to the TCP/IP network or (normally) a Unix server.

Loading the TCP/IP software onto every PC makes sense if you have heavy traffic between the PCs and a TCP/IP remote host. The drawback is that you loose RAM to the resident software and the traffic over the whole local network is increased.

The alternative is to install a TCP/IP gateway—the better solution for a homogeneous network of computers that has occasional need to access a TCP/IP host or network. The throughput of the TCP/IP gateway is normally limited by the speed of the link between the gateway and the TCP/IP network rather than the gateway's processing power. A gateway can connect to the TCP/IP network or host using an Ethernet link, modem link, or X.25. If the gateway links two Ethernet LANs, it is called an Internet router. It is often useful to load two protocols, e.g. IPX/SPX and TCP/IP, onto the same PC. For this, either ODI-compliant hardware can be used or a third-party software solution installed. A popular method is to use the Clarkson packet driver which sits between the network adapter's hardware and the protocol stack. Many TCP/IP software modules will drive or require the Clarkson packet driver to run.

Although TCP/IP is unrivalled as a data delivery system between dissimilar computers, it is limited in what it can do with the data once it has arrived. At this point, three new protocols are used: FTP (file transfer protocol), SMTP (simple mail transfer protocol), and TELNET (a terminal emulation program).

If the software at both ends of a TCP/IP link supports FTP, you can use basic, standard commands to log on to remote machines, list directories and files, and exchange files (FTP will also manage translation between EBCDIC and ASCII formats).

SMTP is a strictly defined script language that allows dissimilar computers to exchange mail messages—the great advantage of SMTP is that the commands to deliver or retrieve mail are the same regardless of the type of computer used at either end.

Interoperability with Mainframes

Downsizing is one of the words most often heard when justifying the expense of a network. Downsizing means throwing out your mainframe or minicomputer and replacing it with a PC or, more realistically, a network of PCs. To justify the time and considerable expense downsizing incurs, it has been realized that it is more cost effective and productive to keep your mainframe and change the way you use it. Now the buzzword is client–server computing.

Client–server computing has been made possible by the arrival of desktop PCs. It has nothing to do with the hardware organization, instead it dictates what the hardware does. In this section, we examine how to link your PC or PC-based LAN to your mainframe or minicomputer and use it more effectively with a client–server distribution.

Mainframes—the old way

Before the PC, mainframes were accessed using dumb terminals. It is estimated that there are still 50 million dumb terminals in use and connected to mainframes. A dumb terminal is little more than a monitor, keyboard, and interface adapter to the mainframe. No significant processing power is incorporated within a terminal. That is not to say processing power would not be useful, but that it is not necessary to interrogate a mainframe and display the results.

The main difference between a PC and a terminal is that the PC can run applications on its processor while the terminal displays the results of applications running on a mainframe. It is this fundamental difference that is redressed by client–server computing.

Mainframes are not inherently bad, or particularly expensive to keep running. There are considerable advantages to running your business on a mainframe and terminal setup: terminals have few parts so they very rarely go wrong; mainframes are in a central location and can be easily tended. If you have more than 500 users, it can become difficult keeping the data synchronized and up to date using a PC-based LAN. Mainframes excel at mass storage of tens of gigabytes of disk and tape storage.

Managing the data is one problem, but if you then ask the mainframe to run applications for each of the users, performance will slow, and productivity suffer. The basis of client–server computing is to give each computer the job they are best suited to.

As an example of the overhead incurred using a terminal to interface with a mainframe, consider producing a report of your top customers from the on-line database. You would need to submit a job request via your terminal, the mainframe would process this and return your report a few tens of seconds later. In this example the mainframe is having to provide you with a command-line prompt, then run the report generator application and the database manager application before sending the data back through a formatting application to present itself to you. Your one simple command has cost a high processor overhead at the mainframe.

Client–server computing changes this. The mainframe is used as a data store—which is what it is good at—and processing power is introduced to the desktop. If a PC is linked to a mainframe, the PC could run the report generator that formats a request, sends the data request to the mainframe, waits for the data to return, then formats the data before presenting it on screen. The mainframe has been spared time-expensive processor cycles. This is the basis of client–server computing and makes your use of the mainframe more efficient while also allowing the user interface to improve by running PC applications on the desktop to query the mainframe data-server. To reach this ideal situation you need to connect your PC to the mainframe.

In its most basic form, you might not want to move to full client–server computing just yet. That does not mean you would not benefit from a mainframe feed to your PC applications. In substituting a PC for your terminal you will not have to change any of the mainframe's software or the hardware connections. Install your PC, install your mainframe connectivity option, and you can set up multiple sessions and access the mainframe data from your PC.

PC to mainframe connections

There are four basic ways to connect a PC to a mainframe. These are via a coaxial cable, using a remote modem, a LAN gateway, or a direct Token Ring connection. We will look at each and outline its benefits, costs and equipment requirements.

If you plan to connect a stand-alone PC to your mainframe, as a direct replacement of a terminal, you are limited to two of the four options: coax connection or modem link.

Any mainframe connection is not a straightforward path between PC and mainframe. All mainframe sites will have a controller and many sites will also have a front-end processor (FEP). The controller acts as a multiplexor, with up to 32 coax links in and a single high-speed channel out to the mainframe. Terminals and PCs on a coax connection can be sited up to 5000 feet away from the controller.

The most basic wiring plan involves nothing more than a mainframe linked to a controller that has links to the terminals. If more than one controller is required, or the controller and its attached terminals are in a remote site, more equipment is required.

The remote site needs a controller connected to a modem—a synchronous modem is normally used since the mainframe is connected to an FEP, which is connected to another synchronous modem; a synchronous link can now be established and maintained by the controller and FEP.

Multiple controllers are likely to be linked using a LAN. Since IBM dominates, the LAN protocol used is the IBM-designed Token Ring. The controller links to the Token Ring LAN, and the mainframe again requires an FEP with a Token Ring adapter fitted.

Neither of these installations need concern you if you want to simply connect a stand-alone PC to a mainframe, but they are worth bearing in mind.

Establishing a link

The simplest way to establish a link between a PC and a mainframe is through a 3X74 controller. This is directly linked to the mainframe and multiplexes up to separate 32 channels in from I/O devices. If you have a coax port in your office, which previously connected to a 3270 terminal, you can connect your PC to it by fitting a coax adapter into your PC and installing 3270 terminal emulation software.

Before you can start using a PC with the mainframe, there are a number of major obstacles that have to be negotiated. The main problem is the incompatibility between a PC and a 3270 terminal. A PC lacks the special function keys of the terminal and its character set misses several graphics symbols. More fundamental is that PCs operate using ASCII codes to represent characters, while a mainframe expects IBM's EBCDIC (Extended Binary Coded Decimal Interchange) to be used.

To cope with these basic changes you will need terminal emulation software— not only remapping the PC's keyboard but translating between ASCII and EBCDIC.

The terminal emulation software needs a link to the mainframe, which is courtesy of a coax adapter that fits into an expansion slot. There are two standards available to which coax boards can comply. The first is to emulate an IRMA board, the second an IBM adapter. The difference in standards has no effect on the output to the controller, but means the software on the PC has to talk to two different APIs. Software products, such as terminal adapters, must support one of the adapter standards, so check if there is a precedent within your company before choosing. Some coax adapters are capable of emulating both IBM and IRMA standards according to DIP switch settings, while software will normally also support both. IRMA adapters have the majority of the installed base, but since IBM launched its own coax adapter card, it is beginning to take the greater share of new installations.

The basic difference between the two adapters lies in their interface with the PC software. An IRMA card is a basic character-based I/O device. Much like receiving data from a serial port, the IRMA card generates an interrupt as each character arrives from the controller. The IBM adapter, in contrast, uses a section of RAM as a short-term buffer and stores data there to be read by the software. The difference results in a performance step—the IRMA card is a little slower than the IBM card.

Adding to the performance difference, the IRMA card supports the older CUT (control unit terminal) protocol for terminal emulation, while the IBM adapter can also support the newer, and more efficient, DFT (Distributed Function Terminal) protocol.

While the CUT protocol will support a single session between the mainframe and a PC operating in text mode, the newer DFT protocol allows up to five sessions to run at the same time and also provides support for graphics display and DISOSS file transfers.

In addition to the protocols described above, there are a number of APIs that are designed to ease a programmer's task when writing applications that run on a PC and access data on a mainframe. IBM's 3270-PC and HLLAPI (High Level Language Application Program Interface) run on the PC and can be accessed from any high-level language such as C. Beware of some APIs, such as APPC, which have to be run on both the PC and the mainframe—but do offer better integration in return for greater effort of installation.

Windows on a mainframe

Terminal emulation software can, if the protocol and link allow, support multiple sessions to a mainframe. This means you could login and view company results then toggle to another session and start a report generator, toggle to a third session and view sales by area. Each session is independent, you can pop up each screen with a hot key. Under DOS this is possible, but hardly convenient. Microsoft Windows makes the implementation of multiple sessions very simple. Attachmate and DCA have good Windows-based emulators that allow multiple sessions in multiple windows to be viewed. This could be useful if you are a network administrator and want to monitor output from IBM's mainframe-based NetView network management application in one window while still managing other users or tasks.

There is a second advantage of using Windows as a basis for mainframe connectivity—one that is aimed at MIS managers and programmers. Third-party sourced Windows DLLs are available that contain all the calls and command sequences to carry out basic operations with a mainframe—from logging on, displaying data, to starting a new session. DLLs are available from IBM (its Windows Connections product) and Attachmate. Attachmate also supplies Visual BASIC libraries so that writing a Windows custom front-end for a mainframe is very easy using Microsoft's Visual BASIC development language for Windows.

The 3270 terminal standard

IBM is dominant in not only the mainframe market, but the terminal market. It defined the 3270 terminal standard and this has become the *de facto* standard across other manufacturers as the accepted interface, display, and keyboard required to connect to an IBM mainframe. The 3270 range of terminals has four most basic models: the 3178, 3179, 3278, and 3279. The 3178 and 3278 have mono displays, the 3179 and 3279 are colour. In addition, there are four models available with four different display options. Lastly, graphics support is built into the G range of terminals, while the 3194 and 3290 displays offer multi-protocol and multi-session capabilities.

14
Protecting Your Data

DISASTER PLANNING

You have installed the network efficiently, tuned the performance to its optimum, and planned your expansion needs. Now, what happens when it all goes wrong?

Users expect networks to go wrong. When yours does, you will be surrounded by less than happy users demanding access to their files. By introducing a network, you are charged with ensuring the safe keeping of all the files stored on it. Unless your users trust the network, they will not be happy about storing their data on it. And if they do not want to do that, you need not have bothered installing it.

The vulnerability of a LAN is only too apparent; when hardware goes wrong, everybody is effected. If you use a peer-to-peer network and the PC operating as print manager breaks down, no one will be able to print. If your network centres on a single file-server PC, what will you do when that goes wrong?

In Chapter 4 the general well-being and safety of the server PC is discussed. If you can implement as many of the suggestions described, you will be fighting a strong defensive position against obvious carelessness. Your network crashing because the PC gets too hot or a cleaner pulled the plug can be easily avoided when siting the PC during installation.

To protect the data your users have stored on the network, and to ensure that they have the greatest possible uptime, you must plan against all possible disasters. Approach disaster planning with your most pessimistic frame of mind. However, if you assume nothing will work perfectly, you will probably spend too much time and money on the prevention. There are no hard and fast rules to follow, and the final judgement on how many preventative measures you implement and how much you spend is down to your budget.

This chapter describes the preventative measures you should consider including on your shopping list, and shows you how to choose and how to use them. The subjects are listed by priority; first is how to back up your data. If you can only afford a few hundred pounds for data protection, you should spend it on a suitable backup device.

The next sections cover the threat of virus attacks and how best to avoid them. More complex hardware solutions to disasters are next on the list, covering disk duplexing, disk mirroring, uninterruptible power supplies, and proprietary systems. At the end of this chapter is a section on how to implement a disaster recovery plan, step by step, in your office. This chapter looks at a subject that is often a pain and a chore, but like the best preventative medicine, it will help your LAN stay healthy.

BACKING UP

It does not matter how horrific the scene that leads to data corruption, from a fire to a single power spike, if you have an up-to-date backup of the vital data, you will have fewer worries.

Think pessimistically, if your database is corrupted, or all your correspondence files lost, and you do not have a backup of the data, then someone will have to key it all back in. For even a small office, this would take years of effort from a typist, with a salary bill of tens of thousands of pounds, not counting lost business. If you need to convince your financial director of the cost of spending a few hundred pounds on a backup device, let them know the consequences if they do not.

Unfortunately, the one part of your PC, be it a workstation or a server, that is most likely to fail is the hard disk. Hard disk manufacturers rate the reliability of their products with a figure for its mean time between failures (MTBF). This rating can be found on many sorts of peripherals, but your hard disk is the most important. You may think that your data is safe because you chose a hard disk with a high MTBF of, perhaps, 100 000 hours.

What you must bear in mind is that there is no way that the manufacturers could possibly have tested this figure. If each new product was delayed 100 000 hours (or 4166 days) before being launched, any competitive edge would be lost. Instead, the manufacturer calculates an MTBF rating by looking at its current product range and how many problems have been reported.

The statistic that you should use when calculating the likely chances of a disk crash and data loss is the disk's power on hour (POH) rating. It describes the chance of your disk drive crashing and should be one important part of the equation when calculating how much to spend on data protection and back-up. A disk's POH is equal to the total time the disk is on divided by the MTBF.

$$POH = \text{total time} / MTBF$$

A server left switched on 24 hours per day for 240 working days per year, with a hard disk drive fitted that carried a MTBF of 100 000 hours would have a POH of:

$$POH = (24 \times 240) / 100\ 000 = 5.8 \text{ per cent}$$

Your server's hard disk has just under a 6 per cent chance of failing in the next year. The same equation can be applied to each workstation, but bear in mind that although they are switched on for less time, the hard disks are likely to be cheaper, with a lower MTBF.

Unless you want good odds that you will suffer a disk crash over the next 12 months, and possibly lose your data, install a backup device.

CHOOSING A BACKUP SYSTEM

There are several ways of backing-up your data. Each has its advantages and disadvantages, with a compromise usually reached between price, speed, and convenience. The most basic method of backing-up data is to use floppy disks. Floppies currently have a maximum capacity of 1.44 Mbytes, with 2 Mbyte disks soon to arrive. If you only need to backup this amount of data, a floppy disk is cheap, quick, and universally compatible. In convenience, it is hardly practical for a single workstation, let alone a server which would see you feeding in tens of disks—and wasting your time.

The second obvious choice would be to add a spare hard disk and copy all files from the main server's drive to the backup drive. In the case of a fire sweeping your office, you will lose both copies unless the hard drive is removable. The answer is a removable storage media that should ideally have the capacity to hold all the data on your server and workstations.

Hardware alone is of little use, and the software you choose has more bearing on the usability of your backup method. If the software is complex to use, the chances are that you will begin to lose interest in carrying out a backup as often as you should; instead, you will skip this chore.

The software, which, if you are lucky, will come bundled free with the hardware (Fig. 14.1), should have an option to operate it from the command line—so that it can be added into a DOS batch file. In stand-alone mode, the software should also be able to execute automatically at a preset time. That way, your backups will be regularly carried out with no effort on your part.

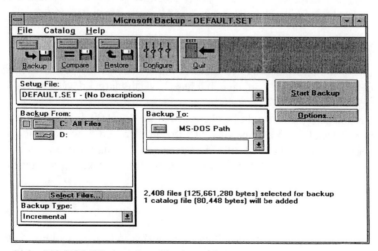

Figure 14.1 MS-DOS Windows-based backup software

Compatibility is the final point. It sounds obvious, but if you buy the hardware and software from different vendors, ask to see them working together before you pay. If you are upgrading your current network, it is worth checking that the new hardware is backwards compatible with your current media.

Hardware Options

Leaving aside the controlling software for later, the first choice is the type of removable media you want to use for backing-up your system. The field splits into two sides with traditional tape-based technology offering high capacity at a low price, against newer disk-based technology that is very expensive.

Tape Storage

Tape technology for PC-based LANs is often the preferred route. The three main tape formats span the requirements of most users. At the low end are DC2000 tape drives. DC2000 drives uses QIC ($\frac{1}{4}$-in. cassette) tapes and both tapes and drives are widely available; the small cassettes are very robust, and cost around £50 each. The storage capacity of these cassettes starts at 80 Mbytes. A DC2000 drive for 80 Mbyte cassettes can be found for under £400, providing the cheapest way into secure backups.

A second advantage is that you need no special adapter card to drive the unit—it works directly from any floppy drive controller; all other tape drives need a special, expensive, controller card. The disadvantage of DC2000 $\frac{1}{4}$-in. cassette tapes is the speed of data transfer; a rate of 2.5 Mbytes/min is typical. For a small LAN of four or five users, with modest amounts of data, a DC2000 unit is a cheap, if slow solution.

DC2000 drives are designed to take QIC-80 80 Mbyte cassettes, but are also capable of using QIC-40 40 Mbyte minicassettes. The theory is that any QIC-80 tape from any drive can be read by any software. Compatibility is not always assured, so check first with both software and hardware manufacturers.

DC600 cassettes

The next price and performance band is the DC6000 cartridge drive. Like its smaller brother, it uses a $\frac{1}{4}$-in. tape, but has physically larger data cassettes—at the same price of £40 each.

The removable media might be cheaper, but the DC6000 drives are three times the price of DC2000. It also needs a SCSI controller card to work, which adds at least another £300 to the total bill. The advantage for small networks is the speed of data transfer. Up to 10 Mbytes/min can be backed up, taking a quarter the time to save your data.

DAT drives

For medium to large network installations, helical scan tape technology is popular. This is a newer technology than $\frac{1}{4}$-in. and, by writing data onto the tape in angled strips packs considerably more data into a smaller physical cassette. Digital audio tapes (DATs) are light and compact cassettes and use 4 mm wide tape. DATs can carry a nominal capacity of 1.3 Gbytes but using data compression software or hardware, many manufacturers claim up to 5 Gbytes can be saved onto a DAT.

New standards for DAT include Data/DAT. Currently, DAT tapes are written to and read from sequentially. If you want to find a file, you must go to the beginning of the tape and search through. Data/DAT will allow random access, like a normal hard disk, so that a file can be pinpointed directly. This improves speed to a degree, but finding a file will still take around 20 sec.

Speed of data transfer for DAT is better than $\frac{1}{4}$-in. tape with a maximum of 18 Mbytes/min typical of many commercial systems. The main disadvantage to this equation is the price, with DATs drives costing almost twice that of a similar $\frac{1}{4}$-in. system at around £4500. The cassettes themselves, however, are slightly less expensive at around £40 each.

8 mm cassettes

The highest capacity data tape currently available uses 8 mm videotape as a storage medium. These tapes are able to store either 2.5 or 5.0 Gbytes of data before either software or hardware data compression is added. The price for this technology is still high, at just under £6000 for the drive. Tapes are available at £40 each. Like Data/DAT, 8 mm will soon provide random access to files, but is even slower than DAT with file access taking around 90 sec. However, 8 mm is the way forward since the International Standards Organization decided to standardize on this as the preferred backup media.

For large networks in which performance over capacity is paramount, high-speed $\frac{1}{4}$-in. tape drives are still hard to beat. With a maximum capacity of 1.3 Gbytes (before data compression), these drives can transfer data at over 32 Mbytes/min.

D/CAS data cassettes

Manufactured by only two companies, these drives might appear to have a limited appeal, especially since they started life with limited storage capacity. Now, cassettes that can store between 160 and 600 Mbytes are available and performance is good thanks to a SCSI interface (as used in DATs and DC6000 systems). Prices are average with the drives costing around £1800 and cassettes around £30 each. The manufacturers have plans to introduce 2.5 and 10 Gbyte tapes within the next year, which makes this potentially the fastest and most cost-effective method of backing-up a large network drive.

VHS videotape

Video machines store data onto tapes digitally, so the technology seems ideal for computers. Video cassettes can store around 14.5 Gbytes of uncompressed data and are extremely cheap—under £15 each. The price and capacity of the media makes this the best choice for a price-conscious buyer with a need for high capacity.

This dream goes wrong when the drive is considered. These are very expensive at around £20 000–£30 000 for a complete unit. They use a SCSI interface which has poor data transfer rates of around 120 Mbytes/min. Not surprisingly, the main manufacturer, Metrum, targets its drives at mini and mainframe sites. If your network is the result of downsizing from a mini or mainframe, you could benefit from the capacity, but only if you want to pay such a premium price for the drive hardware.

- Tape capacity and transfer rate is normally stated with data compression switched on. If you verify as you go, you can halve the transfer rates of a drive.
- Try and buy a drive that can hold the capacity of all your volumes, which means no cassette swapping.
- If price is your main concern, smaller capacity drives cost less—but need more cassettes and more time to backup.

Disk Storage

The alternative to using a tape-based media for backups is a disk-based system. There are two fields that can be exploited for backup purposes: optical technology and removable disk cartridges.

Optical drives

Optical disk technology uses a laser beam to burn data onto a disk carrier. WORM (write once, read many) technology is the more established and cheaper technology, but offers limited practical functionality for regular backups. Its disks (similar to a compact disk) are bought blank and data can be written to them once only. The writing process is slow—similar to a normal floppy disk—but once data is burnt onto the surface, the disk can be read as if it were a normal hard disk, with similar access times.

WORMs are useful to create an archive of current working material or to create an easily distributed database and have a capacity of several gigabytes. However, because they can only be written to once, they are expensive and impractical for a weekly backup.

The alternative, and newer technology, is a WMRM (write many, read many) disk. With similar storage capacity, and with similar read and write speeds to a WORM, WMRM is more use as an on-line storage device, since there is no limit to the number of times that data can be written to it. Currently, both technologies are priced several times higher than DAT tape technology.

Removable hard disks

Removable hard disks might look like thick $5\frac{1}{4}$-in. floppy disks, but have all the features of a standard hard disk. The two most popular units from SyQuest and

Bernoulli have capacities of 88 and 90 Mbytes, respectively. The drive, either a single or double drive unit, has the same footprint as a normal desktop PC, and sits between PC and monitor.

The drives need a proprietary interface card, which takes up an expansion slot in your PC. Once connected, they effectively provide what they claim, a fast removable hard disk. Access speed is normally around 19–22 msec, the speed of a medium speed normal hard disk. There main disadvantages for backing-up networks is the limited capacity, and high cost of the cartridges.

Drives cost between £500 and £800 with each removable disk cartridge adding another £150 to the bill. For transferring large quantities of information between two sites on a regular basis, these units are more convenient than floppies and quicker than a modem link. Because of their speed and capacity they can also be used as primary hard disks, making them a flexible option.

INTERNAL OR EXTERNAL?

Backup devices are often offered as either internal or external configurations. The internal unit fits inside a standard PC chassis, normally taking the space of a half-height floppy drive. Power is supplied from the PC using one of the spare low-voltage power leads that are in all PCs. The internal option is generally cheaper than an external unit since there is no casing or separate power supply required.

It is unusual to find a server that needs more than a single floppy drive, so an internal option saves space and money. It also cuts out the need for cabling—an area of potential problems.

THE HARDWARE REQUIRED FOR YOUR PC

With the introduction of PCs, a standard method of connecting peripherals to the PC was developed. SCSI is the interface standard of choice when high-performance and high-capacity data storage peripherals are being added. Proprietary interfaces or hardware that does not conform to SCSI standards should be avoided. See Chapter 7 for a full explanation of the different interface standards and their benefits.

SCSI is a standard that defines the connection cable and the way the data is sent along it between the PC and the storage device. If your server is already using a SCSI hard drive, you can add a SCSI-compatible tape drive by simply plugging it in daisy-chain fashion after your hard disk drive.

To control any SCSI device, you will need to fit a controller board. These adapters take up an internal expansion slot within your PC and versions are available for ISA, EISA, or MCA bus PCs. As mentioned, if you are thinking of upgrading your server to the SCSI standard, you need only one controller for all your drives and backup units. A popular misconception is that SCSI has a limitation of only being able to control seven devices. By using the full SCSI addressing capabilities, several thousand devices can be daisy-chained and managed from one controller.

SCSI is the prevalent standard, and all storage peripherals are now complying with it. Unfortunately, not all manufacturers believe it is powerful enough and many add their own commands and options. Avoid any system that is not base-SCSI compatible, which applies to controllers and devices.

If you can afford a caching SCSI controller card to drive your tape unit, you will see a immediate performance boost in throughput. Caching controllers carry between 512 Kbytes and 16 Mbytes of RAM on-board managed by their own processor. This improves data flow between your server's hard disk and the backup media and lessens the load on the server's processor.

Installing your new adapter card means you will have to plug it into a free expansion slot in your PC. Normally, you will have to set the controller's interrupt (INT), its port address, and possibly a DMA channel address. These should already be set to default values that are unlikely to clash with other settings in your PC. Before you power up, check that these are not the same as your network adapter cards. On an EISA or MCA server, this is impossible since the setup software will prevent you assigning the same interrupt and ports. If the backup device is being fitted into your local workstation PC, then check it against the settings of your network adapter and VGA card.

If you run a Novell network, typing 'IPX I' at the command prompt will display the current settings of your installed network adapter. You can then see which DMA channels, memory locations, and interrupts your network card is using, and so which should be set on the SCSI driver card.

Installation

Although the physical installation of a backup device, whether internal or external, is important, the installation and organization of the hardware into the network will dictate how useful the backup unit is. There are three methods of installing a backup unit into a network environment. Each solves a particular problem, but requires more resources.

For a network, unless you use diskless workstations, the data on each user's local hard disk is just as important as the shared data on the server's disk. It makes sense that a full backup plan should include the workstations. Without a network, the only way of achieving this would be to fit each with a local backup tape drive—expensive and unnecessary.

With suitable software, your network lets you backup data stored on each workstation and the server onto a single, central backup tape. The software must be sophisticated enough to cope with this, but most third-party packages can carry this out (see later in this chapter).

The main problem facing you with hardware is where to fit it. As mentioned, there are three options. The first sites the backup unit at a workstation—typically hung off the supervisor's PC. Current software allows both remote workstations and file-servers to be backed up. The advantage of this method is that no load is presented to any file-server. The big disadvantage is that the data to be backed up streams across the network, clogging up the available bandwidth and slowing all other network operations. It does, however, mean that you can insert a tape, start the backup, and remove the tape without leaving your desk.

The second method is server based. The drive and software run on a server. This provides the maximum speed of transfer for server-based data and allows any user with rights to the software to initiate their own backup. Like the first option, this method can clog up the network when transferring data from workstations to the server-based backup device. Because the device is housed in the server, which should itself be in a secure environment, the backup data is very secure.

The third and final method is to set aside a dedicated backup server. You have a communications server, and a database server—why not a backup server? The PC picked for this can be any ancient 80286 PC/AT lying around not being used, and lifts the load from the main file-servers. Like the first option, the backup data streams across the network to this secondary server and fills available bandwidth. However, by setting the backups to start late at night, or during quiet periods, the problem becomes insignificant.

SOFTWARE OPTIONS

The most basic function of backup software is to make sure that your data files are copied correctly from the source hard disk to the archiving media and, if required, to restore the files back to the hard disk. Sounds simple, but such a basic system is, in practice, unusable for a LAN environment with the quantity of data that must be managed.

A straightforward backup or copy of all your data files to a tape is very safe, but each backup takes a long time to carry out, and because of the quantity of data saved each time, the process is going to be expensive in new cassettes. The next section of this chapter examines ways to improve efficiency without compromising security by only copying changed or new files.

One of the most useful features of new backup software is its ability to run automatically at a predetermined time. The entire process could then be carried out without user intervention, so there is less chance you might forget, during a quiet period on the network or at night.

Backup software normally presents a menu-driven front-end to the user. You can then easily select whether you want a complete backup of all files, or an incremental backup of changed files or of the contents of a particular directory. Novell's NetWare includes the NBACKUP program. This is a straightforward application with few frills that lets you backup your data to devices installed in the server or to a local DOS-compatible backup device. It is also capable of running automatically at a predefined time and date, and includes the ability to backup the bindery—the vital system files controlling a Novell network.

If your needs are basic, then take a look at the backup software bundled with your LAN software—it could save you money. One of the advantages of using the backup software bundled with your LAN software is that it is, obviously, compatible. Unless specifically written for your LAN operating system, backup software from a third party might miss some of the important points of your LAN's filing system. For example, trustee names (users with specific control over a particular file) should be backed up in a Novell LAN. If you do not, you will find yourself restoring files that need to be reconfigured. Novell's NBACKUP utility can manage these, as can software specifically written for Novell networks.

It is not good enough to use backup software intended for a DOS workstation. DOS files can carry eight file attribute flags, including read-only and archive. A Novell NetWare 3.12 file has space for 16 attribute flags, and under OS/2 names of files can be in capitals or lowercase. If you run a basic DOS backup program, it will not know about all this extra, important, file information and will miss it when backing-up (Fig. 14.2).

If you use backup software that runs on the server, rather than locally on your workstation, the disadvantage is that the software will use up server RAM. This leaves less for normal server operations, and so performance will be degraded very slightly (see Chapter 7, 'Tuning your server'). The advantage is that security is improved, since you do not need to leave a workstation running logged with supervisor privileges, and the software and server are locked away in the server room. Automatic timed execution is easier; since the server is on all the time, there is no chance of you forgetting to switch on your workstation and running the software.

- Do not accept a general-purpose backup software package for use with your LAN—it is unlikely to be able to cope with backing-up LAN user and account information.

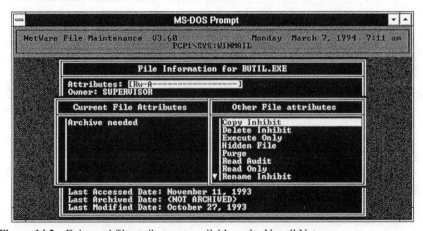

Figure 14.2   Enhanced file attribute set available under Novell Netware

DEVISING A BACKUP STRATEGY

The aim of your backup strategy is to ensure that you have up-to-date copies of your important data files saved in the most efficient way possible. One of the biggest worries of many system managers is 'Am I backing-up often enough?'

There is no fixed rule that you must backup your entire system every Friday. You should know what your users are doing on the network, and be able to judge the importance of the information.

If you are recording new financial data, it might be vital to lose no more than an hour's worth of work—so a backup of the most important data would be needed every hour. For clerical work, it would be a nuisance to lose a day's work, but paper copies exist, so it can be rekeyed. In this case a daily backup would be less expensive.

In these cases, it would be unnecessary to carry out a full backup of your entire system. Only the important files or those that had been changed since the last backup need be saved. The file's archive flag helps here, and its use is explained in the next section.

When starting a backup strategy, remember first to try a complete backup and restore of sample data to make sure that the software and hardware works and that you know how to use it.

Full Backup

As the name suggests, full backups are the most complete you can carry out. Every file and directory structure is saved to the backup device. This makes restoring a complete system very easy. If your hard disk crashes with no signs of life, then plug in a new disk and restore the whole structure. All applications, files, and system information will be as before.

This is the easy way out for system administrators, but is also expensive. Tapes would be filled very quickly and if you exceed the capacity of a tape, the software will just sit and wait until someone replaces it with a new, empty tape. Calculate your total data requirements before setting a full backup running—you might have to wait around to swap tapes. You can get around this using a jukebox of WORMs or WMRM disks, but it is an impossible problem with tapes.

- You should carry out a full backup at regular intervals, typically once a week for a small office network; once a day for a large or critical installation.

Incremental Backups

If a full backup looks like overkill, you are right. For everyday backups a more efficient system is to use an incremental backup. In this, only the files that have changed since the last backup are saved.

Every file that is stored on a DOS, NetWare, or OS/2 machine carries a series of attribute flags. These can be set by the user or the operating system and indicate if the file is read-only, a system file, and so on. One flag, the archive attribute, is vital for incremental backups. Whenever the contents of a file is changed, the operating system automatically turns on the archive flag. Backup software then scans through all the files on your system, backing-up files with the archive flag set. All archive flags are reset after the file has been backed up.

Because only your data files are likely to change (application files should not), an incremental backup will take less time to execute and take less backup media than a full backup of every file. They are preferable as a more time efficient and less costly daily backup solution.

The disadvantage of incremental backups becomes apparent when you have to restore a system. Take an example in which you do a full backup once per week, on Mondays, then an incremental backup every day. If your disk fails on Thursday you will have to restore Monday's full backup, then feed in tapes for Tuesday and Wednesday to restore the system. If a user asks you to restore a single file, you might need to search through a stack of tapes, but good backup software will keep a catalogue of the contents of each tape.

Since you will hopefully be restoring less frequently than you backup, the incremental process takes less time. With the exception of DOS's own BACKUP and RESTORE commands, all backup software should be capable of carrying out incremental backups.

* Your installation and work dictates how often you should carry out an incremental backup. Do not forget you also need regular full backups.

Automatic Operation

The beauty of automatic operation is that you can set up your backup software once, to do an incremental backup on a regular basis, and do it all automatically. You can slope off home or carry on with other work while the backup runs its course.

Before you do set up the automatic timer, you should be aware of a number of disadvantages that could potentially bring down the whole backup strategy. If no one is present while the backup process is being carried, for instance at midnight every night, then a small fault will disrupt your schedule. If the tape fills up, there is no one there to change it. If there is a tape fault or drive problem, no one will discover it until the next morning. If either occurs, you are faced with a dilemma: start the backup again immediately, telling users to wait for an hour during the time, or skip a cycle until the next scheduled backup. Although you will be less than popular, it is safer to carry out a backup immediately. Remember that backup software cannot read files that are currently being used, so users have to stop using their files for the duration.

If you run the backup automatically, make sure that the software is sophisticated enough to do this securely. If it runs on your local workstation and waits until the appointed hour, you lose the use of your workstation. Worse, because many LAN operating systems need a supervisor status user to login, to provide access to every user's files, you are leaving your workstation logged in as supervisor. This is poor security, and anyone could walk up and tamper with it.

The solutions are to site a special terminal in your secure server room or use software that runs on the server. Under NetWare 3.12, NLMs load and run on the server; under NetWare 2.2, VAPs do the same. Maynard and Emerald Systems produce a number of products that will run automatically on the server, without the need for a workstation. Running the software on the server is a more secure and workable solution.

- Automatic, timed backups give you freedom, but should be executed from the server rather than a workstation.
- If a timed backup does not complete, backup as soon as you find this out rather than wait for the next scheduled slot.

When to Carry Out Backups

This sounds an obvious topic, but take a look at your network usage before you commit yourself. If you are running a small office, doing a full backup once a week, do not start this backup as you leave on Friday night. If you do, the tape will sit in the drive all weekend—if there is a fire, your efforts will all have been for nothing.

If your network is busy during normal office hours, schedule your backups when there are likely to be fewest users on the system. Backups can take up server processor time, server disk requests, and cable bandwidth; the net result is a slower service for every other user.

Many backup programs are unable to access files that are being used. If a user opens a document file in their wordprocessor, the backup software will not be able to backup this file.

Tape Rotation

For an efficient and safe method of backing-up, how you organize your tapes or removable disk cartridges is particularly important. There are a few golden rules that you try and stick to, if finances allow. At any one time, you should have at least three copies of data. One up to date, on your server's hard disk. The second, slightly out of date, on tape in a fireproof safe in the office. The third, stored off-site in a bank or similar. This way, you can respond quickly to user demand with the backup data on-site, but protect against fire or theft with secondary data off-site.

The second set of suggestions concerns the number of tapes used. Unfortunately, at around £40 each, implementing a complete rotational method could soon upset your budget. In a small office, a typical scenario would be to do a full backup every Monday, then an incremental backup for each day of the week onto that day's own tape. Five tapes in all. Another five tapes would be used in rotation. The five in use staying on-site, the second set stored off-site.

For a large site, or one with critical data, you might carry out a full backup every morning, with incremental backups onto separate tapes during the day. This could need five tapes per day, with different sets for each day, and duplicates rotated off-site. This soon becomes expensive, but you must make the choice between initial cost and the price of re-entering all lost data.

VIRUS PROTECTION

Computer viruses are small programs that are out to get you and your data. Although typically only 4 Kbytes in size, these programs hide within other programs, replicate themselves onto any floppy or hard disk, and at a particular, and usually inopportune moment, strike. Their effects are sometimes harmless, a message to save the world from a fervent programmer; or fatal, corrupting data and knocking out your system.

On a stand-alone PC, the chances of getting a virus are pretty remote. Unless you regularly download software from small, poorly run bulletin boards, or accept a lot of disks from unknown sources, you are more likely to suffer data loss through a disk crash than a virus attack.

In a network environment, the odds change. Viruses can spread very easily, and if one workstation gets a virus, everyone will get it by the time they next log on. The two main sources of viruses are disks sent in from unknown or unchecked sources and contact with bulletin boards.

If your office is self-contained and, apart from buying shrink-wrapped applications and blank disks, has no contact with the outside world, then you should still, if possible run regular checks, but the chances of an infection are near zero.

If your LAN connects to anything outside your direct control, even another LAN in another office or building, you would be advised to implement a background virus-detection procedure (Fig. 14.3). The tools you will need are software packages and are relatively inexpensive—around £200.

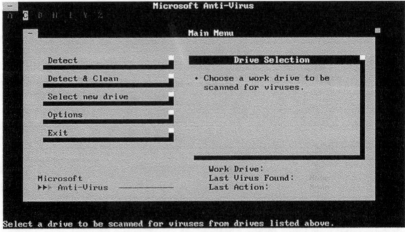

Figure 14.3   Virus scanning and detection using MS-DOS 6's built-in utilities

Strains of Virus

Boot sector virus (BSV)

The boot sector is the first sector of a floppy diskette and, on a hard disk, the first sector of the DOS partition. When you power on your PC, this is the first sector to be read and it is responsible for loading the main operating system. A BSV infects the boot sector, which means it starts up along with your PC. It then takes control of several of the PC's interrupts—normally interrupt 13h (disk read/write). Every time you read or write to a floppy or hard disk, the BSV intercepts the call and checks if it has already infected this new disk. If not, it promptly copies itself over.

Direct action file virus

This strain of virus embeds itself into the code of a program file. This could be a COM or EXE file or even a SYS driver file or OVL overlay. It is most commonly found in COM files, simply because it is easier to write viruses for COM files! The first three bytes of a COM file point to where the program is stored in the file. A DAF virus only has to append itself to the end of the COM file, patch the first three bytes to point to it, and its job is done.

The most effective protection against DAF viruses is to make the program files read only—which is standard practice with networked application files. Novell NetWare's FILER utility will let you change a file's attributes to read-only, as will DOS's ATTRIB function.

The Solutions

There are three possible ways to stop and trap viruses before they get onto your network. These cover the server, the workstation, and the modem—the three most popular ways in to a system.

To convince yourself that there are no viruses on your network, you should carry out a scan of the entire system. Most virus-detection software has two front-ends, one command-line driven so that it can be easily included into login scripts and batch files, the other menu-driven. For a thorough scan of your server, run the check over all volumes. Any corrupted files or files that are infected with any of the 3000 current viruses strains will be reported.

Intel's LANProtect, Symantec's VirusScan, XTree's ViruSafe/LAN, and Fresh Technology's McAfee products are all good products that can identify the majority of virus strains. Keeping up to date with new viruses is important, so check with the publishers how they intend to keep you up to date. Intel, for example, provides a secure bulletin board from which you can download new virus detection routines.

If your workstations are running MS-DOS 6 or above, you can use Microsoft's built-in virus scanning software, VSAFE. This works like other third-party products to disinfect your PC.

If the virus is new or well hidden, how can you stop them? Scanning a PC's disk will tell you if there is a virus present, but if a virus is already running, you need permanent protection. In the case of Symantec and Intel products, a small detection program stays resident. If it spots any virus or rogue calls to the disk, it will stop them and inform you. DOS and OS/2 make it easy to install such applications, but you really need this sort of permanent watch over your server—which could be running a proprietary operating system such as Novell's NetWare.

If you run a Novell network for total protection, make sure that the virus-detection software can be loaded onto the server as an NLM for NetWare 3.x or a VAP for NetWare 2.x. The NLM or VAP will stay resident on the server and keep a permanent lookout for stray and suspicious calls to the disk.

The advantage of loading the virus-detection onto the server is that all network traffic, which passes through the server, will also be scanned. If a virus is detected, the actions taken depend on the software, but normally will halt the disk operation and record an entry into a log file while sending the supervisor a warning message. This real-time file scanning is very effective, but takes up RAM on the server (between 15–40K is typical) and also requires a slice of the processor's time, which could lead to a slight performance drop for other users.

An alternative is setup automatic scans at the entry points to the network. First, carry out a thorough scan of the server and ensure that it is free of viruses—use any of the virus-detection scanners mentioned. Next, include a line into the system login file for each user that will scan their workstation's local hard disk. Now, each time a user logs into the network, their hard disk will scanned, stopping any virus before it can get onto the network.

If your virus-scanning software stays resident on the workstation, any floppy disks or disk reads are also checked before being cleared. As with the server solution, loading a resident scanning program onto each workstation will take up RAM—between 5 and 20K is typical. If your workstations are fitted with expanded memory, you can load this resident program into high memory, so that there is more free RAM available for your user's DOS applications. See Chapter 7 on 'Improving Performance' for other ways of saving RAM on your workstations.

The last point of entry for viruses is by a user downloading software using a modem. Apart from prohibiting the use of modems, there are two less harsh solutions. The first is create a batch file that scans the download subdirectory used by the communications package immediately when the user quits:

```
CROSTALK.BAT
CD C:\CROSTALK
XTALK4
SCAN C:\CROSTALK\DN_LOAD
CD C:\
```

The second, more subtle method, is to use a communications program such as FireFox HyperAccess5, which scans files as they are being downloaded.

How Viruses Really Spread

The previous section discussed the two main types of virus and their basic mechanics. But how do viruses spread through buildings, cities, and onto your PCs? Although a prime suspect is software downloaded from bulletin boards, consider who else goes near your machines. If a seller comes around with a demo disk, he or she might have installed the disk at another company that was infected. Or your maintenance or hardware engineers who have a master disk to fix any problems with your network cards. Both have been around other sites, and you are letting them in.

However, the chances of catching a virus are still very small. Your data is in far greater danger from a user typing DEL *.* by mistake or a disk crashing than a virus taking its toll. Both these can be minimized with a regular backup procedure. It might be boring and bothersome to carry out, but like a regular scan for viruses, it could save your data.

UNINTERRUPTABLE POWER SUPPLIES (UPSs)

Once users start to rely on your LAN, you will need to ensure that there are as few interruptions to the service as possible. In a sentence, every server in your network should be connected to a UPS. It does not stop there; if you have 10Base-T cabling, you might also need to protect the hub with a UPS—if the hub shuts down, so does your network. But before we look at the ways to protect a server, the types of UPS and the size of UPS you will need, it is worth examining what causes the problems in the first place.

The Problems with Power

The electrical power supply delivered to your office is susceptible to five different types of problem. Each has is its own solutions and you should consider the various solutions before you pick a UPS.

- *Brownouts*, also called sags, are short-term decreases in the electrical supply's voltage level. Brownouts are the most common power problem, accounting for over 80 per cent of all electrical problems. Brownouts are normally caused by the power company lowering the voltage in an area to compensate for extraordinary power demands. Brownouts do not necessarily cause the computer to shut off, instead they will challenge you to find the problem by causing keyboard lock-ups, system crashes, and drive errors. The end is the same, with data corruption the likely result.
- *Spikes* are an instantaneous increase in the voltage level on a power supply. Spikes are normally caused by a lightning strike, damaged power cable, or faulty equipment. As you can imagine, a sudden voltage spike, several times the normal mains voltage level, can damage or destroy electronic components. The end result is the possible loss of data, but with the extra effects of damaging components. Just over 7 per cent of all electrical power problems are spikes.
- *Blackouts* are the total loss of power. This normally occurs very rarely, and is often due to natural causes such as lightning or storms. Blackouts account for just under 5 per cent of all power disturbances and their effects can be disastrous. If

your computer loses power during a disk or cache write, or during a reindexing operation on a file, you could corrupt the entire file or destroy the file allocation table (FAT) in a DOS system, or the Bindery in a NetWare system.

- A *surge* is a scaled-down version of a spike. The voltage level increases for a few hundredths of a second when nearby electrical equipment is switched off. High-power heaters, pumps, or motors on the same circuit will cause a voltage surge every time they switch off. Computer power supplies are designed to dissipate small surges, but if the surge lasts a long time or is a particularly high voltage, the electronic components in the computer could be damaged or destroyed.
- Noise is very common in installations where several large electrical devices are operating near each other. Noise is caused by electromagnetic interference (EMI) and radio frequency interference (RFI) and disrupts and distorts the normally smooth sine-wave of an electrical supply. Large electrical devices, especially motors, generators, and other computers, that are not properly shielded can generate noise on the mains supply. The effect of noise is to cause small, single-bit errors in data, either in RAM or on disk, which can corrupt a program or data file.

The solutions

There are a number of different types of equipment that will go some way to solving some of the power-supply problems described above.

- A full UPS normally provides all of the solutions described below, including generating an electrical supply from built-in batteries. If a blackout occurs, the UPS will instantaneously switch in its mains supply and send a signal to the server warning it that it is operating from batteries.
- Surge suppressors prevent spikes and over-voltages from getting past. They are often incorporated into distribution blocks or fitted in-line between a mains outlet and the computer mains supply cable. They do nothing to stop voltage drops.
- Internal UPS systems fit inside a computer, or more often are manufactured as part of a computer's casing. Although well integrated with the computer, they do not offer protection for other peripherals such as a monitor or network hub. They are also limited in power to the space available in the computer and can cause problems if they go wrong—you will normally have to shut down your server to remove the internal UPS and spend more time removing the device.
- Voltage regulators make sure the power supply arriving at your computer is at the correct voltage. They cut out surges and some brownouts, but do not act as a UPS. They fit between the mains outlet and the computer's power-in cord.
- AC filters are small and cheap, and work to remove noise from a power-line. They do not work as a UPS, nor do they normally protect against power surges or brownouts. If your computer works on the same circuit as a large generator or motor, you should fit an AC filter as in the line, close to the computer, to remove any noise.

Selecting a UPS

The makers of UPS may try and convince you that their UPS is best because of some neat function, but there are really just a few things that you need to keep in mind when shopping for a UPS. The first is its power capacity. If there is a blackout, would it supply all your vital equipment for long enough to provide an orderly shutdown? Second, is it capable of communicating with your server, to let the server know it is operating from its battery and to initiate an orderly shutdown. Extra functions could include monitoring the status of the battery's charge and viewing the incoming line condition, but these are not crucial.

It is vital for you to know the power supplied by a UPS—there is little point in buying a UPS that cannot provide enough power to support your computer. The power of UPS is measured in V-A (volts-amps). Computer equipment, in contrast, is rated in watts. The calculation is as follows:

$$\text{watts} = \text{volts} \times \text{amps}$$

The rating of a UPS, in V-A, does not take into account the power factor of a device. This power factor is a number, between 0 and 1, which indicates the amount of useful energy used by a device. For example, a light bulb has a power factor of 1—it is a rare case. Most computer equipment has a rating of around 0.7. Because of this, the V-A rating of a UPS is always larger or equal to the watt rating of the computer equipment it is supplying.

To calculate the size of UPS you need to power a server and monitor, look at the labels on the back of each. These will normally either give the power rating of the equipment in watts or the amps drawn.

$$
\begin{aligned}
\text{Computer + monitor amps} &= 3 \text{ amps} \\
\text{AC voltage} &= 240 \text{ volts} \\
\text{Total watts} &= 720 \text{ watts } (3{\times}240) \\
\text{Power factor} &= 0.7 \\
\text{UPS V-A rating rqd} &= 504 \text{ V-A}
\end{aligned}
$$

Interfacing to a Server

Make sure that the UPS has an interface socket to connect to the server. There are three types of interface commonly used. If your server is an ISA-bus PC you can connect a Novell UPS adapter card (also available from some UPS vendors). This connects to the UPS using a two-wire cable to the UPS's connector. The second method is to connect the UPS directly to the RS232C serial port. This interface is supported by Banyan VINES, LAN Manager, and NetWare. Lastly, if you are running on a server with a PS/2-style mouse port, NetWare can monitor the UPS through the mouse port. By default, NetWare 3.x includes an NLM that will monitor for a power-failure signal from a UPS and then execute a controlled shutdown. LAN Manager similarly monitors the serial port, broadcasts a warning to all users, then shuts down when it detects a power-failure signal.

If you connect more than one server to the UPS, you should buy a Y-splitter, available from the UPS vendor, that lets you connect the status port outlet of the UPS to both servers.

OTHER FORMS OF DATA SECURITY

Disk Mirroring

One of the best ways of protecting your data is to make a backup. This is fine until your entire hard disk fails and you have to order a new disk drive, then reload the backup data. NetWare, along with many of the other high-end network operating systems offer disk mirroring as a means to protect against the failure of a hard disk. When setup, disk mirroring makes an exact duplicate of a NetWare partition on another hard disk. Mirroring is a cheaper, but less secure way of protecting data than disk duplexing—the disk controller card is still common to the multiple drives and is a possible source of failure.

Disk Duplexing

Disk Duplexing offers the most effective means of protecting your data. Not only is the data written onto multiple disk drives, but each drive is controlled by separate controllers. Therefore, if one drive or controller fails, the second complete disk subsystem is still operational. To mirror or duplex a NetWare partition, run NetWare's DISKSET utility and move to the Available Disk Options menu. From here, you can insert new drives to and indicate to which other drives they should be mapped.

If you are running multiple MFM or ESDI controllers within an MCA-bussed server, be careful in setting up. The controllers cannot share interrupts and may not work at all. The best solution would be to change to multiple SCSI controllers—which are recommended for NetWare servers.

Some disk controllers include disk duplexing and disk mirroring as part of their feature list. Be careful, since you are again relying on a single controller card that might fail. It is often safer and easier to find spares for a setup that uses multiple standard, non-cacheing SCSI controllers rather than a single controller that aims to do everything.

RAID

One of the most popular methods of boosting a server's fault tolerance is to use a disk array. RAID (redundant array of independent disks) is currently a common addition to many dedicated server PCs. RAID has six levels of operation: RAID 0 through to RAID 5. RAID can be compared to NetWare's own software implementation of fault tolerance, i.e. disk mirroring and disk duplexing described above. The different levels of RAID allow you to implement data stripping (i.e. spreading blocks of data across different drives) together with mirroring and duplexing. RAID also provides facilities for error correction. In this case, one of the drives in the disk array is dedicated as a parity drive and stored data is spread across the remaining drives. If one drive fails, the parity bit allows the stored data to be reconstructed.

NetWare's internal fault tolerance is often considered to provide better performance than a hardware solution. NetWare's solution uses look-up tables to maintain parity and drive mapping information and is hardware independent. NetWare's internal system also has the great advantage that it is free. RAID for NetWare servers is often a slower, more costly method of fault tolerance that can also tie you to a particular brand of drive or controller. However, RAID is ideally suited to other operating systems, notably Unix.

Novell's TTS Protection

To boost the protection afforded to your data, Novell included its Transaction Tracking System (TTS) with NetWare 3.12. TTS first appeared in SFT Level II NetWare, then became incorporated as System Fault Tolerance NetWare 286 and 386. Although it is built into NetWare, TTS often causes more confusion than it should.

In a TTS scenario, programs can treat groups of write operations as a transaction. This way, TTS can track exactly what was written to disk. Its main task is to keep a copy of what was originally on the disk before the write operations have updated it. For example, if you are in the middle of writing to five records as part of a transaction and the file-server crashes, TTS will have kept a complete copy of the original data. You can back out of the transaction. Effectively, unless an entire transaction is completed, TTS will ensure that the original data is not changed.

TTS does not happen automatically. Firstly, the TTS system will only track files that have their transactional flag set. To do this, use the FILER utility or the FLAG command line. For example, to set the transactional flag on all .DBF files in a directory use the command:

```
FLAG *.DBF /TRANSACTIONAL
```

Once you have flagged a file as transactional, you cannot delete or rename it. To do either, flag the file as a NORMAL file, rename it, then set its transactional flag again. If you use a backup program, check to see if it copies these extended flags (of which the transactional flag is but one) during a restore operation—if it does not you could be running your data with a false sense of security.

TTS makes more of a demand on the server's system cache than the vanilla operating system. If the cache buffers are set at too low a level, the system could start to thrash. You should assign at least 8K of disk cache buffers per station.

If you do install TTS, bear in mind the possible overhead that is imposed on disk resources. If you have a 30 Mbyte file that is truncated during a transaction down to 12 Mbytes, TTS will still need an 18 Mbyte work file. If you do run out of disk space, TTS will be disabled automatically and the supervisor will receive a message that reports to this effect.

PLANNING YOUR DISASTER RECOVERY

We started this chapter with a discussion about how to backup and the backup devices that are on the market. Once you have a backup drive installed, worked through the virus prevention techniques discussed, and bought a UPS and duplexed drive, what is left? The documentation is the last, and often forgotten, chore left in this disaster recovery plan.

You should write down exactly how you have implemented every step of your data protection and fault tolerance scheme. Write down step-by-step details on any particular installation problems you had with duplexed drives or mirroring, and include which drives are mirrored to which. Sticking little numbered labels on each physical drive might seem a obvious step, but it could help a replacement supervisor. Your disaster recovery has to plan for your own fault tolerance. If you setup a complex system, without documentation, and are then run over by a bus, your replacement administrator will be lost. On a more serious note, do keep detailed records that describe how you setup your data protection plans.

Lastly, you should create a book (with several copies) covering what to do in the case of a disaster. These will contain step-by-step instructions that a novice can follow in case a server goes down during your holiday period, or when you are away. Label each section clearly: what to do if there has been a power cut; what to do to recover a deleted file; etc. Tell the office manager where these manuals are, and make sure that several other users in the office understand how and when to use them.

Glossary

10Base-T A cabling and connection standard used to carry Ethernet signals. 10Base-T is the offspring of the generic Ethernet specification which defines data transmission of 10 Mbps using 802.3 data packets over twisted-pair cable with telephone-style RJ-45 connectors. Unlike Thin-Wire Ethernet, 10Base-T has a physical star topology that makes it more robust and more secure than its predecessor. However, it needs a central hub. Simple plug-in connectors and 10Base-T's robust and flexible cabling is now finding its way into many more sites than the older coaxial cabling.

Address book List of names and mail addresses of network users. Address books can be shared by an office or be personal. The full list of all available users is called the global address book.

Alias Simple name for a user or group of users, interpreted by e-mail software. Using an alias means you do not have to remember complicated mail addresses.

API application-programming interface; standard set of commands that will control an application. The application in this case would normally be a low-level product such as the mail-server software or the operating system.

Attachment File linked to an e-mail message, and sent at the same time.

Bridge An interconnection device that can connect LANs at the data link level so allowing similar LANs using different transmission methods, e.g. Ethernet or Token Ring, to talk. Bridges are able to read and filter the data packets and frames employed by the protocol and use the addresses to decide whether or not to pass a packet.

Brouter Brouters combine the functions of bridges and routers in connecting two LANs. A brouter will route data packets if the protocol is known and bridge them if the protocol is unknown.

Bus One of the simplest network topologies in which a single length of cable connects all network devices. It has a definite start and end—in contrast to a ring or star topology. Thin- and Thick-Wire Ethernet use a bus topology. Bus networks are easy to implement, but one break in the wire brings the whole network down. Star topology networks (such as 10Base-T) avoid this problem using one central connection point—the hub—with lots of short wires to each node.

Cheapernet A jargon name for Thin-Wire Ethernet—because it is cheaper than Thick-Wire Ethernet.

Client Network workstation that communicates with a server; an e-mail letterbox.

Client–server A computing system consisting of networked 'clients' which request information and a central 'server' which stores data and manages shared information and resources. Client–server software, or architectures, are trying to reduce the amount of data traffic flowing over the wires between clients and server. It does this by processing data at the server as well as simply retrieving it. For example, a client PC with a simple front-end application asks the server to find all contacts in south London. The server trawls through the database and only returns the correct matches. The alternative is for the client to request the entire database to be sent, which it then searches. The difference is subtle, but is the new design on which server-based SQL databases and similar work. The network is not stressed so heavily, though the server does more by having to run an application in parallel with the NOS.

Directory synchronization Way of bringing all mail directories (which hold each user's mail) up to date on a WAN.

Distributed processing A technique to enable processors or computers to share tasks among themselves most effectively. Each processor completes allocated subtasks independently and the results are then recombined.

Duplexing A technique to increase the fault tolerance of networks. In a duplexed disk system, there are two identical controllers and disk drives. Data is written to both via a separate controller. If one goes wrong, the second device is switched in under software control with no effect to the user. This is a more fault-tolerant system than disk mirroring.

Ethernet One of the earliest networking architectures which normally refers to transmission of packets of data at 10 Mbps over coaxial cable with BNC connectors. It defines how the packets of data are formed, using IEEE standard 802.3; variations include the 10Base-T standard which uses twisted-pair cabling and various proprietary high-speed networks. Thomas-Conrad Corp.'s proprietary alternative to FDDI is non-standard and lacks industry support, but does operate at 100 Mbps.

Gateway High-level interconnection device which passes packets of data from one type of networking system, computer, or application to another by converting the protocols and format of the packets used.

Gateway (e-mail) Interface between different e-mail systems; gateways convert protocols to connect dissimilar networks.

ISO OSI reference model The Open Standards Interconnect (OSI) definition was published by the International Standards Organization (ISO) in 1977. It describes seven layers of network function from the lowest layer (physical), which deals with physical connections such as the wires, connectors, and electrical signals, to the highest layer (application), which provides the user interface to the lower levels. OSI offers guidelines for developers, enabling them to design networks and related products which can talk, regardless of their make and use.

LAN Local area network. A group of workstations (PCs or Macs) that are physically and electronically linked using cabling. Network software allows each workstation to share files and resources, such as a printer.

Mail-enabled application A normal application from which it is possible to send mail without specifically calling up your e-mail package. Lotus is mail-enabling new releases of its Windows packages to automatically call up cc:Mail; WinMail supplies macros to mail-enable standard applications.

Mail server Central hub of mail network, from where messages are routed. Can be the LAN server, or a separate server.

MAPI Microsoft's open Mail Application Programming Interface.

Mapping Linking a directory path to a local drive letter, enabling a user to log directly onto a server's network drive without having to select volumes, directories, and files individually.

MHS Message Handling Service, Netware's store-and-forward message transfer mechanism. Some packages use this as the message transfer system (BeyondMail, WinMail); others can access it through a gateway.

Mirroring A means of improving fault tolerance in a network. In a mirrored disk system, two separate hard disks are connected to the same controller. The same data is duplicated on the two drives by one controller. This offers cheaper, but less secure, fault tolerance than disk duplexing.

Naming services An important development within the last couple of years, spurred on by the importance of WANs. It simply dictates that within a network, each node has a unique address and name and any server or workstation can reach and communicate with any other. NetWare 4.0, DECnet, and VINES employ global naming services.

NetBIOS Network Basic Input/Output System is a low-level software interface that lets applications talk to network hardware. If a network is NetBIOS compatible, it will respond in the same way to the set of NetBIOS commands, accessed from DOS by the int 5Ch interrupt. NetBIOS was the *de facto* standard, thanks to a lack of international standards, but its limitations and age now make it near redundant.

NetView NetView is IBM's network management and control architecture. It is one of the most expensive management suites, one layer of which runs on networked PCs gathering data about the state of the network and its nodes. This data is relayed to the main NetView program, which runs on a mainframe, to provide constant network reports, control, and analysis. The software to gather the information runs under both DOS and OS/2—with DOS it requires a dedicated PC.

Packet The basic unit of data sent over the network during intercommunication. A packet includes the address of the sending and receiving stations, error control information and check procedures, and, finally, the information itself.

PROFS IBM mail standard, built into OfficeVision, allowing gateway users to communicate with 3270 terminals.

Protocol Rules covering format and timing of messages on a network.

Receive log Tracks total mail received at that point, whether on a mail server or a client.

Remote client User accessing mail without being connected to the mail server's local network. The user can be elsewhere in a WAN, or access the mail system via a modem link.

Router An interconnection device similar to a bridge but operating at a higher level within the OSI reference model. Routers detect protocols rather than the data they carry and use the destination address to work out the best route for the packet through a complex network. Typically used within WANs, intelligent routers can select whether to use telephone links, LANs, or particular shortcuts through a network.

Shared folder Mail folder accessible to more than one user, functioning as a bulletin board.

SMTP Simple Mail Transfer Protocol. The Internet protocol for e-mail transfer.

Store-and-forward Method of transferring mail by moving copies of the messages, rather than pointers to the messages on the server. X.400 and MHS are store-and-forward systems.

TCP/IP Transmission Control Protocol / Internet Protocol is a set of communications protocols developed by the US Department of Defense, originally for use in military applications. TCP/IP bundles and unbundles sent and received data into packets, manages packet transmission, and checks for errors across networks. Originally found binding Unix networks together, its flexibility and portability are making it a *de facto* standard for any LAN and WAN.

VIM Vendor-independent messaging. The common API set established by IBM, Borland, Novell, and Apple, and built into OS/2 2.0.

WAN Wide area network. Multiple small, linked local area networks or a network with multiple servers linked together using public telephone circuits, leased lines, or high-speed bridges.

X.400 CCITT standard: application layer OSI mail transfer method.

Index